Lloyd

MW01699278

WHAT ARE THE ODDS?

A MEMOIR:

Family and Unique Construction in the Pacific Northwest and Beyond

by Lloyd Huntley Kessler

2015 Edition

ELDERBERRY PRESS, INC.
OAKLAND

ACKNOWLEDGMENTS

I am most grateful to these people for their contribution to this effort:

Lyn Z. Page—my ghostwriter, organizer, designer and new friend.
Heather Deringer—also my ghostwriter and new friend.
Rex Jackson—son-in-law, with his many computer graphic skills, improving the quality of old photos as needed.
Joanne Ruth Kessler—youngest daughter, whose interest in our family's genealogy helped to provide research into mysteries generated by my memory gaps.
David George Kessler—younger brother who provided updates to his own life's history, some of which I didn't know.
Christine Lewis of Ohio—who scoured the Internet for hours in pursuit of long-lost data and many possibilities, all for someone she has never met. Chris knows the value of family research and her time was valued.
My family members—who blessed my life through their presence from my early 20's on into their own adulthood, and then gave me grandchildren and great grandchildren to delight and renew me as I age.
My wife Millie—for the sixty-plus years of partnering, pampering and persistence in making a better man of me by her presence as my wife, and for being a fine mother to our children. Even though we lost her to Alzheimer's on July 3, 2014, she is still the woman who persevered beside me through all the events that tested us over the years. I am indeed a lucky man.

It takes a lot of time and effort to put together a whole book—much more than it appears to require when the idea first makes itself known. This book is no different. What started out as a book about my life's work turned into one about my family as well. Along the way, it was clear that in order to tell you about my work, I must also include those who assisted and influenced me along the way. Gathering, identifying, researching and selecting information that was no longer residing in my memory also required help from others.

FOREWORD

I can hear my bones talk back to me today as I ask them to move a little easier. I'm aware that they do that sometimes. On my last birthday I turned 86. It could be better. I could be 90.

I've had an interestingly good life, and I thought others should know my history. I never planned out anything in my life, but my dreams often gave me previews of future construction projects before I even knew about them. As a result, I've met the challenges well, for the most part. So here I am, putting my life of remarkable coincidences out there for all to read. This road I'm on allowed me to live this good life, and propelled me forward into my twilight with many blessings. I'd like to tell you how I did that and what I learned along the way. What are the odds that all these events would be so coincidental? Is it fate? Is it Divine intervention? Is it paranormal? Or is it what dreams are made of? Coincidence? IS there such a thing?

I wonder.

I say I've been very lucky to be blessed with a loving family and a successful life. A series of connections from one job to another made for unusual progress toward my very good fortune. Many people made my life worth living, along with the chance to thrive doing work I loved. I can say that I did my best.

What ARE the odds of all this happening to me?

Table of Contents

Chapter 1

MY EARLY YEARS

I started out as a baby. Yes, I know; so did you and everyone else. However, I was Lloyd Huntley Kessler, born June 19, 1928, weighing in at just the right heft for me to become the elder brother to two brothers and a sister before I was 20: Thane Couzen, born a year later; Ardis Ruth, arriving six years later; and David George, finally here 19 years later in 1947. I'm indeed lucky.

Lloyd—1930.

Thane and Lloyd—1930, the cones are vanilla—the only flavor our folks bought.

Right: Lloyd in 1931—about 3 yrs. old. Eel River at Red Mountain Creek confluence.

Lloyd and Thane—1931.

Thane and Lloyd—1932.
We spent a lot of time around the water.

Lloyd and Thane—1932.
What do you suppose Thane was laughing at—those cats?

My first memory dates back to age 3 or 4. I can yet remember wading on my own in the Eel River in northern California, with my brother Thane.

Thane and Lloyd in the Eel River—1934. We spent most of the daylight hours at the river, digging in the sand and paddling around. Picnic lunches always came with Mom when we played there.

Dan Hutchinson (cousin), Thane and Lloyd—1934.
Three-wheel races were often held in the driveway.

1934—Lloyd—1936.

Cousins:
Harry Wuner, Bob Underwood, Dan Hutchinson, Thane, and Lloyd (in front)—1934. We spent a lot of time together in those years, with a normal amount of mischief among us.

CHAPTER 2

MY SIBLINGS
Thane Couzen

1934

Thane was 13 months younger than I. We rough-housed at home, like most brothers, and although I was stronger and could beat him up, he would never give up—or admit that I was hurting him.

One afternoon when we were 11 and 12, we raced our bikes down Oak Avenue, a steep road toward the Willamette River near our home in Oak Grove. Thane flopped over and slid a long way on the rough-paved road. One side of his body was severely lacerated from ankle to shoulder, but he would not let me help him. We made our way home in spite of his pain, where mother dressed his wounds. Not once did he let out a whimper. I admired that quality in him. He was tough.

My brother and I, from early on (first grade or so) were allowed to roam and explore the wooded area adjacent to our homes. My parents made sure we understood the boundaries. They let us out of their sight and expected us to take care of each other. They also expected us to be back at a pre-determined time. We always were, and they never had to look for us.

Thane graduated from Milwaukie High in June of '47 (one year after me), becoming part of the post WWII 1947 "Happy Group" that replaced the wartime "Serious Group." There was still a draft, but we were headed for better times. He had wilder friends, and did more reckless things, like passing cars on the right, and setting off a firecracker in a theater in Oregon City.

In the summer of '47, I got him a job as a laborer on the road project I was working on for the Bureau of Public Roads at Glacier, Washington. That fall, he joined the Army Airborne, spending most of his time in Japan. He managed to survive a parachute jump-gone-wrong. He landed hard, seriously bruised and banged up. It took him a few days to recover, but it could have been much worse.

Lloyd and Thane—April 25, 1949—North Richland, WA.

Thane's tour of duty ended at Fort Ord, California, the same week the Korean conflict started. (June 25, 1950)

He started college at University of San Francisco that fall, and graduated later from a different university in 1954.

After college, he made his early career selling life insurance, and sometime later owned a State Farm insurance agency in Hayward, California. He retired at age 64, and died of cancer a year later.

He had lived one kind of American Dream: college, military, marriage, children, career, business owner, and success. I loved him.

Thane's favorite car—1987 Porsche 944.

Thane and his wife, Maine-born "Ris"—short for Evarista—raised four sons: Ron, Alan, and twins Charles and Mike, the youngest. Thane was a dedicated father who kept the boys involved in sports, and took them fishing at every opportunity. In high school, Thane was on the cross country track team. The hobby he pursued throughout his life was running marathons. He ran them up until a couple of years before his death. I admired that in him also.

His son Charles originally received a back injury while working for a construction company shortly after high school. California's settlement to his case put him through college. He was a super door-to-door salesman in later years, offering a variety of meats as his product.

As the economy failed, he had to expand his territory. One day, as he was driving slowly down a street near his home, a woman driving an SUV crossed the center and hit him head on. He stopped prior to impact but suffered severe damage to his arms, wrists and back, severely limiting his ability to lift and drive. The woman was texting on her cell phone and never saw Chuck's truck. He is still dealing with the aftermath of that crash as he handles the claim himself against the insurance company today. Good luck, Chuck.

Thane Kessler Family: Charles, Thane, Ris, Mike. In front: Ron, Alan—circa 1963.

Thane lived a good life, from July 11, 1929 to Dec. 3, 1993. He is buried in Hayward, CA.

Ardis Ruth

Lloyd, Ardis and Thane—1936. In the background is a 1936 Willys, the only new car George H. Kessler and family ever owned.

My sister was 6 years younger than I, so there was not much interaction with us, the big brothers who didn't really care about her girl-stuff. According to HER, we were kinda thorns in her side!

As a teen, Ardis was very rebellious. Our parents enrolled her in St. Helen's Hall in Portland, an Episcopalian boarding school for girls that was established in 1869, and was known for its ability to stem the rise of exciting young women's rebellious behavior. For a year or two, that was her home.

The family then moved to Belmont, California, where she attended Notre Dame High School.

She had the capacity to be a good student, and graduated from Diablo High School in Concord, in 1952. She married a furniture salesman, Bill Gregory, whose parents owned a furniture factory in Portland. They raised 3 kids in Fullerton, California: Daniel, Christopher, and Elizabeth.

Ardis, like our father, was a very strict disciplinarian. She was very opinionated and had a loud mouth too. Millie did not like her much up close, but preferred their interactions to be by long distance phone calls and letters. They got along best that way. When Ardis and kids came to visit, they went shopping with our kids, telling them that they always stole something when they shopped. Our kids never stole, of course.

Gregory Family: Bill, Ardis, Elizabeth, Danny and Chris.

By the time Ardis' kids finished grade school, her husband had become a full-blown alcoholic. They split, leaving Ardis as the primary provider. Her kids started high school, but soon drifted away. Dan bummed around and worked just enough to survive and get involved with drugs. In his early 20's, he was stabbed to death on a park table somewhere in Colorado.

Chris worked summers for a few years as a smoke jumper with the US Forest Service. He later took up residency on an Indian reservation. (It's not clear to me what his purpose was for doing that.) He now lives with his wife somewhere in Iowa.

During high school, Elizabeth, like her brothers, drifted into drugs and all the related problems. She too, did whatever it took to survive. When desperate, she came to Ardis for help. She eventually got a job in a convenience store in a small town in Iowa, where she now resides.

Ardis had an outgoing, warm personality, but in family matters, she was the alpha female. When she passed away in 2006, she bequeathed Elizabeth and Chris $120,000 each from the proceeds of her real estate holdings. She wanted them to have a good future, too.

Ardis' last rites

I used to think that wakes were all about the sadness of losing a loved one. Now I don't think so. Wakes are about the celebration of the life that was. Her memorial service was held at St. Wilfred of York Episcopal Church in Huntington Beach, California, and it was anything but solemn and dull. Ardis was a strong woman, sometimes too strong, but with many friends. Whatever dark disposition that strength sometimes brought her was quickly erased by the laughter she no doubt orchestrated at her wake. There was much more laughter than tears. Even those shedding tears were smiling. They continued to both laugh and cry at the outdoor reception. The perfect weather marked one of only two days it had not rained that September. After the reception, most of the immediate family boarded the boat to prepare for the burial-at-sea ceremony, which consisted of a prayer on deck and the offering of flowers along with her ashes, both cast upon the sea.

The waters were calm on the cruise down the Newport channel. My brother Dave and I hit it off well with the boat captain. He told us that most of the time he had to keep his "undertaker's face" on during these ceremonial excursions because most people are somber as they go to sea to bury their loved ones. This is his craft's only business, so it was important not to offend his passengers.

Not this time. We laughed and joked with him, admiring the bikini-clad women riding sailboards as we cruised down the channel. We met the Coast Guard cruiser, captained by a beautiful woman, who helped us navigate past the sailboards. We discovered during our chatter that our boat captain and she were lovers. Unhindered by that information, we proceeded out to sea for the burial, giving us closure amid our mirth. The whole funeral wake ceremony was a very fun time. I felt guilty, but this was exactly the way Ardis had planned it. Of that, I'm sure.

She lived from April 15, 1935 to August 23, 2010.

ARDIS RUTH WHITE Obituary

White, Ardis Ruth April 1935—August 2010 Resident of Fountain Valley, after a two year battle with cancer, Ardis passed away peacefully at her Fountain Valley home on August 23. Born Ardis Ruth Kessler April 15, 1935 in Nice, California, Ardis has lived in Orange County since 1965. The third of four children born to the late George and Naomi Kessler, she was the beloved wife of Charles White until his death in 1994. Ardis was preceded in death by her brother, Thane (Russ) Kessler and her oldest son, Daniel Carlos Gregory. She will forever be remembered by her brother, Lloyd Kessler and his wife Millie; her brother, David Kessler and his wife Carmela; her children, Christopher Paul Gregory and Elizabeth Ruth Gregory; her grandsons, Ronald Daniel Gregory and Cody Allen Gregory; as well as her nieces, nephews and countless friends who were blessed to know her. She will be especially missed by her "adopted" family; Joan Tucker and her three daughters Patricia, Anne and Nicole. Ardis was a long time active member of St. Wilfrid of York Episcopal Church in Huntington Beach, where she served as a lector. She was also active in the church flower guild and baby basket committee. An ardent world traveler, Ardis was always planning her next trip. Her favorite destinations were Europe, Hawaii and the Caribbean. She was an active member of the Monday Morning Club, Harbor Singers and the Bixby Twilight Golf League where she formed many lasting friendships. In addition to travel, Ardis enjoyed singing, golf, volunteer work and visiting with friends and family. With her ready smile, sense of humor and can-do attitude, Ardis brightened the lives of all who knew her. Friends and family are invited to attend a Memorial service for Ardis on Saturday, September 25 at 10:00 am in St. Wilfrid of York Episcopal Church, 18631 Chapel Lane, Huntington Beach, CA 92646 (714) 962-7512. A reception in the church hall will immediately follow the memorial service. The family requests that all donations be made to the St. Wilfrid Flower Guild, 18631 Chapel Lane, Huntington Beach, CA 92646.

Published in Orange County Register on September 12, 2010

David George

David Kessler with his cap pistol in 1949—age 2—nineteen years my junior.

Out for a walk with Mom, Naomi.

Since David is so much younger than I, it was difficult for me to keep up with his childhood as I forged my own adulthood. However, he is no less loved than his siblings were. He's been good enough to fill me in with some details I had not remembered about him.

Waving 'bye.

Eagle Scout.

As you can see, he earned his Eagle Scout badge by age 17. Everyone was proud of him, including me.

In the spring of 1968, sometime after high school graduation, he served a tour in Vietnam in the U.S. Army, becoming a Flight Engineer on Chinook helicopters as an E-5. During the Vietnam War, he served at Camp Holloway in Pleiku, a mountain city in the center of the country. During his second tour in Vietnam, he moved to the Army base at Phu Hiep, just south of Tuy Hoa Air Base, on the China Sea.

He made many flights into the war zone. One day he told his CO, "I can make these Chinook transmissions better if I spend more time on the ground." Those particular transmissions were known to be unreliable at the time, and were thought to have been responsible for many crashes. David convinced the CO that he knew how to make them more dependable. The CO agreed, so David spent the rest of his tour on the ground, making sure that no one else rode in unreliable seats, powered by unpredictable equipment. He arrived safely at home in the spring of 1970, after two tours of duty in Vietnam.

David has excellent mechanical engineering aptitudes, abilities, and experience that helped him to solve problems on Sikorsky Air Cranes, as well as other aircraft transmissions and engines, including the Super Guppy, over the span of his career.

In 1973, he worked as a crew chief for Erickson Air Crane, a company that flew the Sikorsky for helicopter logging, BPA highline construction, and demolition. One Air Crane could remove 18 or twenty towers in a shift, compared to a conventional crew's ability to move just one.

The helicopter could also move and transport towers back to the staging area for dismantling in one move, unlike the less cost-efficient manner used by conventional crews, which dismantled each tower separately at the tower site. The parts then had to be trucked to the staging area.

One of David's projects was the Super Guppy—Santa Barbara, CA.

During 1980-'81, David worked with Aero Spacelines, where the wide-bodied cargo aircraft, the "Super Guppy" was assembled. It is used for ferrying outsized aircraft components. His job there was Contract Administrator for their agreement with UTA French Airlines.

Today David works for a Santa Barbara firm called Yardi, where he is Vice President, Affordable Housing. He is responsible for the development and support of Affordable Housing Projects (HUD).

David and his wife Carmela have one daughter, Stephanie, married and now in her late 20's, who has had their first grandchild, Carina Cheyenne Lebate, born July 4, 2014 in Santa Barbara, California. Stephanie is also employed by Yardi, and travels a lot, troubleshooting for their clients.

Carmela recently retired as a counselor from the Lompoc School District, and was recently elected as a Member of the School Board.

David has both a good mind for mechanics and business. As such, he was executor for Ardis' estate. We don't see each other often, because he lives in Lompoc, California, but we keep in touch regularly.

CHAPTER 3

MY PARENTS AND EARLY LIFE

Naomi Ruth Underwood Kessler and George Huntley Kessler

May they rest in Peace.

They taught me respect, responsibility and self-preservation.

Naomi Underwood in Flaming Geyser Park November, 1926.

Naomi, her sisters, a sister-in-law, and five nephews—1932—Thane and Lloyd sit at the right, Standing L to R: Viola, Florence Underwood (sister-in-law), Naomi, Frances; Middle row: Delores and Yvonne; Front row sitting: Bob, Dan, Harry, Thane & Lloyd.

Naomi and older sister Viola Hutchinson—1932.

Mom was congenial, but not a big hugger, as many are today. Many women were like that in those days, but their love was shown in other ways. Although Mom asked for a kiss from us boys regularly—and we'd give her one—it was without much enthusiasm. I guess we just didn't like anything "mushy" at that age!

The retaining wall along the Eel river—1930—one of Dad's projects.

George Huntley Kessler—1947.

Dad's personal style in work clothes extended to his riding britches, boots, Stetson hat and a dark tie. He always wore a shirt with two pockets, and always had his sleeves rolled up.

This is a postcard from my dad while he was in Afghanistan:

"Big Son, this is the hyena Mother wrote you about. 1 shot, 450 yards, 7:30 p.m. @ dusk. 30-06 rifle, Stith riflescope. First one seen around here for about three years." Afghanistan, Circa 1950.

Dad was a warm person, especially when he first came home from a job. He smoked cigarettes, so the smell was always there. I didn't much like it, but was always glad to have him home. Even his sometimes-painful bear hugs to me (and everyone else) were still one of many ways we knew he loved us. He always worked long hours. Time didn't mean much to him, but he was seldom late for dinner. It was the one time we all had together—when we all sat around the table for our evening meal. For at least an hour, we talked about current events and other things of interest to us. It was an important tradition for our family.

If and when Mom and Dad argued, it was usually at dinner time, and because he disciplined us with too harsh a scolding for our misdemeanors that day. But there was never any profanity spoken in our home. The strongest exclamation I heard was "Confound it!" Mom would say "darn" once in a while. I remember that Thane's favorite expression was "Don't be a jerk." Dad's choice phrase for those he didn't appreciate was

"That guy's a pain in the neck." I don't remember any of Ardis' quips. No cussing examples there. I didn't use profanity until my late 20's, and it took me another 40 years to really make an art of it!

Those meals also were the breeding grounds for our indelicate efforts to learn good table manners. Mom and Dad had to start early and practice often in order to teach us. But we managed to catch on over time without thoughts of rejecting the lessons when we got older. That decision paid off during future years. Potential in-laws notice those things.

At home full time, my mom was a good cook. Her labor on Sundays often filled our home with the inviting aroma of her roasted chicken. To this day I remember how it made us hurry home when we knew it was in the oven. From Jennings Lodge, we practically had to crawl home on hands and knees because the aroma made us weak when the wind was just right and we could smell it down the street. Holidays were filled with good traditional foods and those same wonderful smells.

Before she married, Mom worked as a secretary. Maybe that's where she learned to be efficient and to know what it takes to get young boys to learn discipline. (I didn't enforce that with my own kids. Sigh.) Respect for elders and for authority were just a part of our upbringing. In our household, there was no such thing as getting up and leaving for school without the bed being made.

I remember more about Mom after my 6th grade year in school. Things like her not liking to do housework (but doing it anyway), and that she was a very good cook. Laughter was a little on the lean side in our house, but for the most part my family was congenial. No drama to speak of, other than the normal squabbles families have that are usually resolved with some 'meetings of the minds.' Our immediate family didn't have much real adversity or big traumas. Again, I was lucky. My folks were social people, if only on occasion. Dad didn't have much free time from his civil engineer duties, but he liked to fish, and taught us boys his own methods. Mom worked for a couple of years at a fabrication plant making metal and other parts for the war effort. Other than that, she worked hard in our home.

My folks were also generous people. Our friend, the widow Mrs. Kingsbury, fell very ill at one point, her family of 6 kids depending only upon her. My folks took in her daughter Ruth for a period of time, but I don't remember a lot about that except that she was the same age as Ardis. Hmmm. More girls in the house. We boys just did our own thing.

Washington, Marriage Records, 1865-2004 record for George H Kissler

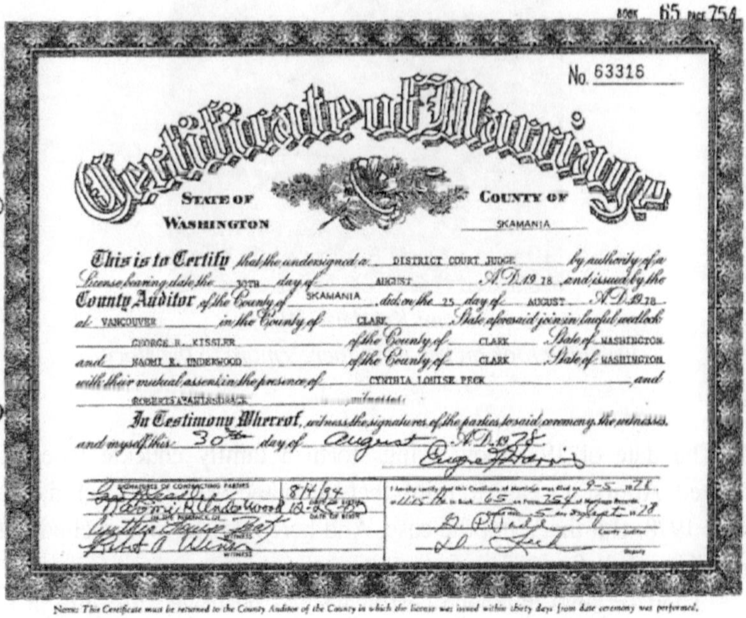

BOOK 65 PAGE 754

No. 63316

Certificate of Marriage

STATE OF WASHINGTON

COUNTY OF SKAMANIA

This is to Certify that the undersigned a DISTRICT COURT JUDGE by authority of a License bearing date the 30TH day of AUGUST A.D. 19 78, and issued by the County Auditor of the County of SKAMANIA did on the 25 day of AUGUST A.D. 19 78 at VANCOUVER in the County of CLARK State aforesaid join in lawful wedlock GEORGE H. KISSLER of the County of CLARK State of WASHINGTON and NAOMI R. UNDERWOOD of the County of CLARK State of WASHINGTON with their mutual assent in the presence of CYNTHIA LOUISE PECK and ROBERTS A. WATINSDRACK witnesses.

In Testimony Whereof, witness the signatures of the parties to said ceremony, the witnesses, and myself this 30th day of August A.D. 1978.

Note: This Certificate must be returned to the County Auditor of the County in which the license was issued within thirty days from date ceremony was performed.

cord Index

Name: George H Kissler
Spouse: Naomi R Underwood
Marriage Date: 30 Aug 1978
Marriage Place: Skamania
Date Recorded: 5 Sep 1978
ference Number: swskmmcbook65_754

Source Information

Record URL: http://search.ancestry.com/cgi-bin/sse.dll?h=1742029&db=WAMarriage&indiv=try

Source Information: Ancestry.com. *Washington, Marriage Records, 1865-2004* [database on-line Provo, UT, USA: Ancestry.com Operations, Inc., 2012.
Original data: *Washington State Archives.* Olympia, Washingto Washington State Archives.

Did you notice anything strange about this marriage certificate?

Naomi Kessler—1977.
From the look on her face, there's more to the story.

The date of 1978 now brings forth a family chuckle when it's spotted. At first it's easy to think that Mom and Dad didn't get married until 1978. But that's not the case. And here, Kessler was spelled with an "i" instead of an "e" on the certificate!

Their original marriage certificate was destroyed in a fire at the courthouse in Aberdeen, WA, where they were first married in 1927. So, to satisfy the Veteran's Administration's need to have a marriage certificate in order to ensure that Mom could be buried in Willamette National Cemetery beside Dad, they quietly went to Stevenson to get married once again in 1978. That satisfied the VA, and it was, in another sense, a recommitment to each other. No fuss. No muss. Just clearing out the obstacles to something they both wanted.

Naomi and George—1965.

George H. Kessler—Circa 1960.

Childhood Memories

I started my first day of school (first grade) in a Garberville, California, in a three-room schoolhouse. My parents seldom took vacations, but this year they chose the first week of school to go, leaving me with friends. That was during the Great Depression. At that time they dressed me in a red sweater and corduroy pants. All the other kids word blue bib overalls and blue shirts. Some were bare-footed. All went well until the first recess.

Because one third-grader didn't like my style, I learned to fight early. I gave him a bloody nose. The teacher made me go stand on the school porch until noon. Because I couldn't get to the rest room, I peed my pants. That was my second biggest first grade event.

I enjoyed some fun childhood highlights, though, like all kids do...and I gained some insight into how life works, and took the information forward, feeling lucky to have discovered the pitfalls before they discovered me, or left me skinned or broken. I was a fast learner. Well, most of the time.

There were several 'incidents" over the years in which my fists did the talking. Since we moved around a lot to follow Dad's jobs, I didn't make a lot of friends in school. We weren't there long enough.

Once again I got into a squabble, this time over a girl. I was in 6th grade in Oak Grove, Oregon. Guy Stevenson and I were dressed up in white shirts and blue pants for some school function. I don't remember how it started, exactly, but I cleaned his clock. After being pulled apart, we went back to being good friends. That was one of our first clues about girls and their effects on boys.

Donner Pass

During the summer of 1937, my Dad, a civil engineer for the California State Highway Department, was supervising a highway project at the summit of Donner Pass (elevation 7,056 ft.). At this time, our family was camped at the exact same place where the Donner Party camped in February of 1847, at Donner Lake. We lived in three tent houses with wooden floors.

Donner Pass in the Sierra Nevada Mountains of California. This King Survey photo took place in the 1870s, long after the 1847 crisis but long before Lloyd's trek.

Donner Pass—showing original route. For more information, see http://en.wikipedia.org/wiki/Donner_Party.

Mom, Ardis and Dad slept in one tent. Thane, our dog Pal and I slept in a second. One night Pal had been out chasing coyotes, but when they turned back on him he headed for camp. I heard him running through the gravel outside the tent just before he jumped over the tent house door, landed right on my bed, and dove under the covers.

The third tent was used for cooking and dining. Our water source was Donner Creek, which flowed past camp. Thane and I fished the creek or climbed the mountainside on the south side of camp, leaving after breakfast, climbing on top of salal brush, and over the huge boulders that were a constant reminder of the area's geology. We were not to go past the railroad tracks. My folks decided that was far enough for us to roam, and we honored it. We were always to be back in camp in time for lunch.

■ ■ ■

My Dad gave me a Model 69-22 caliber Winchester rifle for my 13th birthday (1941). About the time school started that fall, Dad enrolled me and Thane in a gun club at 65th and Johnson Creek Blvd. (See the map.) To get there, we had to walk ¾ mile from our home in Oak Grove to the Oak Grove street car stop, where we boarded it to Portland. We then exited at Waverly Station and transferred to the Gresham-Estacada route, de-boarding at the 65th and Johnson Creek Blvd. stop. From there, we walked the short distance to the Gun Club. When the club meeting was over, we reversed the route, carrying the gun with us each way. No one ever questioned us, or even blinked.

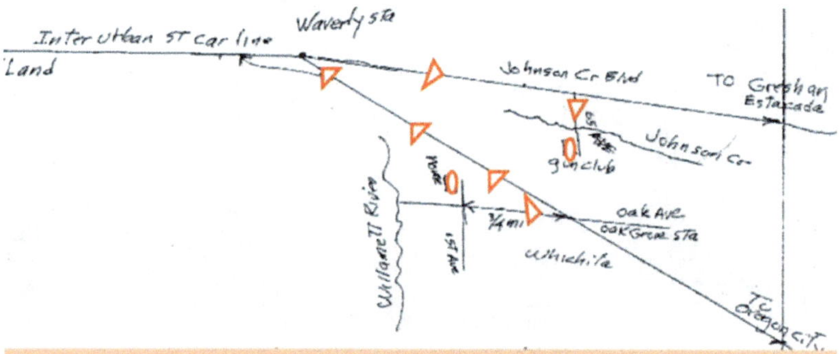

Can you imagine doing that today in 2014? With a gun?

An Adventure with the Kessler Brothers

After my 8th grade year (1942), we moved to Bay Ocean. My Dad had become the resident engineer for construction of the Tillamook Blimp Base.

The Air Museum is now housed in a rare World War II Blimp Hangar, the only one left, and the largest wooden structure in the world! You can see their web site at http://www.tillamookair.com/html/bldg.html.

As a part of that move, Thane and I rode the train with our bikes from Portland to Astoria, and then journeyed south, riding them along Hwy 101 to Seaside, and from there on down to Garibaldi. By ourselves. This was our pre-determined destination.

Before we arrived, Dad had decided not to rent the house there after all. He knew we'd get the pre-arranged note at the postmaster's office, which instructed us to ride our bikes on down to Tillamook. That was a total of nearly 70 miles from Astoria! We camped out at night during the three or four days it took to get there, but we made it!

Dad then rented a house at Bay Ocean, one of two houses left on high ground, about 10 miles west of Tillamook. The rest had been washed away by winds and high tides over the years.

Our collective adventures during those years of 1942 to 1944 weren't spectacular, but mirrored the ones our peers also enjoyed. It was a safer world then for two boys sharing such experiences with the total confidence of their parents that they would arrive safe and sound from such long distances.

Typical of many of our weekly Saturday routines, Thane and I rode our bikes the 10 miles to Tillamook to see the matinee. That was normal for us (and a lot of other kids) in those days.

In another venture, Dick Kingsbury, Thane and I decided to ride our bikes from Bay Ocean to Camp Meriwether. It was wartime, so no one was there but a caretaker. We helped ourselves to his eggs since he wasn't home to protest. On the way out we ran into him, and were pretty sure he was suspicious, but we just headed home as fast as our legs could spin those wheels. We heard no more about it, but Dick's conscience bothered him for the rest of his life!

■ ■ ■

High school held some other events that weren't so bright. After what I thought was a bad call from a ref in a basketball game in my senior year, I caused an event to happen that marks a bad day in my life. I jumped up from the bleacher seat I was in and ran down toward the floor to make my complaint. Everyone else thought to do it too, and the bleachers collapsed. One lady's leg was severely injured. The diplomacy between my high school principle and my dad and I was not much fun. I got off easy. I wasn't suspended. What I learned from that incident is what my dad always told us, which was "Don't put the other guy in harm's way."

■ ■ ■

As seniors at Milwaukie High School in 1946, bunches of us liked to ski Mt. Hood, but there was no snow that year at Government Camp, so what little we did ski was done at Timberline, much higher in elevation. We all brought food with us, but the homemade butter Bob Morse brought was really bad-tasting. Bob was six feet tall, 200 pounds, and was the tackle on our football team. That night, I made an indelicate comment, and lost the ensuing fight. Bob had sore knuckles from pounding my head.

CHAPTER 4

MY EARLY JOBS SURVEYING

While I was attending Milwaukie High School, I took auto mechanics classes in Clackamas, Oregon, at Camp Withycombe, a military base that had been partially converted to a trade school. I felt pretty good about my skills, so after graduation I ventured out to several shops on Union Avenue in Portland, the largest city in Oregon. As I stepped out of one of the shops, a brand new 1946 red Plymouth convertible pulled up to the curb. On board were friends from my high school graduating class: Cresson Baxter and Ted Corbett.

If I had stepped out one second later, I would have missed them, and my destiny might have been different. This turned out to be the beginning of my life's journey.

Cresson's father was a successful florist, and bought him the car as a graduation present. They were on their way to Bonneville Power Administration to sign up for a survey crew. Ted's uncle was a civil engineer for BPA, and it was his lead we were following.

When the personnel manager learned I had some surveying experience from the times my dad had taken me along on his jobs, he asked if I wanted to sign up. I did.

Cresson decided not to take the job, so I was hired as a chainman, and Ted and I traveled by train to Skycomish, Washington (courtesy of BPA), where we worked on a crew that was surveying the first transmission line over Stevens Pass. A "chain" is a measuring device used by surveyors to measure distances from point to point. A Party Chief runs the crew; an Instrument Man runs the activities of the Chainmen, whose job it is to work with both ends of the chain. The device measures in hundredths of a foot, rather than inches like a carpenter rule.

It was cold and dangerous work...dangerous in that it required using an ax to cut brush. One day I chopped into a small fir tree that didn't agree with the force of my swing. Unceremoniously, it let my ax force its way through the trunk and into the top of my foot. For once, I felt the physical revenge of my own AX-shuns.

After driving myself in the Government station wagon to the nearest hospital in Leavenworth—I got 4 or 5 stitches as my reward.

I was unable to work in the field for a while, so they put me to work in the office. There I learned how to do the essential paperwork that goes with running a business and/or a crew. I use those principles even today in running my own business.

In future years, the foot wound made me uncomfortable on occasion, but never did impede my ability to work!

Grayback Forest Station—1944—I was a Junior in high school and employed by the U.S. Forest service. The job was digging out (ribes) goose berries and wild currant for blister rust control near the Grayback Forest Camp, a few miles from the Oregon Caves.

Lloyd, 1944, at Grayback.

Higher Education—1946-'47

While Thane went to San Francisco for college, I enrolled in Oregon State College at Corvallis. It was an agricultural college then, later renamed a University. They're now the Oregon Beavers from "Corn Valley," which even has a set of FAQ's for the town: Corvallis: (aka Corn Valley, Cornchester):

- 220' above sea level
- Daydream capital of the globe
- Great place to live but I wouldn't want to visit
- Paradise for men and dogs, hell for women and horses
- Where men are men and women don't care
- Best kept secret—bored, nothing to do socially incestuous
- 50 miles from the mountains
- 50 miles from the desert
- 50 miles from the coast
- 50 miles from the airport
- 50 miles from Eugene
- 50 miles from just about any place you'd rather be
- It's nice when you're not there

Here in Corvallis, I thought at the time, there is not too much fun. I had to work in the school cafeteria to pay my room and board. My bills were due on the first of the month; college paid on the 5th. I was fined a dollar a day for every day after the 1st. The lady who ran the cafeteria liked me, and let me cheat on my time to make up for the five-dollar fine each month.

During my second semester I became ill with strep throat, sweating profusely for weeks. I was treated with penicillin and/or sulfa, but it didn't stop the condition. I had to quit school. Never went back. Went home and didn't work for 3 months from weakness that seemed endless. I didn't fully appreciate my health until I recovered from that miserable time.

That summer, after I recovered, I worked awhile for the Bureau of Roads in Glacier, Washington, (1947), as a chainman on a road construction crew. I was getting more and more skilled at my job.

When the work season was over, I bummed around for a while and then found a job at Crown Zellerbach Paper Mill in West Linn, a small city adjacent to Portland, Oregon. That was September of 1948. In the wood mill section, we were all in danger. All the time. Sharp hooks, knobs, saws and chippers often literally took their pound of flesh from the men. My job required sawing off knots and removing bark with rotating chipping knives.

It might have been my intuition, if not my logic, that made me realize out of the blue that I was the only person who had done this job for 6 months or more without injury.

I told my supervisor that it was time for me to move on. He agreed. And I did indeed move on that September day of 1948. After a day or two, I breathed a little easier. I still had all my fingers.

What were the odds of THAT? Most everyone else of tenure had sustained wounds, some really bad.

Next I discovered another crew of surveyors to join at BPA, so my chainman duties moved to Forest Grove to work the transmission line surveys, the same type of surveying that I did in 1946 at Stevens Pass. I got even better at my job in the 3-1/2 years I worked for BPA.

Our crew was called J-Party, and consisted of a couple of office men, a party chief, two instrument men, a couple of chainmen, and maybe an ax man or two. From Forest Grove we were transferred to Vancouver, Washington, where we surveyed and constructed a power line called "the Alcoa Tap." ALCOA was the acronym for Aluminum Company of America, based in Pittsburg.

The plant in Vancouver was described by the Port of Vancouver as:

Alcoa—Proof of the "Possibilities"

ALCOA Plant (looking east), March 1941.
December, 1939—After ten years of the Great Depression, Clark County received some very welcome news: The Aluminum Company of America will locate to the Vancouver Lake lowlands.

Lloyd and Wally Stadter—1948.

Leonard "Snuffy Smith" Baumgartner—1949.

Morrie and John Stemke—Is that a diaper or a fake chastity belt?

Our "Prairie Schooner," the BPA station wagon—1949.

Lloyd in front of barracks at Arlington airport—1949. J-Party singles were housed here, as well as aircraft-and-engine students.

Kessler & Goodmunson. Forest Grove—late 1948.

I worked for BPA until February, 1952, and then was hired by Pettijohn Engineering. They were doing the preliminary surveys for the Pelton and Round Butte Dams on the Deshutes River near Madras, Oregon. Then, in the late summer of 1952, I went to work for Lee Hoffman Construction, building BPA power line footings for the Columbia River Crossing between Portland and Vancouver—and beginning the adventure of a lifetime.

Chapter 5

MILLIE'S EARLY YEARS

Millie Wille—1931.

Millie started out as a baby. Yes, I know; so did you and everyone else. However, she was born Mildred Irene Wille, in Deer River, Minnesota, just in time to become the little sister of Clifford Robert, and daughter to Bob and Inez Wille on August 29, 1931.

Millie Wille –1931.

Brother Clifford and Millie—circa 1937.

Wille family home near Vancouver Lake.

Donna Hill, Millie Wille and Diane Hill—Millie and Queenie—1945 circa 1945—Butte, Montana.

Millie & cousin Dickie Lee.

Bob, Millie and Inez Wille—1944.

Millie—September, 1948.

We are fortunate to have pictures of her long before I met her.

The Vanport Flood

Memorial Day, May 30, 1948. Some 40,000 folks lived in Vanport City, known today as Delta Park, a flood plain on the Columbia River just south of the Interstate Bridge (I-5) linking Portland, Oregon, to Vancouver, Washington. The railroad fill that was used as a dike broke, flooding Vanport. Many people still living there lost everything. It was the second largest flood in the Columbia's recorded history.

By early 1948, about half of the wartime workers had moved away since most jobs had evaporated with WWII's end in 1945. However, many jobs were replaced by post-war industry. That brought more people to the area, creating another housing shortage, making Vanport housing attractive again. The post-WWII economy was booming, and housing was in short supply. The service men were catching up on four years of lost love lives and jump-starting the Baby Boom.

One of my best friends, Raymond Young, his wife Polly, and baby daughter were living there. Ray was standing on the railroad fill "dike" when it broke. He ran to his car and got away safely.

My friend Jack Webber and I had dates with two girls who lived in Vanport to go to Seaside that day. We had a great time at the beach. On the way home we learned of the flood, so we took the girls to a pre-arranged address just in case their homes got flooded.

I only learned recently, Feb. 2013, that Millie's best friend Marty Friar was on a train from Vancouver to Portland that made it across the breach. Marty was a star player on a semi-pro softball team sponsored by Lind Pomeroy Florists of Portland. The team was headed for San Jose, Phoenix, and other towns in the southwest for a series of games. Two of Marty's teammates lived in Vanport, and had already packed their bags for the tour. They were the World Championship teams of 1947 and '48.

Neither Jack nor Marty knew each other at that time, nor did I know Marty and Millie. But later on, Jack was Best Man at our wedding, and Marty was Millie's Maid of Honor.

Many other areas in Portland-Vancouver flooded. One of them was Vancouver Lake, where Millie lived.

These images are historic, taken by the Wille family at the time.

Cliff's wife Dorothy, Cliff and Millie Wille—on Vancouver Lake during the flood. The Diamond's home is in the background.

Millie & Isabelle ("Izy") Friar—Vanport Flood on Vancouver Lake—Millie's back yard.

Mille in doorway to Wille residence—May 30, 1948.

For more information about this event, see: http://en.wikipedia.org/wiki/Vanport_City,_Oregon

My father's firm, Cunningham and Associates, helped design Vanport. In his report to the government, Dad specifically stated that the railroad fill would not protect the city of Vanport from flooding. Since it was wartime, the warning was ignored. After the flood, it was a matter of warnings not being heeded and preparations not made for such an event.

It was basically understood at the time that all housing projects in the area were temporary, and would be dismantled once the war effort was complete. However, some people are still living in many of those temporary houses today, some 70 years later, mostly in The Heights, an area in Vancouver surrounding Mill Plain Blvd. that was replaced in part during the 1970's with new developments. On McLaughlin Blvd, running NW from Mill Plain to Grand Blvd., many of the old houses still linger, several times remodeled, but still recognizable by those who knew the housing styles from that era. Their outsides haven't changed much over the years, except for a new coat of paint, an occasional addition, or a bigger window for the front room. Somehow that street's homes defied the promise of "temporary", and became a permanent part of that neighborhood. It was the same for the Fruit Valley Neighborhood.

CHAPTER 6

MY MILLIE

I did not know Millie during the time of the flood in May, but met her in October of that year.

Here's what she wrote in her diary shortly after we met:

"Tuesday, Oct. 19, 1948—Went to school. At night, Marty came down with Jack Webber, Larry & Loyd (sic) Kessler. Had met Jack & Larry last Sunday. I went with Lloyd—Went to Castle. Got Mary Lewis for Larry.

"Friday, Oct. 22, 1948—This is homecoming week. Had planned to go to dance but went out with Loyd (sic) Kessler instead. Had an awful lot of fun! He's from around Milwaukie."

Millie in 1949—This is the picture that Lloyd still carries in his wallet.

In 1949, Rock'n'Roll hadn't yet been created, so we danced to the big band sounds of the late 40's, like Freddie Martin and Tommy Dorsey, and the pop songs of Doris Day, Bing Crosby, Dinah Shore, Spike Jones, Dick Haymes and The Andrew Sisters, Muddy Waters, Eddy Arnold, and, of course, Frank Sinatra.

Our peers watched movies like The Red Shoes, Treasure of the Sierra Madre, Twelve O'Clock High, Adam's Rib, with Spencer and Hepburn; All the King's Men; Batman and Robin; The Great Gatsby; Ma and Pa Kettle; On the Town; Abbot and Costello Meet Frankenstein, and Key Largo. (However, I must admit to having seen none of those movies to this day, except Twelve O'Clock High.)

Millie—with her 1937 Plymouth, which carried her to high school and home.

Millie's Parents—Bob and Inez Wille—1948.

Silly Millie Wille, the show-off.

My beauty—Just goofing around—1949.

Lloyd (who is bleary-eyed here), Millie, Marty and Irv—1949.

1949

In the meantime, after the Tap was completed in Vancouver in 1949, J-Party moved to Pasco, Washington, where we did surveys on four or five power lines, including North Richland, Priest Rapids, Ice Harbor and Kennewick. Most of the crews commuted to Portland on weekends, but after a couple of months, I stayed in Pasco most of the time, only going west occasionally.

During May of 1949, J-Party was transferred from Pasco to Arlington, and I commuted on weekends to Vancouver and Milwaukie to see Millie and friends. We wrote letters to each other weekly, and had a lot of fun doing that. Millie's letters are full of fun and frivolity. For instance, this one:

June 15, 1949—letter: "Boy, Mom bawled me out about sleeping on the couch!! I suppose you know that from now on we're to go right to bed. Only you go this way ← and I go this way → !"

We were very fond of each other by that point, and had a lot of fun writing back and forth. On weekends when I wasn't going to see her in Vancouver, I explored Eastern Washington and farther east.

These letters highlighted our courtship up until May of 1950, a couple of months before we were married. She then put them into a shoe box, where they remained unread for the next 62 years. It was only when Millie went to live at Highgate, a residence for Alzheimer's patients, in May of 2012, that I discovered them, and began this journey through my memory banks.

■ ■ ■

On June 6, 1949, Millie graduated from Vancouver High School, the only one in town at that point in time. (Today there are four.) Here is her Senior picture.

Mildred Wille—1949 Graduate.

Millie and Marty—Best friends—Seaside, Oregon—April, 1950.

Chapter 7

REVELATIONS

At one point during our courtship, I had mentioned that I didn't want to impose on Millie or her family. She quickly responded, "Don't you ever think you're imposing on us. I want someone here to eat my cooking!" The joke was that no one else would eat it!

During those early days of our courtship, I had buddies working for BPA in Sand Point, Idaho, I decided to go and visit them one windy day in March, 1949. I stopped in Spokane for the night, where nothing seemed to be "happening," so left the next morning to see my friends. There were 18 bars within 2 blocks there, and we did our best to drink 'em dry.

Coming and going.

The next day I decided to drive to Noxon, Montana, the nearest town to the border. In my next letter to Millie, I wrote "I have now been east."

She surprised me by saying "What do you think of MY Montana? I used to go hunting with my dad only 21 miles from Noxon. We have some relatives living there. I have a daughter living close to there, too. Let's see. She should be close to 4 years old now. (I know why you went east—just because Idaho and Montana are 'wet' states, aren't they?... not that that would make any difference to you.)"

I had never been to Montana before, and I ended up in the very place where Millie's daughter lived! What are the odds of THAT? To me, it was a fateful turn of events.

During this time I was working in Pasco, I was also chasing girls around, and prowling, like all good boys do, even while I was corresponding with Millie.

One weekend, I decided to go visit Millie in Vancouver. We went out and had a real good time. But when I returned to Pasco I discovered that I had received an unwelcome gift from an anonymous donor. My reward was a case of gonorrhea.

I wrote Millie in May of '49: "I tried to call you this morning, but I couldn't get through. I'm not sure how it happened but I soon will. I hope you did what I told you to. We moved to Arlington this week. Bye now, Love, Lloyd."

The news shocked her, of course, but she couldn't answer that letter. There was no return address on mine.

I wrote her again, and this time she answered to my then-current address, telling me that it would be a week or so before she could go for the test, but that she had read up on the subject and found that symptoms should show up within three days. And for her, none showed up.

As it happened, the night before I'd gone to Vancouver, I'd attended a western dance, or barn dance, and the girl I'd been dancing with followed me out to my car. The rest is easy to fill in, dear readers.

But the results surprised both Millie and me. I was ashamed of my behavior for being so reckless. Millie took it in stride. And I was cured of that behavior.

She wrote back to me on May 16th, "I know the girl in the doctor's office. It's going to be embarrassing. I hope she isn't there when I go in."

I, at the time, had my serious side, and this situation was very serious to me. I didn't see the humor in it then as I do now. In those days, it was mortifying for a young girl to have to explain to someone she knew (the receptionist) that she might have VD, much like it was embarrassing for a young man to buy condoms, particularly if the pharmacist knew him —or even worse, if you happened to know his daughter. Or, if you were a stranger in the community.

CHAPTER 8

CARS—THE ONES I LOVED

At the beginning of my junior year in high school, I purchased a 1932 Ford V/8 2-door sedan from a chiropractor. His office was in downtown Milwaukie. I met him when I was taking a physical exam required by my high school for sports participation. It was war time, and medical doctors were in short supply.

The car was in excellent condition, except for the engine. I took it to the trade school where I was learning auto mechanics, and spent most of my junior year overhauling the engine.

While the '32 was being overhauled, I discovered a 1937 Graham in a lady's yard, where it was sitting up on blocks. The lady's husband had gone to war. She never had liked the car, and it had become an "attractive nuisance." I revisited it soon.

I rode back and forth from Milwaukie High School to Camp Withycombe (the military base that had been partially converted to a trade school), with other classmates who were also taking classes in auto mechanics, machine shop, and welding.

It was wartime; gasoline was rationed, and so were tires. I had very little money.

Every car owner was issued gas ration stamps:

"A" stamps—for pleasure driving—each stamp was worth 2-5 gallons per week, depending upon the availability of gasoline.

"B" stamps—depending on the number of miles the vehicle had to travel back and forth to work each week—each stamp was good for 5 gallons.

"C" stamps—each stamp was good for 5 gallons, depending upon the number of miles the commercial vehicle drove each week.

"T" stamps—same as "C" stamps, but for trucks.

At the time, my family lived at 55th and Johnson Creek Blvd., in a moderately dense neighborhood. Gas stamps were a hot item on the black market. My brother and I rode our bikes around the area at night and stole gas stamps out of car glove-boxes. It was amazing how many people left their cars unlocked. We never took "A" stamps. We would take a few "B" stamps out of the ration book and leave the rest. We knew the people could get more if they were desperate.

I sold the stamps to my friends or classmates for $2 each. Some of these guys had part time jobs at the *Oregonian* and *Oregon Journal* newspapers. They would re-sell the tickets to the full time employees for four bucks each. This gave me enough money to pay for gas and admission for weekend ball games or movies.

As luck would have it, one of my buddy's girlfriends worked at the Ration Board in Oregon City. Her job was to tear the excess stamps out of the Rations Book. When we visited her, he talked to her as I retrieved the discarded stamps out of the waste paper basket and "recycled" them. Having stamps made me very popular.

One day in October of 1944, after second period, I was walking down the main hall in Milwaukie High School when a couple of wise guys yelled, "Hey, Kessler, ya got any gas stamps?" just as I was passing the principal, Mr. Byers. I wasn't sure Byers heard him, but my survival instincts lit up. I decided not to sell anymore stamps to anyone at school.

Soon after, I got a weekend job along with three or four of my classmates, cleaning passenger trains. I then had a new source of money. I did not sell any more stamps, but hid my stash in the attic of my bedroom closet. It was sort of a reserve—or insurance fund.

Many months later, WWII ended, and the next day rationing also ended. I committed the stamps to a bonfire. Fortunately for me, my folks never learned of this endeavor.

However, during the fall /winter of 1945, my friends, classmates and neighbors, Al Lucas and Chuck Clark, prowled around with me at night, stealing tires, wheels, tools and car parts, and anything we thought we needed. This included a set of red leather car seats. Most of this stuff was stored in my parent's garage, which was not attached to the house. Mother seldom looked into it.

One day, shortly after I got home from school, I was working on the '32 Ford in the driveway when the sheriff showed up. He was very pleasant, and we talked about my problem with the car. After a while, he asked to see the inside of the garage. I didn't argue, although I was a bit apprehensive. He asked me where I got the red leather seats. I told him I got them from a Graham, which was still up on blocks in a lady's yard. He also questioned me about the other loot, and asked me if I knew where my buddies Al Lucas and Chuck Clark were.

He said, "I'm going over to see if they are at Chuck's."

Just as he started to leave, Al and Chuck drove in. They knew what was up. The sheriff talked to all three of us, and upon conclusion, he said, "I want to see you guys tomorrow at 10 a.m. at the courthouse in Oregon City." And then he left.

Believe it or not, all three of us arrived the next day—on time. In fact, we rode together in Chuck's 1936 Ford, three-window coupe. When we got there, the sheriff and his deputy put me in one room, and Al and Chuck in another for questioning. They were able to get the information they wanted in such a way that I didn't have to rat on Al and Chuck and they didn't have to rat on me.

In conclusion, the deal was that I was to return the red leather seats to the Graham and apologize to the owner. I did so, and bought the car for $200. We were also to return the rest of the loot to the rightful owners. We did—well, most of it.

Al and Chuck's parents never found out about the caper. Nor did my dad. Al, Chuck and I remained friends for life. I've always suspected that the sheriff's best clue came from my mother.

What are the odds?

▪ ▪ ▪

My next sweet ride was the 1937 Graham Supercharger, a fast, heavy, 4-door Sedan with red leather upholstery (I was in high school, so don't judge me!). That made the girls leap into my lap when they hit that cold seat. Yes, it was the one I bought from the lady from whom the seats had been stolen, and subsequently returned by our deal with the sheriff.

▪ ▪ ▪

The third gem was a 1932 La Salle Touring Car, complete with an ice box built into the back of the front seat. It had a V-12 engine, with dual updraft carburetors and hydraulic brakes. It had black leather upholstery and locks on the steering column, dashboard and transmission. I bought it at a time during WWII when I could only buy 4 gallons of gas per week. I never had enough gas in the tank to get the car into high gear!

One late afternoon, a State cop chased me up River Road hill in Milwaukie. As I topped the hill, I ran out of gas and steered the car into the hazel brush to the right-hand side of the road. The cop went on by. I jumped out of the car and hid; the cop came back and forth a time or two. The next day, I sold the car to a woodcutter for fifty dollars. The last time I saw it, he had chopped it off behind the back of the front seat and it was carrying a load of wood. I had driven the car a total of maybe 20 miles!

■ ■ ■

My Dad also owned a 1937 Graham that he bought in 1941. In 1946, we lived at 55th and Johnson Creek Blvd., next to the street car track. Dad usually rode the (interurban) street car to work. One day he decided to drive the Graham to work. On the way home, he rear-ended another car and did severe damage to the front end of the Graham. He never did repair it.

A few days later, he borrowed *my* Graham. Again on the way home, he rear-ended another car and did extensive damage to the front end. I had the engine rebuilt and repaired the structural damage myself.

In September of 1946, I was driving to Corvallis to sign up for OSC, but when I reached Jefferson, I threw a rod. I left the car and hitchhiked the rest of the way and got in line with 7,000 other students to sign up for class. (The most OSC had enrolled before was 3,000.) Most of those signing up were veterans going to college on the GI Bill.

It was then time to retrieve the car. I called my brother Thane, and he got his friend John Sitton, who drove a beat-up 1935 Ford, to come and hook the tow rope onto the Graham. With me steering, we headed for home. We soon caught up to slow traffic. John stuck his arm out the window, gave a right turn signal, and passed a couple of cars on the right, which meant we were driving on the gravel shoulder. Scary, even if you're not towing another car. He did this several times. I felt lucky to survive the trip home!

As it turned out, the engine overhaul company had not cleaned the filings out of the crank shaft oil passages. Between 1946 and 1948, I spent a lot of time working on the Graham. In January of 1948, it was running well, and I sold it. But one day in 1953, I happened to be in Stanwood, Washington, and there was the Graham! I spoke to the owner, who said it was running well. I was pleased.

▪ ▪ ▪

Then came my 1932 Essex Terraplane. It was a beauty. It was powered by a newly rebuilt 1936 Hudson engine. I bought it from Jack Webber in 1948. Few of these coupes were built. I owned the only one I had ever seen.

1932 Essex Terraplane, purchased in 1948.

Lloyd 1949—with his Essex Terraplane.

After I painted it maroon and added a side mirror, I sold it back to Jack in February of 1949, and bought his 1940 Ford convertible, which I drove for six months. It was a great car, but I decided I wanted a new car. So I sold the '40 back to Jack in May of 1949, and started saving money for a new one.

1940 Ford convertible—sold to help buy an upgrade: a new 1949 Chevy convertible.

That left me afoot. In order to commute from Arlington to Vancouver and Milwaukie, I had to take the train or bus, or beg a ride with friends who happen to be going that direction. It was always a long trip; one time I was late getting to work because of it. Some weekends I didn't get back to Arlington until 10 or 15 minutes before work started. A couple of times I had to walk 8 or 10 miles.

Since foot travel wasn't so much fun, on October 1st, 1949, I bought a new Chevrolet convertible from Peterson Motors, the Chevrolet-Oldsmobile dealer in Arlington. Shortly after I bought it, Millie and I decided to go steady. It must have been the car!

Millie in the 1949 Chevy convertible.

But within a short time—one week—it was obvious that Millie didn't want to go steady anymore. It was cramping her style. She was having a lot of fun. She wasn't ready to marry and neither was I. Although I felt bad for a day or two, I soon got over the breakup and went back to Arlington to work. That was the worst I'd ever felt, and I made up my mind that I would never allow my feelings to be hurt over a girl again! So, as a result of that vow to myself, I spent even more time chasing girls and commuting to Milwaukie to see friends—or I traveled to Vancouver, B.C., where I partied on weekends with my friend Leonard Baumgartner.

At the time, I thought it was probably a good idea that we broke up. I doubt if our relationship would have worked out had we been married then.

However, my love affair with cars continues into the new millennium.

The Jaguar

On August 2, 1973, as Bob Rice, an underground contractor, and Mike Collins were returning from an eight-martini lunch, they spotted the Jag in the show room window of the Monte Shelton Dealership in Portland. Bob was enthralled, so Mike said, "If you have any balls, you'll buy it."

He did. On the spot. For $12,000. He put 42,000 miles on it over the next two years, driving to his widely-scattered job sites.

One night after getting plastered at the Gas Light Bar in Vancouver, he rear-ended another car at the intersection of 78th St. and Interstate 5. The bonnet and engine suffered severe damage that took many months to repair.

In the meantime, Bob fell on hard times and the IRS was breathing down his neck, so he hid the Jag at various friends' places over the next six years. One day in 1980, he said to me, "I have to move the Jag. Do you want to buy it?"

"How much?" I asked.

"$7,000" was his answer.

I told him that if it ran okay, I'd pay him $3500 then and the rest in 30 days.

It started right up, but ran roughly, so I said, "I will drive it to my shop to check it out." In my own mind I was sure what the problem was, so I reset the timing and it ran perfectly! Much to Bob's chagrin, the top had disappeared. But that was no big deal; I bought a new one for 500 bucks.

Once the new top was on, it was time for fun. Millie and I drove to Manzanita (Oregon coast) to visit our friends Lindy and Katy Albreci. We made a trip to Ocean Park, WA to visit Marty (Millie's best friend) and Al Carrol. Then we drove up the Columbia Gorge to Stevenson and Hood River. And, we showed off at my Milwaukie High School class reunion. Over that period (1980-1998), as I was working away from home, these trips only totaled about 4000 miles.

One evening in 1990, I was driving to Portland at 70 mph in the fast lane when the brakes locked up three miles south of the I-5 Bridge. Using full power, I was able pull to the right side of the freeway. The

1973 Jaguar XKE E Type—and Lloyd (2014 photo).

brake repair by a Jag specialty shop cost me $2000, but the brakes were not repaired. They still locked up.

The car sat in our shop until 1998, at which time I decided to repaint it the original factory blue, for which I budgeted $6000 .While shopping for blue paint at Full Spectrum Paint & Supply, I discovered Pearl Paint. Looking at the color samples, I decided that "Caribbean Mist" was the perfect color for the XKE, and suddenly all the body parts were disassembled and in the dip tank. By the time the car was ready to drive again, every part had been repainted, repaired or replaced: a 100% restoration, and much more. My original budget was only short one zero!

I enjoyed a show car with a paint job that could not be repaired. I did not dare park it anywhere that it could be scratched or marred. Not much fun. Millie and I did drive it to the Skamania Lodge (up the Gorge) once, and also to another high school reunion.

The brakes continued to lock up, so I took it to two different "Jag wizards" who claimed they road tested and cured the problem. Each time they locked up just a half mile after I left the shops. More money wasted.

Due to a freak accident caused during a job we were doing near his home, I became acquainted with Tony Briski, a brilliant engineer with many talents. He analyzed the brake lock-up problem and proved that the brakes as designed could lock up even if the brake pedal was not activated.

Tony's hobby is building race cars. In 2014, he has nearly finished manufacturing a Cobra, a British sports car with an American engine by Ford, produced intermittently since 1962.

Tony began his hobby some twenty years ago and keeps up with the latest technology. He went online, found a newly-invented "electric-over-hydraulic" brake system, and installed it on the Jag.

The car is now finally drivable—and that is just what I'm gonna do! I bought the car to have fun, and if it gets a ding or two it won't change its racy look. I can have fun being a show off—once again!

Once again, what are the odds of me finding Tony?

CHAPTER 9

MILLIE'S LIFE-CHANGING EVENT

After some time apart from Millie, I received a letter from her mother on Dec. 8, 1949. The bad news was that Millie had been in an auto accident near Monmouth, Oregon. Millie and Lyle Inman (Don's college roommate, Millie's blind date for the night); and Mary Lewis and her boyfriend Don Blakeslee, were returning in heavy fog from a basketball game in Albany. Lyle was driving; Millie was in the front passenger seat; Mary and Don occupied the rear seat.

The two-car, head-on crash left Millie with a cracked pelvis, fractured left hip socket, two missing front teeth, a cut on her lip, and two pretty shiners. The doctors didn't think she'd pull through, but she did.

We don't know the model and make of the car Millie was riding in. We do know that it was totaled.

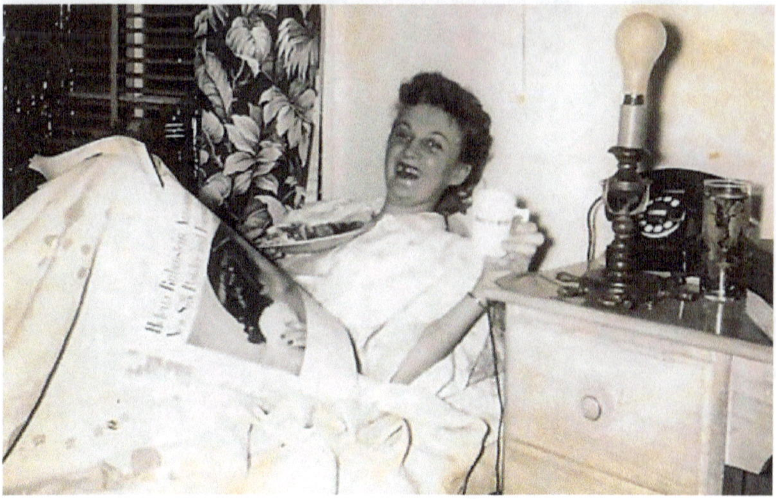

Millie after her accident—1949.

What are the odds of her living through that crash? All of our lives would have been changed by a worse outcome or had she died. She was lucky. And so were we.

CHAPTER 10

MARRIAGE

1949-1950 were two busy years for Millie and me.

This was taken on April 30th, just before we decided to get married. Never mind the banana. It was her attitude that interested me!

Lloyd and Millie walked down the aisle in St. Paul's Lutheran Church in Vancouver, WA. Saturday, June 24, 1950.

Driving away with a concrete block attached to our tail was unexpected. When we turned the first corner, it went flying into pieces, leaving the other "ornaments" still tied to the rear bumper.

We went on a honeymoon trip down the Oregon Coast into California along the Redwood Highway (Hwy 101). We spent one night at the Ben Bow Inn, a landmark that was then built like our modern motels, and where my parents took us as kids. We proceeded on to San Francisco, staying the night at the Mark Hopkins Hotel, where we went with Larry and Shirley Hein to the Merry-Go-Round Room. They had been married the week before and were honeymooning, too. Princess Fatima was the main attraction there...and her huge diamond ring cast awesome colors on the walls as the room rotated. We had a great time.

Millie in Northern California—Castle Crags Mts. in background.

From San Francisco, we drove to Fort Ord to visit my brother Thane. He was in Headquarters Company, in charge of payroll. His three-year enlistment was complete, and he was being liberated.

As he was standing in the discharge line, an officer stepped in front of him and said, "Everybody in front me is being discharged. Everyone behind me is going to Korea."

Thane thought quickly and said to the CO, "Wouldn't you prefer to discharge me since I'm in charge of issuing your check? You wouldn't want your pay delayed, would you?" The implication was for potentials "errors" to be made if he were not discharged then.

Thane left his Army days behind him at that moment.

We traveled from there to Las Vegas, Boulder City, Cameron, Arizona, the Grand Canyon, Zion Park, through the Nevada desert, and over Donner Pass.

We stopped at the site of the Donner Party's camp (with a little nostalgia on my part), and then traveled on to Mt. Lassen and back to Millie's folks' home in Vancouver, Washington. We traveled four thousand miles in all. Gas was 30 cents a gallon. We were gone 14 days for the trip, and it cost us about a thousand bucks. Memorable.

Alcatraz Island provided this background.

Me in a suit. THAT didn't happen very often!

At this time, I was working for BPA and was stationed in Enumclaw, Washington. Morrie Berry and I were renting an apartment there. The day after our wedding, Sunday, June 25, 1950, the Korean War was (not officially) declared. Morrie, who was in the Marine Reserve, was called up and sent to Korea. This made the apartment available to Millie and me.

CHAPTER 11

THE KESSLER'S—ALL FOR ONE AND ONE FOR ALL

Maxine Lynn's Arrival

On Feb 1, 1951, our first daughter was born at Enumclaw General Hospital. We named her Maxine Lynn Kessler. We resided in Enumclaw until April of that year. When our BPA survey crew was transferred to Kent, Washington, we moved into a cottage at Wilson's Resort, on the shores of Lake Meridian. Our marriage was going well. I was working all day and going to school a couple nights a week. That left Millie with a 4-1/2- month old daughter to talk to most of the time.

A Startling Announcement

One day in June, 1951, after I got home from work and after finishing dinner, Millie said, "Lloyd, a guy named Eric moved into the cottage next door today. He is divorced, unemployed and lonely." The fact that she told me at all was her signal that she wanted me to know they had "made love."

The resort cottages were next to each other and shared the same courtyard. The weather was sunny and warm, perfect for romance. He was about 30, unemployed, and recently divorced. Millie was a beautiful young woman of 19. I was 22. To this day, I cannot remember his name, features or his face.

Fate dealt me the hand to play. My job required teamwork and full concentration. My only resource was my paycheck. Millie and Maxine had to be cared for. In order for me to focus on my job, I put the affair to the back of my mind—where it remained for many years thereafter. I simply had to adjust to the situation and move on. I loved her, and we had a family to raise.

The Road to Anacortes

In July 20, 1951, J-Party was directed to Anacortes to establish and set up control for laying the first ever underwater high voltage transmission line. This "66KV" line extended BPA's northwest power grid from Sunset Beach on Fidalgo Island to a substation on Jones Island, a distance of about nine miles. From here, the underwater transmission line would connect to other more populated islands. We at J-Party were excited to be a part of this history-making event. It was a welcome break from our every-day surveying. BPA put us up in the Anacortes Hotel, which also acted as our temporary office. We spent a few days establishing control and rehearsing the cable-laying operation.

The night before the cable-laying, we celebrated in the Anacortes Hotel Sucia Reef Bar, named for the island about ten miles north of Anacortes which is shaped like an island in the Pacific Atolls. When we left the bar, Don Marx directed the hotel night clerk to wake us up at 6:30 a.m. I woke up a little early. (I always do when I've been drinking, because I'm afraid of over-sleeping and being late for work.) I ate my breakfast and headed to the boarding area. It was almost departure time, but there was no sign of Don or Murray Olds. I ran back to the hotel, woke them up, and hurried back to the boarding area, telling the superintendent that Don and Murray had been delayed, but would be there soon.

It was crucial that Don and Murray were aboard the cable-laying vessel to plot the actual final location of the cable.

The superintendent said, "We must sail now. I will have a fast boat taxi Don and Murray to the cable-laying vessel."

For the heads up, Don and Murray were ever-thankful to me, and the whole cable–laying operation went perfectly because they were on the job, and on time. It was a shining example of what cooperation and teamwork can do for the benefit of not only the job, but the relationships between crewmen.

I didn't know it then, but the Anacortes Hotel Bar was a harbinger of things to come. If only I hadn't been out drinking at the tavern...

Maxine was a beautiful child, especially to us, so during her first year we took LOTS of photos.

Maxine, at 5 months, learned to crawl in one hour chasing the live duckling. The duck wasn't so lucky. A weasel got him that night.

The tiny figure in the lower center is Maxine, quite content to be in the soft summer weather at our Lake Meridian cottage.

Maxine and Thane.

M & M's—at Lake Meridian.

Millie and Maxine at Fourth of July Parade, Lake Meridian, 1951.

In 1951, the Wilson Resort on Lake Meridian looked like this. The cottage we lived in is on the far left.

Maxine, five months old at Happy Hour.

My Uncle Lloyd and The Howler—This was Maxine's first vacation, June, 1951.

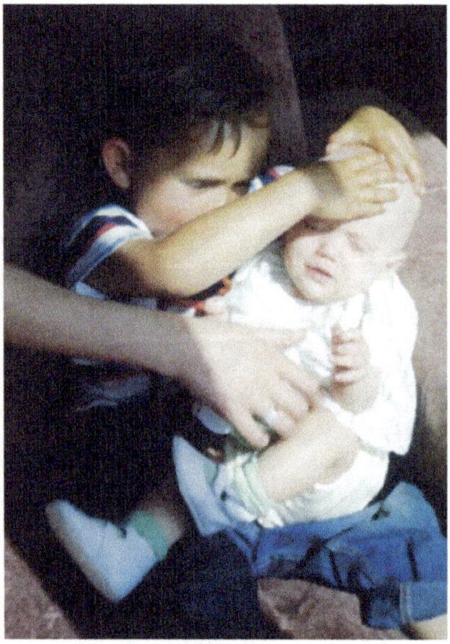

Uncle David baptizing Max.

Maxine in 1956 at home by Vancouver Lake.

1964—Chelan, WA—8th grade.

1965 Shumway Jr. Hi—Vancouver.

There's always something special about the first child born to a couple. And we welcomed Max (as she is fondly referred to these days) into that place in our lives, with joy.

Maxine was always a dynamo, and liked the boys from the time she was a freshman in high school. Although she connived, plotted and planned a lot of missed school-time during her junior and senior years, she still managed to keep decent grades, and graduated with her class.

She excelled as a gymnast (called "tumbler" in those days), and provided half-time entertainment at her school's basketball games.

After high school graduation, she worked at Tektronics, doing piecework with plastics until she developed allergies to the materials and needed to move on. Later on, she worked for me doing bookkeeping and office duties, but is now working for Sharp Electronics in management for the research division.

She is married to Rick Adams, and even with two grown children of their own, Amanda and Ricky, plus two siblings from Rick's former family, Joe and Jenny, Maxine maintains her role as the family organizer, and takes control of most of the gatherings we have at our home at the lake.

Amanda has two children, Adelaide Janell (Addie), and Elizabeth Lynn, our 6th great grandchild. Ricky's son is Elliott Michael. Each new addition is a welcome member to our family.

Karen Sandra

We think that Karen Sandra Kessler, born March 16, 1952, in Vancouver, Washington, at Memorial Hospital was (and is) a special addition to our family. She wasn't planned, like so many other happenings in my life, but she was welcomed with open arms and hearts.

1952

1953—Karen was determined!

1953, North Richland.
She rode a teeter-totter like a seasoned veteran!

A well-behaved child, she was! But if scolded, we would never see her cry. Not her. She defied the idea that anyone would see her vulnerable. Strong. Like her mother.

Although she was fond of gymnastics, she didn't excel, preferring to involve herself in the art world early on. The many wall hangings in our family home now are the result of her artistic interests and skills. She took training in pottery from the Archie Bray Foundation in Helena, Montana, and continues her artistic projects in painting and ceramics to this day.

There is one rather ironic memory that has stayed with me all these years: on Karen's wedding day, just as the pastor spoke of the difficulties the young couple may face in real life, there was heard a huge clap of thunder at that exact moment. No rain. Just that statement from the sky. It seemed so out of place, but was perhaps an omen of things to come.

Karen, Pastor Theodore Hartig, and Brian Surbert.

The marriage didn't last, but her son Collin came into the world, and he has since blessed Millie and me with three great grandchildren, Melanie, Aile, and Naomi.

Karen has remained a socially warm and open communicator, and now continues her private practice as a Shiatsu massage practitioner in Vancouver. Her warm sense of humor serves her well.

Of her art, she says:

"When I begin a piece of art, it usually stems from a story about my own life. When I am finished, the work is more about my emotional responses to the whole world. The figures in them are not people I know. They are often recurring entities from my dreams, and sometimes they will combine as a character with someone I know from the real world, or with myself. The finished work is not my own history, but a fiction I have created. I nearly always work figuratively, partly out of love for the human form, but mostly because of the added dimension that is created when the viewer decides what a figure thinks and feels.

When I make the initial contact with the paper, plate or canvas, I usually have a finished work in mind, but nothing is for sure. I make art because I love the interaction with the materials, the unplanned insights, and process of figuring things out.

My dance series is about what is joyful. I use dancing to maintain my sanity through the hard parts of life. Dancing doesn't take away the obstacles, but it helps me get around them more gracefully, and it reminds me of what it means to be joyful.

During my wildest illusions of grandeur, I feel that when I'm making art, I'm solving the problems of the world. During my most humble moments, I know that I'm just filling in space with colors."

Karen and son Collin—1972.

Douglas Lloyd

Although there are no pictures of Douglas Lloyd Kessler in his infancy, we did take many of him later on. He was born on September 10th, 1953, in North Richland, Washington. After two girls in the family, he was a welcome addition! But we men were still out-numbered with feminine counterparts, the opposite of my own upbringing. The ratio took some adjustment on my part, but I loved them all.

Mom and son Doug—1954—Vancouver.

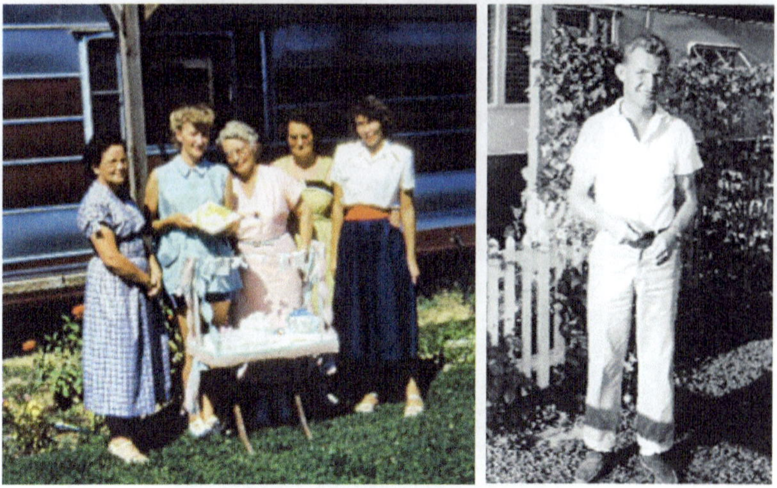

Neighbors gave Millie a baby shower for Doug's arrival in North Richland, and I looked like THIS!

1954, beside the trailer home in North Richland, among his abundant box of toys.

1954

Taken just 6 years later (1960), you can see the twinkle in Doug's eye as he sits with me, who is NOT paying attention to the clues those eyes portend!

From bridge-sitter to tree-hugger—1964—He was fearless about climbing.

Doug, as a boy, was like most others in that he was a rough and tumble sort of kid. His personality is laid back, much like mine, but he interacted with his sisters in a good way. If there were any tussles amongst them, they didn't last long. The kids seemed to like each other, a real bonus for busy parents.

Doug progressed through Cub Scouts into Boy Scouts, advancing nearly to Eagle Scout status by his high school years.

He and wife Beverly, a teacher, have two sons, Owen and Nicholas. Although he is still active in my business when new projects allow, he is also an art student again, taking classes at Pacific NW College of Arts. He and Karen have shared several art classes as colleagues over the years, but drawing nudes is his main interest in art at the moment.

One of the things I like best about him is his dry sense of humor, often demonstrating how nice it is to have at least ONE more male among the quartet of women making up this family!

Joanne Ruth

Baby pictures don't get much more endearing than these.

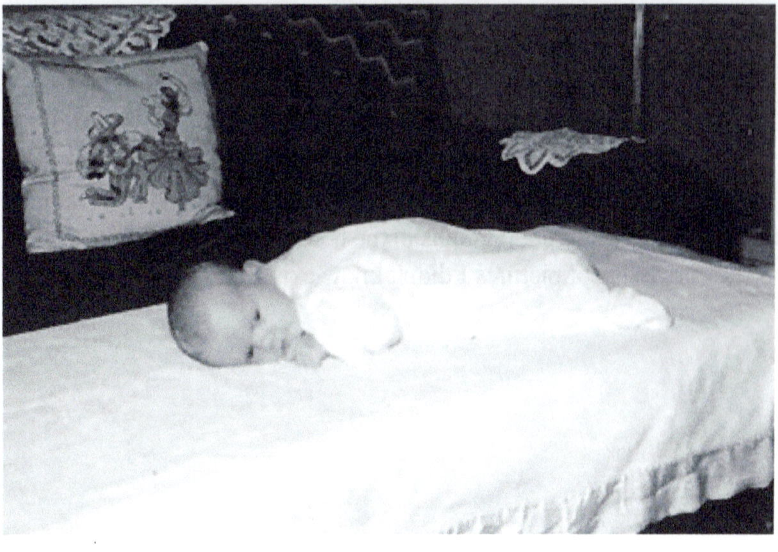

Then, about the age of five, when her front teeth begin to disappear to make room for bigger ones, she remembers this about her photo session:

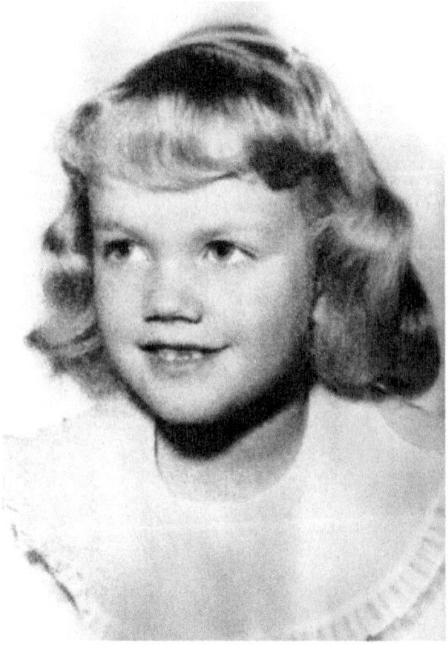

"I remember the day clearly. Mom took me to the City Center Motel on 6th and Broadway in downtown Vancouver, where a photographer had set up in a rented room. The dress was a pale lavender taffeta with white trim around the edge of the collar. I know I hadn't yet started kindergarten yet, which I did in the fall of '61."

She transformed into a beautiful young woman through her teens. There aren't as many photos of her in her childhood, for which there remains some regret by Millie and me, but she was always the same delight for us that the others were…and are. We did find these among the many stashes of photographs in the house, where many new discoveries were made of pictures I didn't know existed.

Chelan, Washington—1964, age 8.

With two daughters, Jill and Jana, and no grandchildren just yet, the youngest of our four children has the mellowest personality. She was almost never in trouble as a child, and easy to be around. She liked school and was a good student, so she didn't embrace her older sister's tricks for skipping classes. To this day, there's no drama when she's around.

1970, Age 14, Shumway Jr. High.

1973—Cheerleader—HBHS.

Joanne worked for The Columbian newspaper in Vancouver for decades, but now works as a sales associate for Audio Group, selling hearing aid advertisements and serving her customers well. She says this about her childhood:

"Growing up by the lake was an adventure. Our house was near the dead end; along the same street were the homes of our grandparents and great aunts and uncles. It was a wholesome existence, where a bike ride or a walk along the lake felt safe and free...except when being chased and barked at by the neighborhood dogs. Those brief moments struck terror into this little girl's heart.

Sunny days and rainy days were good for exploring outdoors. Walking along the shore, on a trail or the road, the smell of the cottonwood trees was always present, and June meant tufts of cotton blowing through the air, covering our yard with summer snow. There was always something to discover on those walks—a mud puddle, patch of stinging nettles, a fish skeleton, or a field of grasshoppers. I would imagine myself as a one-girl Corps of Discovery.

When I was younger I'd ride my blue bike as far as "the STOP sign," an intersection about a mile away, where our road connected with Fruit Valley Road. That was where our neighborhood ended and the rest of the world began. Later, I'd pedal on into Fruit Valley to visit my friends who lived "in town."

My time indoors was spent reading and sewing. Using the money earned from picking berries, the rest of the summer left plenty of time for sewing clothes. We girls made most of our outfits, taught how by Mom. She was quite a seamstress. She was also a busy chauffeur, and always got us to the library, church, swimming lessons, tumbling lessons and many extra-curricular activities.

One of my favorite memories of growing up by the lake was watching the sky and the water in the evenings. Rings would appear across the calm surface when catfish came up for bugs. The sun would drop behind the hills on the west side of the lake and turn the sky amazing colors. To this day, when I see a beautiful sunset, I'm transported back to my childhood and find myself thinking about Mom and Dad, and the house by the lake."

Each of our kids has his/her own talents and accomplishments these days. But in the 1950's, they were still blooming. We took many pictures to mark one occasion or another during those years. Like most other families of four kids, they had their ups and downs with each other, but mostly were in harmony with their siblings.

Maxine and Karen, riding double just outside our trailer house parked in North Richland, Washington, in 1953.

Maxine and Karen, 1954, on Grandma Wille's front porch.

Doug, Maxine, and Karen: "The pedals are too far away, Doug!" 1953—North Richland.

Karen, Maxine and Doug in our trailer home, 1954.

Those days everybody had a simple swing set.

Karen and Maxine—in their homemade dresses—1955.

Maxine, Doug, Karen and Fritzer, the dog—1956, at home at the lake.

San Diego Zoo—1958.

Christmas, 1959—Joanne, Millie and Doug's back. Maxine is behind Millie's elbow and Grandma Wille, also called "Grandma Wiggy," is standing to the right. Karen sits on center right.

Doug, Maxine, Karen and Joanne—1960—by the lake.

Doug, Joanne, Maxine and Karen—Circa 1961—at Grandma's house.

Grand Coulee Dam—1964.

Doug, Joanne, Karen, Maxine and Supercat—1965.

Karen, Maxine, Doug and Joanne—1969.

These are my children. I am proud of them.

CHAPTER 12

LESSONS LEARNED

On Being Productive

In Feb. 1952, I quit BPA and went to work for Pettijohn Engineering in Madras, Oregon, doing preliminary work on the Pelton and Round Butte Dam sites.

Millie, Maxine and I purchased a 35' house trailer and parked it at the best fishing spot on the scenic Deschutes River, about a mile upstream from the Warm Springs Bridge. The owner of the property, a Native American man named Chester See, along with his family, allowed us to live there rent-free because they liked helping young people. We became good friends. We lived there until June of 1952.

It's a beautiful site on the Deshutes River, and the fishing is good!

1952—8'x35' Kit House Trailer.
Millie holding Karen; Maxine is standing. June, 1952—we were parked next to the best fishing hole on the Deshutes.

Millie, Karen, and Maxine, 1952, taken the same time as the picture above.

In early June, I went to work for Millie's father, Bob Wille, who was superintendent for Lee Hoffman Construction. Hoffman was constructing concrete footings for BPA highline approach towers for the Columbia River highline crossing. The work was on the Portland side of the Columbia River known as Smith Lake. We developed a good working relationship, and over time, he taught me how to look ahead and how to make every movement count. We finished the job in half the time, with a crew half the size of that of another contractor building the same size project next to us. I had always wanted to work construction, so I was glad to have the chance to work with Millie's dad. Those lessons served me well in future years.

Millie's dad was a productive leader; Bob enjoyed top production from his men. He had been a hard-rock miner in Butte, Montana. Bob and his partner hold the record for the most tons of ore put out in one shift. His record stands today in the museum showcase of the Montana School of Mines.

After the Smith Lake project was completed in the fall of 1952, I went to work settings footings on a BPA highline over Lolo Pass for Charles T. Parker Company, near Zig Zag, Oregon. After winter shutdown, I began work settings footings for Montgomery Electric, near Enumclaw, Washington. The work was completed in February of 1953.

▪ ▪ ▪

Hanford

When my work for Montgomery Electric was completed, I applied for a job with Kaiser Engineers in North Richland, Washington. Kaiser had a firm-priced contract with the Atomic Energy Commission to build two atomic plants on the Hanford reservation in Eastern Washington. Dollar-wise, this was the largest contract ever awarded in the United States: $106 million. These two plants were known as 100KW (west) and 100KE (east).

I was hired as a Head Chainman and assigned to a layout crew run by Instrument Man Louie Olsen. We laid out roads and utilities that serviced the various building sites. Three weeks later, I was promoted to Instrument Man, handed a huge roll of blueprints, and assigned to a cooling water structure.

I hadn't had much experience with blueprints up until that time, but I was forced to read them. Learning to read the prints gave me the tools to do construction layout on heavy construction projects. This knowledge helped me throughout my career.

I was now running my own layout crew. Our job was to lay out the foundations concrete utilities and all embedded items for a huge square tank that would be used to cool water from the reactor. When forming was completed, we checked again to make certain that all forming was correctly done, and that all embedded items were correctly placed prior to the scheduled pour date.

AEC (Atomic Energy Commission) policy was that we were not supposed to talk about what our part of the whole project was. It was considered to be secret, but one day a prominent magazine showed a full-page color picture of the reactor and a description of how everything worked.

Kaiser Engineers were very well organized. They scheduled the work to ensure that all materials, equipment and craftsmen were available to meet the work schedule. In later years in the construction industry, this was called "Critical Path Scheduling". This type of scheduling often allowed the contractor to speed up the work, which advanced the completion time, which equaled more profits.

When I started contracting, I used the same method and consistently out-performed my competitors, giving me much larger profits than the average contractor. I use this method to this day.

■ ■ ■

About Unions

During the early days of the Kaiser project, wages for layout men were very low compared to the other crafts, all of which were union. As a result, the Technical Engineer & Architects Union got involved in organizing the Layout Engineers. This was a very long and tedious process that took a year or more. The business agent for the Technical Engineers was able to use the $3.00 per hour wage scale that was being paid to Instrument Men (the foremen of footing setting crews) as an argument to support prevailing wage rates.

This union agreement was finally agreed to in the latter part of the Kaiser project, late in 1953. And was paid retroactively to an earlier date. All the layout engineers received back pay checks. Some of the lower paid chainmen received as much as two thousand dollars. We also got travel time and paid holidays, sick leave, and vacation time.

Wage ranges	Before Union	After Union
Rear chainman	$65 (per week)	$105 (per week)
Head chainman	$85	$110
Instrument Man	$90	$120

The average 1953 wage was about $4,000 per year before the agreement, and $6,000 after.

Footing Setter Crew

Consists of:

- Foreman—No union affiliation, but paid prevailing wage (same as union) because of Taft-Hartley Act, which required it.
- Rodman—also called Chainman; Non-union until the Kaiser contract. Paid prevailing wage.
- Operating Engineer—Union member
- Laborers—two or three on a crew, depending upon needs—(Union)

The Footing Setter, or Layout Engineer, often referred to as the Engineer, was also the Foreman of the entire setting crew, and was paid the prevailing wage of the operating engineer. In 1953, this was $3.00 hr. The Rodman was paid the union labor scale, $2.50 per hr.

In the early 1950's, BPA had numerous transmission lines under construction in Washington State. Most were built by union contractors, and all were subject to certified payrolls. The information was public knowledge.

This agreement set the stage for more union contracts in the future, the next being the Bechtel job at the Anacortes oil refinery. The same type of negotiations went on the Bechtel job, but in a much shorter time frame. The precedent had already been set. We got good union wages for the job.

■ ■ ■

One day in May of 1954, I read in the Engineering News Record that Shell Oil Co. was getting ready to build a refinery in Anacortes, Washington. As the Kaiser project at Hanford was winding down, I decided to drive to Anacortes to see if I could get a job. When I arrived at the refinery site, there was no one there, but as I was walking around looking at the site, a car drove up.

The driver was the front man for Bechtel Corp. Bechtel was the general contractor for Shell Oil. He had been sent there by the project manager to recruit layout engineers for the project and to get started laying out the project boundaries and the proposed railroad that was to serve the refinery. His name was Witt Taft; we talked at length. I explained the Technical Engineers Union agreement with Kaiser in depth—that it was the first and only union agreement that had been signed to date in the State of Washington. The technical engineers union was now a bona fide union, recognized by the AFL (American Federation of Labor) and the NLRB (National Labor Relations Board).

Witt Taft replied, "Good. Bechtel operates as a union contractor and we want to have union layout crews on this project."

I told Witt that I knew most of the top quality layout men on the Kaiser project. Again, Witt said, "Good! You're hired! I want you to recruit enough men from Kaiser to man four 3-man crews. I will also need a fifth crew, but I will need to fit in a couple of my C.I.O.'s from Southern California. (C.I.O. stands for California-Improved Oakies.) I will pay the same scale that the Kaiser project is paying."

I agreed, and had just become the first one hired for the project.

Just as we finished our agreement, a station wagon drove up. The driver was the owner of a land surveying firm in Salem, Oregon. He was looking for work. Witt and I talked to him for a while. He was very well educated in civil engineering as well as surveying. Witt said, "I want to get started on the layout, but it will take a day or two to get the plans. You guys mind hanging around?"

We agreed to wait for the plans, which arrived the next day. Witt said, "Let's get started." All the necessary tools were in the station wagon. We started the preliminary layouts, starting with the railroad.

When the weekend rolled around, I returned to North Richland, hooked the '53 Ford to our trailer house, loaded Millie and the kids into the car, and towed the trailer to Anacortes.

This was the first time we had towed the trailer with the '53 Ford. It was equipped with overdrive, giving it six speeds forward. This made it easy to accelerate to cruising speed, and was good for climbing grades. It also allowed for going down grade under compression.

The trip went well. We parked in the City of Anacortes' trailer court. Our address was 1109—24th St., Lot 3.

A few weeks later, our friends from North Richland, Butch and Grace Ludke, parked to the right in Lot 2, and Earl and Mary Skow parked to the right of Ludke in Lot 1. The back door of our trailer was only a few steps away from a home in the City of Anacortes Housing Project.

We became very good friends with Kenny and Donna Childs, the family living there. They had two children a year or two older than our kids. Sometimes Donna would babysit our kids. Kenny operated a tender vessel for a local fish packing company. He was part Indian, was well known for his navigation skills, and he *did not drink*. He helped Earl and me find a specialized craftsman to caulk the Reinell, and a couple of times he took me with him on the tender. Donna was 24, the same age as Millie. Kenny was 34, and a WWII Air Force Veteran.

I also recalled that one morning Kenny gave Millie the center section of a huge King salmon he had caught just a couple of hours earlier. She baked it with a special recipe of tomatoes and spices. I had invited my friend Leonard Baumgartner for dinner that night, and when he arrived, he said to me, "Millie sure looks good." He had not seen her since before we were married.

He also said, "I hope we are not having salmon." Of course, I knew we were. We sat down to dinner and there was the huge salmon roast. Leonard took a bite or two to be polite. Then he took another one, and then another one. After an hour, we had devoured the entire roast. Leonard said to Millie, "That is the best meal I have ever eaten." After he left, Millie said to me, "I was HOPING to have salmon for a couple of more meals."

One night Millie had gone grocery shopping while I was watching the kids. I stepped outside the trailer just as Millie was walking the path from Kenny's house toward our trailer. When Millie saw me, she said, "Kenny asked me to buy him some oatmeal."

I asked her where the car was. She said, "I parked in Kenny's driveway. I do not want to walk in that mud puddle between the house and trailer." (The parking lot could not be seen from the trailer park.)

I asked, "Where are Donna and the kids?"

Millie replied, "They moved into Donna's parents' house to give full time care to Donna's ailing parents."

Kenny was a good navigator in more ways than one!

At the time, I had 20/20 vision—but was totally blind.

■ ■ ■

Anacortes

In May of 1954, the Shell Oil refinery job got off to good start, and all was going well. Earl and I bought an old 20-foot boat, a Reinell—powered by a 10-horse Wisconsin engine. We planned to use the boat for hunting and fishing. We did take a couple of overnight trips in the San Juan Islands in the summer of 1954, but didn't do a lot more with it.

By the end of summer, several hundred construction workers were employed at the refinery. The town was booming. After work, many headed to the Anacortes Hotel Tavern. These guys were making big bucks and drank hard. They would drink beer 'til closing. Every night.

After dinners with our families, Earl, Butch and I joined the parties at the tavern. It became a habit. Although we tried to break the habit by playing basketball, the drinking continued. Our wives were not pleased with any of us.

During this time, Millie took good care of me and our 3 children, a son—1 year, and daughters, 2 and 3. But because of my drinking, Millie and I weren't getting along very well. We were civil, but not acting as good friends. One day I brought home a Vargas Girl calendar. Millie got so mad that she insisted that I take her and the kids back to her mother's house in Vancouver.

Wounded, I went back to work in Anacortes. I prowled around for a week or so, and went out with one girl, but didn't have any fun. I did play strip poker with Earl, Butch, Grace and a few others, though. Innocent fun. Mary Skow and kids were in Tri-Cities. (That was probably a good thing. Mary was unhappy with Earl for the same reasons as Millie was with me.)

I was losing—and lost—my shorts in that game. I was a fair poker player. Hmmm. Grace insisted that I take them off. She actually called me "chicken"! But I refused. I was afraid that someone would blab and Millie would find out. (And those were the days before Facebook and Twitter!)

After a week or so, Millie and I made up. We spent a Saturday night at Timberline Lodge, and returned to Anacortes on Sunday. It was one of the memorable nights of my life. This was the first time we had been alone together since our honeymoon. It was a great mini-escape from the kids, even at Christmas time in 1954.

▪ ▪ ▪

Don Marx

In May of 1955, we moved to Umatilla, Oregon, where I went to work for Zuber Brothers, laying out a BPA switch yard. When my work was completed there, I was recruited by my former boss from BPA, Don Marx, to do a contract power line survey for BPA near Roseburg, Oregon.

Don had been my mentor for several years. He had worked for his father's surveying firm, gone into the military, and later on was employed by BPA. In 1949, he became Chief of J-Party. Don was a hands-on leader. He knew the days when he had to produce before he got paid!

We tied property corners to the main location line, or L-line, as well as the access road locations. He and I, as a two-man crew, could outwork many 3- and 4-man crews, even when we had to trek in three or four miles over rugged territory to our site, and then out again. He was ten years my senior. He liked the way I, as head chainman, chose the route. He showed me shortcuts, new techniques and a good work ethic. I learned much from his two years of tutelage.

CHAPTER 13

THE WRECK

By the end of July of 1955, the Roseburg job was completed. Don was hired by a different firm to do another BPA contract survey at Forest Grove, so we moved again, lock, stock, trailer and barrel.

The day after we finished the Roseburg job (a Saturday), we were towing the trailer house, to Forest Grove. We inadvertently got on a back road and were side-swiped by a logging truck. The truck took the driver's side mirror off the 1953 Ford, and tore a full-length panel from the side of the trailer.

The 1953 Ford Victoria that was towing our house trailer when wrecked. The 1939 Packard belonged to my dad. This photo was taken with my Argus C3 camera in 1959 at Long Beach, Washington, when we were visiting my Aunt Yvonne, who lived in Ilwaco, Washington.

The yellow-lined area shows the full length side panel that was ripped out.

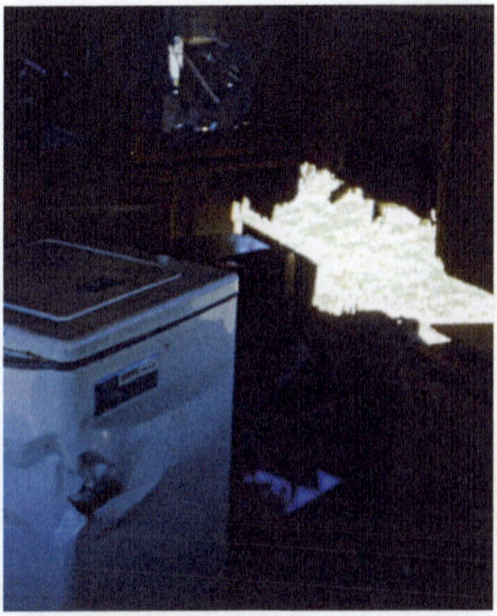

Washing machine shows damage done to the interior through the gash in the lower panel of the trailer.

All five of us had been riding in the car. Fortunately, no one was hurt.

We towed the trailer to Millie's folks' place. They lived near Vancouver Lake in Vancouver, Washington. Gratefully, we stayed with them; I commuted daily from Vancouver to the Forest Grove job.

The next day (Sunday), Millie's folks mentioned that there was a house for sale down the street. As Millie and I walked down the long driveway, I asked her if she wanted the house. She said, "I'd like to see the inside first!" I knew we were gonna buy it!

I had promised Millie that when the kids got ready for school, we'd settle in Vancouver. I had not planned on moving here until that very moment.

As it turned out, the trailer wreck gave me no cause to do any planning! After all, I hadn't done any SO far!

What are the odds of enduring the devastation of our trailer home one day, and finding the perfect home with the most beautiful view on the shore of Vancouver Lake the next day?

Chapter 14

1955-1967
PROJECTS AND MISERY

We finished the Forest Grove job in late 1955. Most of the crew was then hired by a firm from Seattle to do a BPA contract survey on a highline from Olympia to Aberdeen. We completed the project sometime in March of 1956.

I was again employed by Lee Hoffman, and worked for Millie's dad, Bob, on a fish ladder project on the Kalama River near the town of Kalama. That job was complete in mid-May of '56.

A few days later, the union called me to work for Bechtel Corporation on Swift Creek Dam, the same union contract I had helped negotiate when working on the Shell Refinery at Anacortes. The wage scale was very good.

Working there for three years, from May '56 to May of '59, I was exposed to all types of construction and crafts. We laid out earth work in tunnels, dams, concrete, generators, dikes, roads, and switch yards. Bechtel's management team was excellent, from project manager, project engineer, office engineer, chief of parties, right on down to the five survey crews. This helped prepare me for my future work as a general contractor. Management made the project very enjoyable.

When laying out the Swift Creek switch yard at Powerhouse #2, I did some side work for The Brandon Co., the contractor doing the site work on the switchyard.

■ ■ ■

May, 1959. After the dam project was done I didn't work for six weeks, and drew unemployment...the first and only time in my career. There simply was no work available.

After that period I again returned to the work force, beginning with land surveying with Don Marx around Gresham and Beaverton until the fall of '59. From there I was employed by L.H. Hoffman Construction to lay out and construct a new paper machine at the Georgia Pacific Paper

Mill in Toledo, Oregon, working there until the project was completed in May of '60. I then went to work for Lee Hoffman Construction (not to be confused with L.H. Hoffman) as a laborer for about a month (a fill-in job for me) on a sewer line project in Oak Grove, Oregon. (Millie's dad was the superintendent on that job.) These were interesting projects and paid very well.

The next month I went to work for The Brandon Company, setting footings on a highline between Ellensburg and Wenatchee. The Brandon Company was owned by long-time power line contractor, Red Brandon, and his sons. They were headquartered in Red's home at the north end of Lincoln Ave., about a mile from where I live here in Vancouver. They had a subcontract for the tower footing portion of this contract. I was glad because Red had a reputation for fair play. His word was his bond.

His son Jerry was in his twenties and still learning. During this job, they sometimes rode with me from Vancouver to Ellensburg on Sunday evenings. We stayed in the same hotel.

The company staging area was at the Ellensburg airport. To get to the job we had to drive ten to twenty miles on gut-shaking, ball-busting, BPA service roads.

The footings I was setting were known as "rock anchors". This required drilling a four-inch hole into rock. The hole had to be drilled to a precise angle line and grade. Our main tool was an air-driven wagon drill, which had to be precisely set up. This was a hard and tedious process, and required a crew of five or more men. Most of our crew were miners who had worked in the Roslyn coal mines. Nothing was too tough for them.

Jerry had also hired two cement finishers whose job was to grout the anchors. They mixed the grout in a small portable cement mixer. This required hauling a 50-gallon drum of water in the crew truck each day. Most of it was used to clean the mixer.

The finishers were a pain in the ass, and were always in the way. When I picked them up at the restaurant (tavern) in the morning, they would just be finishing a glass of warm loganberry wine. After a couple of weeks of this, I got mad one day and shoved the cement mixer over the bluff. It so happened that Jerry came by and saw it. He was very angry at me, but before the day was over, he had canned the two finishers. Our production increased drastically, and from then on the project went very well. I don't know if Jerry ever forgot about his precious cement mixer.

We finished the project early, and both Brandon and I made money. Our work was completed in October of 1960.

For the following ten months, until August, 1961, I worked for various contractors, including Morrison-Knudsen, doing layout work on the Wanapum Dam on the Columbia River near Vantage, Washington, and L.H. Hoffman, on paper machines jobs in Camas and Longview, Washington, and West Linn, Oregon.

The paper machines were "shut-down" jobs (the machines were shut down while we rebuilt them, so we worked seven twelve-hour shifts per week. All work over forty hours was double time, creating fat paychecks!

▪ ▪ ▪

Millie's miscarriage

While working swing shift one night in February, 1961, for Morris/Knudsen on the Wanapum Dam project, my boss, Clyde Olmstead, said, "Kessler, head for home. I will finish up." Clyde had a great rapport with the night superintendent, and would often let us leave early as long as there was no more work to do, yet pay us for the full shift. So at 9 that night, I headed for home. Normally, I would have stopped in Sunnyside, had a couple of drinks and eaten dinner. This night, however, my instincts told me to get home...FAST.

When I got home, I knocked on the back door. Millie opened it and promptly collapsed into my arms. She had just experienced a miscarriage, losing a lot of blood in the process. I scooped her up into my arms and hauled her to Vancouver Memorial Hospital, where they replenished her blood supply. Millie was scared, but stayed stoic and matter-of-fact during the ordeal. No hysterics for this strong woman.

It made me wonder what might have happened had I arrived much later—at the normal time. I was grateful that I had listened to that intuitive voice that told me to get home in a hurry.

What are the odds of me "knowing" that something wasn't right at home?

My Pilot Experience

I had always wanted to fly. I began my training in 1960, but didn't get my license until 1964 because I was working in several different locations and just couldn't make the time and money conform to a schedule that allowed me to go straight through flight training.

Over the years from 1960 to 1989, I owned two different aircraft: a 65 hp Taylor Craft side-by-side, a 1945 model that I refurbished myself; and later, a 1974 Cessna 185.

The Taylor Craft had a high-time engine that was about run out. The air frame was solid, but needed T.L.C. I gave the engine a major overhaul and completely renovated the air frame. The work took many weekends and evenings for about a year, but once completed, I had a brand new bird! This also allowed me to log more training hours as I flew myself back and forth from Madras, Oregon, to Vancouver on weekends while I was working on the Round Butte Dam—when the weather cooperated.

Taylor Craft 95604 & 1953 Ford Victoria at Chelan airport, 1964.

Unfortunately, this aircraft was totaled out in a wreck when the tie-down cables failed at Pearson Airport during a severe wind storm in 1965. This was sad because these same cables held tight during the Columbus Day storm of 1962, which wreaked havoc on many secured planes.

After the wreck, I did not fly much until 1982, when I purchased the Cessna 185 from fellow contractor Ron McCain for $32,000 cash.

My Cessna 185-1042F at Madras Airport.

Shortly thereafter, in the summer of 1982, I partnered with McCain to do a large US Forest Service project at the world's largest logging camp in Thorne Bay, Alaska. The job was accessible only by boat or float plane, and Ron wanted to put amphibious floats on the 185, but I vetoed the idea. This turned out to be a wise decision. It was much more cost-effective to use the local air services, which were based in Ketchikan. Not only did they deliver the daily mail, but they were in and out of Thorne Bay four times a day.

We finished the Thorne Bay project in May of 1983. I was then able to use the 185 to fly around the northwest in search of new jobs.

In the late summer of 1983, we bid, and were awarded, a US Forest Service contract to build tree coolers at 15 sites in Idaho and Montana.

The 185 proved to be very useful in transporting our personnel to and from our base in Vancouver. It was also very beneficial in transporting parts and equipment to the remote areas where we were working. The 185 gave our company an added dimension, which made us much more diverse, and as a consequence, increased our profits.

This Cessna 185 came from the factory equipped with amphibious landing gear. Sometime before McCain purchased it, the landing gear had been damaged. The plane had been sitting near the water, and had not been flown for a long time. Due to inactivity, water accumulated in the fuel. When the owner did decide to fly it, he did not check for water in the gas, so when he took off, the engine quit, causing the plane to make a hard landing, severely damaging the landing gear.

A decision was then made to equip the aircraft with wheels only. It was also decided to equip the plane with Robinson® Short Take-Off and Landing equipment. STOL is an aftermarket procedure that is not endorsed by the Cessna Aircraft Corp. STOL requires modification to the aircraft as further explained: Conventional 185's come from the factory with three notches of mechanical flaps. STOL requires an additional notch. This fourth notch mandates the flap lever to move further toward the rear of the plane. This extra distance places the lever in an awkward and difficult position for the pilot to manipulate.

After May of 1983, once I was flying on a regular basis, it became evident that the aircraft was not trimming out properly. It was time for its annual inspection, and I had the A&E (aircraft and engine specialist licensed to test the annual requirements) address the trim problem. Once the annual was complete, I flew the plane and found the trim better, but still not right. My instincts told me not to fly the plane. "If something's not right, then something must be wrong," I often said, after learning lessons from long ago.

However, I had Don Hall, a trusted and very thorough A&E redo the annual. Up until this time, Don had been trained by his father, who was a highly respected A&E. Don discovered that when the STOL kit had been installed, the control cables to the rudder (controls right and left motion of the plane), and the aerolons (controls up and down motion) had been improperly installed. They had been connected by two cable clamps that did not meet regulations. One of the clamps had already failed. The other clamp could have failed at any time, causing the plane to crash. However, Don completely replaced and re-rigged the cables, and as a result, the plane trimmed out perfectly.

More projects

During the middle five months of 1961, I again worked a short time for The Brandon Co. on another BPA highline between Ellensburg and Wenatchee, Washington. Brandon joint-ventured this project with the prime contractor that he had been doing footings for during the previous season. Jerry Brandon had learned a lot under Red's and my tutoring. I also learned a lot about production that would help me later on.

The job started out very well, but one Monday after about three weeks, I informed Jerry that I had to take the Friday-after-next off. He replied, "We have to get this job done."

The next Monday or Tuesday, the scenario was repeated. I made it clear to Jerry that I was taking Friday off. Jerry's mind was on other business. As I was the foreman and layout man, there wasn't much the crew could do when I was not there. However, I set things up with the crew so they would be able to keep busy on Friday.

I was scheduled to have a vasectomy at 6 a.m. Friday morning. Due to emergencies, the staff kept me gowed up (anesthetized) until noon, at which time they performed the operation.

Feeling good, instead of going home as advised, I went flying in my Taylorcraft. As it turned out, this put stress on the incision. The next morning it had not healed properly and started bleeding.

When Monday morning rolled around, I decided to fly to Ellensburg. (I was fearful of driving all the way and rattling around in a hard-riding 4-wheel-drive to the job site.)

As I was landing at the Ellensburg airport, I could see the crew leaving the staging area. There was no way I could communicate with Jerry or the crew.

As the day was lost, I decided to fly to Madras, Oregon. I had heard that the Bechtel team that I had worked with at Swift Creek Dam was getting ready to start the Round Butte Dam. Bill Anderson, my boss, Chief of Parties at Swift Creek, was setting up a temporary office in Madras.

He said, "Kess, we won't be starting for about a month, but I would like you to line up enough union men from Swift Creek for two crews."

I flew home to Vancouver.

That night, Red Brandon called and asked me if I was coming back to work. I replied, "No, my condition won't allow me." I felt I had let him down. It's not easy to find a footing setter on a moment's notice.

Red retired soon after that. Jerry went on to be the top highline constructor in the country. He made a fortune.

A few days later, L.H. Hoffman called me to do another shut-down job in Camas. That took about a month. I then went to work for Bechtel at Round Butte. I worked there for another two years.

At that point, the union called and sent my crew to work for Paul Hardiman Corporation on the Green Peter Dam near Sweet Home, Oregon. Hardiman was Richard Nixon's brother-in-law. This was the first hard-money contract they had been awarded. Most of their previous work was cost-plus, mostly on missile silos. In my opinion, they were not cost effective. They had people in the parking lot directing traffic.

Again, in my opinion, their Chief of Parties, who was a Canadian, didn't understand construction layout, and had poor people-skills; nor did he understand the union contract. Due to hot weather and fire danger, we started work at 6 a.m. At 10 a.m., my crew stopped for lunch and laid back for a few minutes, trying to recover from last night's booze.

He walked up one morning and said, "What are you doing?"

I replied, "Taking our lunch break."

He said, "It's not noon."

I replied, "The union contract says it is. If you want us to work through this period, you have to pay us time-and-a-half."

At the end of the week, he and I parted company. The rest of my crew stayed awhile longer, but they jumped at the first opportunity.

A couple of weeks later, in September of 1963, the union called and sent me and Doc Jones, who was on my crew at Green Peter, to work for Bechtel Corporation on the Wells Dam on the Columbia River near Pateros, Washington. This was supposed to be a three-year-six-day-a-week job. Basically, or so we thought, it was like Swift Creek and Round Butte Dams. The crew consisted of Louie Olson, Instrument Man; Doc Jones, Head Chainman; and Johnny Cloud, Head Chainman, and me, Instrument Man.

This job was called a hydro-combine. The dam power house and switch yard were in a single structure. This innovation shortened the average construction time for a dam by a year or two. We worked for the Engineer, and our job was to measure quantities, check alignment and controls, and check the prime contractor's lines and grades.

A month or so into the job, I decided to move Millie and the kids to Chelan. We rented a diamond-shaped vacation home on the north shore of Lake Chelan, about three miles from the City of Chelan's center. To reach the house, we had to drive through a long-established apple orchard owned by the Dodie Family. He and his wife had children about the same school age as ours. The road to the house was very steep. When it snowed, we had to park a long way from the house. This meant having to carry groceries and supplies up or down a steep trail.

Another problem was that the main heat source was in the daylight basement where the four bedrooms were. The only way to heat the living area was to build a fire in the Danish fireplace. This meant keeping a constant fire burning during waking hours.

The good part of living there was that we were only a ten or twelve-minute drive to the local ski area. We joined the ski club, and were able to outfit the four kids for a total of $120. The ski toll fees were a dollar a day for adults and 50 cents for children, a total of four dollars for our family. There was skiing two nights a week and on Saturday and Sunday.

One Saturday, late in the ski season, the truck rear end that powered the ski tow overheated, boiling the #90 oil out of the differential. That meant shutting the tow down until it cooled off. After this happened a few times, one of the members walked up and said, "I think maybe I can cure this." He dumped two bottles of STP into the differential. This cooled the oil down so that it did not overheat for the rest of the season.

This same day, after the tow started up, my son Doug came flying down the mountain on his skis, shushed into the end of the tow waiting line with such force that he broke the tibia in his right leg. The pop the break made sounded like a pistol shot. We hauled him to the hospital and put his leg in a cast, which ended his ski season. The rest of us continued to ski and had a whole lot of fun that winter, in spite of Doug's calamity.

When the ski season was over, Millie got fed up with the house on the lake and rented a house in town. This made us neighbors with some of our survey friends, and put us within walking distance to schools, stores, bowling alley and bars. Living in town made life a lot more fun.

Bechtel Corporation only had one survey crew. Our boss, Chief of Party's name was Arnie Comber. His survey knowledge was somewhat limited. His wife and the project manager were very good friends, (probably) a big factor in why Arnie was working there.

The first few months of the job we were very busy doing the project layout of railroads, roads, dry land excavation. We worked very closely with the prime contractor's survey crews. We also did the layout for the first phase of the Coffer Dams. Once they were in place, we measured the rock that needed to be excavated to reach foundation sub-grade. Same thing for the dry land excavation. All went well. There was a push to get this work done, a portion of which the prime contractor had to complete by a pre-determined date in order to collect a million-and-a-half dollar mobilization bonus. The contractor beat the date.

Sometime later, Arnie got the notion that the contractor was being paid way too much for the rock excavation. The contractor had bid the job based on the original core samples taken prior to the contract solicitation. The contractor, also known as the "risk-taker," bases his costs on information provided. If there had been less rock, his costs per unit would have been more. Arnie told our crew and me, the recorder, to show the rock two feet lower than it actually was. I did as I had always done: I recorded the rod shots as they were called out. This meant the earth contractor (Degerstrom, Kuney and Crick) got paid for the units to which he was entitled. Degerstrom had a bonanza, but he had gotten to sub-grade ahead of schedule. This speeded up the project and was a small part of the project's overall cost. All parties, including Bechtel, retained their integrity, and Arnie never knew the difference.

Near the end of the first year, Bechtel threw a party for their employees. Our survey crew and their wives were sitting at a table when the project manager, Ed Draeger, asked Doc Jones' wife Donna to dance. Donna replied, "Ask Millie to dance." He turned and walked back to his table.

Millie said to me, "I sure didn't want to dance with *him*."

This incident cast a gloom over the party. It couldn't end soon enough for our group. This was reminiscent of a couple of parties that

Bechtel cast for us back when we were working at Swift Creek Dam.

One day in October, Ed Draeger got mad at our survey crew and laid us all off. During World Series, no less! That was a bittersweet moment for all of us. Could it have been because of what happened at the party?

Louie Olson and Doc Jones went to work on missile silos in Montana. Johnny Cloud went back to the Tri-Cities.

Bechtel hired two survey crews to take our place. A few months later, one of Bechtel's inspectors told me, "These guys had to have their hands held all the time."

I took a job for Munson-Nash, who was doing the flow-line boundary work for the dam and the relocation of the town of Pateros. The office was there. The wages were poor, and in my opinion, so was the company. We accomplished very little for each day's work. What it did was to keep bread on our table that winter.

■ ■ ■

Mossy Rock Dam

In February of 1965, I went to work for Dravo Corporation on the Mossy Rock Dam near Mossy Rock, Washington. This was a very good job. We had two four-man survey crews. I was the Party Chief of one crew. My Head Chainman, Kenny Cave, and I stayed in Mossy Rock, commuting home on Wednesdays and weekends. Quite often after our shift ended, we were called to the job to set a point or explain a layout to a foreman. For this, we were paid four hours at time-and-a-half, plus a day's travel pay. We often worked six days a week, and sometimes seven.

The dam itself was a double arch concrete structure. When the contractor bid the job, he had planned on having four survey crews, and forty office engineers to calculate the dam's control points. Because of the dam's unique configuration, there were no two points on the same line or grade. Because of this, it took many hours to calculate a single control point. My boss, Carl Pharis, and I spent two days calculating one point. When we got done, Carl said, "There's only one problem; we don't know if we're right."

At this time, Tudor Engineering, a renowned engineering firm from San Francisco, offered to calculate all the control points for the dam, for a total of $8,000. They had just completed a computer program and were anxious to show it off. Dravo accepted the offer. This meant that Dravo only needed four instead of forty office engineers, and also eliminated the need for two of the four survey parties.

Lloyd, Party chief; Tony Hirt, Instrument Man; Johnny Wise, Head Chainman; John Concannon, Head Chainman.

The job went very well, and kept two survey parties very busy for most of the next three years. In addition to the dam, there were also tunnels, roads and bridges, which made the job even more interesting. After three years, the project was nearing completion. Again we continued to learn and move forward.

CHAPTER 15

1968-1970
FROM WAGES TO OWNERSHIP

Sometime in September 1968, I stopped at the Mossyrock tavern after work as I always did. The bartender, Barbara, introduced me to her sister Betty who had come from Centralia to visit. Barbara explained to me that Betty was ill, and asked me if I would take her home. I did, and a few days later she was back at the tavern. I took her to bed. She became a pest. She would call the job site. This didn't go over well with management, and it became a joke for everyone but me. Fortunately, she didn't know where I lived.

One day, Pee Wee Boyd, my boss, was driving past. I waved him down.

I said, "Pee Wee, cash me out."

He said, "Who are you mad at now?"

I said, "Nobody. I've been doing this for 22 years, and I can't stand it any longer."

He said, "Okay," and cashed me out the next day (Friday).

I went home to Vancouver and tried to figure out my next move.

A couple of weeks after I got home, the phone rang in the breakfast nook while the family was having dinner. It was Betty. My Head Chainman from Mossy Rock, John Concannon, had told her I lived in Vancouver with my father. I stammered and got her off the phone. Millie didn't look very pleased. When dinner was over and the kids had gone upstairs, I tried to wiggle my way out of it.

Millie said, "She called me last night and told me that she had jumped in bed with you a few times."

The next day, Millie told me that she and the kids had taken a vote; they decided to keep me.

In 1964, I had built an addition onto our house, just before I went to work on the Wells Dam. The addition was complete except for the flooring. A friend of mine told me that he was working for a company that installed Torginal seamless floors. I looked at some of the work that he had done and liked what I saw, so I installed them in the addition. They turned out very well, so I asked the installer, Bill Deschner, if he could teach me the trade. He suggested that I buy a Torginal dealership and attend their training school for the product. I did and we began working together.

Torginal Seamless Flooring was a liquid applied material; a complete application took two and a half days.

The school taught us how to keep a job card, cost our materials and track our profit. It was a very good system. I started out by helping Bill. Then I travelled around the county on weekends when I wasn't working, looking at houses that were under construction, and getting acquainted with the owners. I even sold them floors on occasion.

In order to finance this operation, I took out a loan on my house, which was paid for, in the amount of $17,000. That first year, we ate a lot of beans. I also had a CPA set up my business. He figured out how I could pay every conceivable tax ever generated on labor, materials and equipment. I had paid my 1968 federal taxes. The second year I started making money, according to my CPA. I had a large tax bill, but I didn't have any money to pay it, so I didn't do anything. At the end of the second year, I became severely allergic to the cyanide that was in the floor glaze, so I knew I had to get out of that business. I turned my contracts over to Bill to complete. Bill died of cancer a few years later.

■ ■ ■

In the summer of 1970, I saw an ad in the paper for a US Forest Service trail maintenance job. It was 50 miles of trails near Carson, Washington. So my son and I went and looked at a portion of the job. We saw the easy part. I was low bidder. The contract amount was $3,000. My son and daughter, my father-in-law and I did the work. I paid the withholding taxes on my son and daughter, who made $500 each. I paid my father-in-law $1,000 and paid myself $1,000.

In early 1971, I bid two more trail maintenance jobs, and was low bidder on both. One (a total of 200 miles) was in the proximity of Mineral, Morton, Randall, Packwood and The Pacific Crest Trail in the

Goat Rock Wilderness Area, all within the Gifford Pinchot National Forest area of Washington. The other (a total of 50 miles) was in the vicinity of the upper Lewis River and Quartz Creek.

■ ■ ■

Sonny and Me

When this season's trail works started in May of 1971, Millie's dad said to me, "You need to get a horse," so I started looking for one. I read in The Columbian about one for sale for a hundred bucks, and went to look at him. He was owned by the daughter of a logger. She was about 18 and had raised the horse from the time he was a colt. His name was Sonny, a blaze-faced Arabian gelding. She had ridden him in competition, but was now off to college. Her dad, owner of Wilson and Sutton Logging Company, had just built a new house atop a unique knob a few miles up the Lewis River from Woodland overlooking Lake Merwin, and did not want to take care of a horse. He told me he had used Sonny a few times to hunt deer and elk. He also told me that he was hard to load into a truck, and that he and his hunting buddies had to "persuade" him. However, he said his daughter never had any trouble loading Sonny into her trailer.

Wilson was a friendly guy. I drank with him and his crew a few times at a Woodland bar. He loved to play high stake poker with the local gamblers.

I paid the hundred bucks and his daughter loaded Sonny into the trailer. No problems. My lessons in the cost of owning a horse had begun. Horse: $100; trailer: $1,000; saddle: $400: all kinds of advice from horse experts: free. First advice: you need to get an A-frame pack saddle.

So I did, along with two pack saddle bags. It was important to load the bags so that each side weighed the same. If one side was heavier, the bag would slide down the side of the horse and trouble would begin. After my first venture with Sonny and the pack saddle, I got educated.

During the first season with Sonny, this is what I learned:

1. Never tie him high or short, whether in the horse trailer or the field.
2. Never tie him with half hitches.
3. Use a halter when riding him; never use reins or bridle.
4. Make sure no one is behind him when loading him into the horse trailer. Otherwise, he will not go in.
5. Tie him to a tree in the field; do not tie him to a log.
6. Use a long line—50 feet is okay.
7. When he looks like he is a tangled up in the rope, stay away. When he sees food he will untangle himself, nod his head and nicker. ("See how smart I am," he seems to be saying.)
8. Mounting left side, right side, over the end—Sonny doesn't care.
9. Always allow him to talk to any other horse you meet on the trail.

Sonny, ready to pack out.

When we started the Lewis River trail, the crew and I began on the upper end. The first morning, we worked our way in three miles, where we came to a blow-down (ten or twelve logs all intertwined across the trail). I realized that it would take me a couple of days to saw them out. We had packed our sleeping bags and enough food to last for two days onto Sonny.

This trail was ten miles long, and the work should have taken two days or less. In order to maintain progress, Doug and Karen had already gone ahead. I decided to lead Sonny around the blow-down, which meant that I had to lead him a considerable distance out through the brush to get him past it.

As I was coming back on the trail, something spooked him. He broke away and ran down the trail. Stuff was flying out of the pack bags as he disappeared around the curves. Problem: I had no way to know how far the crew was down the trail—or whether or not they would walk back for lunch (unlikely). I decided to walk the three miles back to the trail head, and take the pickup/horse trailer to the downstream trail head.

When I arrived, neither Sonny nor the crew was there. By now, it was late afternoon. I walked in about a mile and met the crew coming out. They had not seen Sonny. We drove to Cougar and spent the night at the motel.

The next morning we drove to the trail head. No sign of Sonny, but his hoof marks were on the trail and it was obvious that he had come to the trail head and then gone back up the trail. I told the kids to walk back to the blow-down and watch for him. I drove back to the upper trail head and walked into the blow-down. There was Sonny, munching grass, the pack saddle hanging under his belly – empty. He was happy to see me. I removed the saddle as he continued eating. I started logging out (removing the logs that were across the trail).

A few hours later, Doug and Karen arrived with the sleeping bags and a couple of cans of tuna fish. The only other sign of food was a couple of bread wrappers. Sonny had eaten everything else. It was time to improvise.

I went to a tentmaker and had him make a pair of bags that would fit over a western saddle. I instructed him that I wanted the lower part of the bag covered with leather to protect them when rubbing against trees.

I also had him make a leather chainsaw scabbard that could be attached to the bags. The inside of this scabbard was to be made of sheet metal to protect the leather from the saw's teeth.

These new bags worked very well (to hell with the "experts"), and also allowed me to ride on the horse when going from one log to the next. I could fit any tool I needed, such as a rock drill, into the bags.

It was fun to see the baffled and dumb-founded looks on the faces of "horse experts" and packers when they saw how we were outfitted.

Another time when we were about six miles from the trail head, I tied Sonny high to a tree like the experts advised. He dug a big hole in the ground, untied the knot (a pair of half hitches), and went to the trail head. I did a twelve-mile round trip hike to retrieve him. From then on, I never relied upon ANY more "horse-expert" advice.

One Thursday afternoon, the fourth day out, we were heading back to snow-grass camp. We had been logging out and had covered about twenty miles that day. Sonny was barely plugging along when he looked across the meadow, thought he saw another horse, and headed toward him.

I could see that it was a bear—coming right toward us, but I let Sonny keep on going, and when we got to within about 20 feet of the bear, it did a 180, and so did Sonny. I almost fell off. He hot-footed the remaining four miles back to camp and did his usual buck-off ritual to celebrate being back.

▪ ▪ ▪

In July, 1971, good weather allowed us to start the two hundred mile trail section of the maintenance job. For the most part, this job went very well, but we did have some hectic moments. One day near Mineral, I came to a blow-down; the crew was on the other side. It was getting close to lunchtime, and I decided to lead Sonny around the blow-down. By this time, he would follow me anywhere. The terrain was very steep. As I was leading Sonny up the steep slope, he slipped, knocked me down and landed on top of me. Fortunately, he only weighed *eleven hundred pounds*. When he jumped up, he stepped on the top of my foot. Ouch. Nothing broke, but it started to swell. I laced my boot as tightly as I could, gritted my teeth, and carried on.

I tied Sonny up and started cutting the logs, expecting the crew to come back for their lunch. I wasn't paying much attention to Sonny, but I did notice that he was nodding his head. When the crew showed up, I figured out why. He got his nose into the bags and had eaten everything except a can of tuna fish and a couple of candy bars. The crew survived on short rations.

I didn't take my boots off for the next five days, but my foot hurt off and on for many years to come. It was the same foot I injured with my ax at my first job with BPA in 1946.

One day, Sonny and I came to a trail bridge over a creek near Packwood Lake. There was no way around; we had to get across. There were several planks missing from the deck of the bridge. It was like a cattle guard. Sonny followed me across, tip-toeing over the missing planks.

Another time, Sonny and I were going cross country. We came to a blow-down of large logs that were lying mostly flat on the ground. In order to get across, we had to walk on top of the logs. Sonny followed me right across.

We finished the 200-mile section in September, 1971. I netted $8,000, a 50% profit.

Sonny and I worked together until he retired in 1980, at the age of 21. He spent his retirement on Sauvie Island, the largest island on the Columbia River, about ten miles north of Portland.

■ ■ ■

Rogue River—Blazing New Trails
Contract Amount: $10,385

The next month, October, 1971, I was low bidder on a trail re-construction job. The contract was for that last 15-mile section of the Rogue River Trail that runs west from Galice to Illahee, in southern Oregon. The Rogue River job was in a banana belt and could be worked all winter. We started our work at the Illahee trail head, and worked upstream. I boarded my crew at the Illahee Inn: my son Doug, my son-in-law Brian Surbert, and me. The rest of the crew were Locals.

Before I started work, I asked at the Agnes Store if there was any good help available. The proprietor replied, "If you want good help, you'll have to get it somewhere else."

As I was leaving the store, I struck up a conversation with a local logger who was between jobs. He had two friends, one who lived across the river from the store and made his living raising tomatoes (a variety which ripen earlier than others), selling them in Gold Beach and other coastal towns. The other was a local, semi-retired logger. I hired them both and we started the work.

The Illahee Inn catered to fishermen who drifted the Rogue River in their McKenzie drift boats. They hated rubber rafts, and hated jet boats even more.

I hired a local jet sled owner to haul our crew daily to the upper portion of our job. His name was Francis. His boat was powered by a 350-horse inboard motor. He was 70 years old or more, robust, and *everybody* hated him. They said it as only a matter of time until he was going to sink the sled because he would ram it into the rocky shore when loading or unloading.

I mentioned this to him one day. He said, "Don't worry, and don't tell anyone. My son used to work for Boeing and he procured enough titanium to cover the bottom of my boat." I never did tell anyone.

This whole matter was somewhat of a public relations problem for me. The Inn didn't want to lose my business, and I didn't want to annoy the other guests. Getting along turned out to be of mutual benefit to all parties. However, Francis' status remained unchanged.

The work required removing numerous trees, most of which were madrone (aka madrona) and live oak. This meant getting rid of the stumps, which we dug out by hand. It was extremely hard work.

I realized it was time to get my Explosives License because part of this job was going to require blasting rock, and it's much easier to shoot stumps than to dig them out by hand.

Spike (who was called the Tomato Baron), when hiking into the job, wore his rain clothes. When he got to the job site, he took off his rain coat and rolled a dry sweatshirt into it. He then worked all day in the rain without a coat. At the end of the shift, he took off his wet sweatshirt, put the dry one on, and hiked out.

I told Spike about the store keeper's saying that "if I wanted good help I needed to get it someplace else."

Spike said, "That son-of-a-bitch. I buy a lot of beer there, and so do the other Locals. We sit outside around the Heidelberg Tree and drink it."

This happened in the days of the pull tabs, and there were tabs piled about a foot deep all around the tree. In 1964, a new bridge had just been completed across the Rogue River at Agnes. Spike was afraid it was going to wash out, so he bought two cases of beer at the store, and headed back across the river. He didn't think he was going fast enough, so he dropped one case. Just as he reached the other side, the bridge collapsed. He had worked on the bridge with some of the other Locals. It was determined later on that the reason the bridge fell down was because there were so many beer cans in the concrete. It had nothing to do with the twenty-foot wall of water raging down the Rogue, of course!

We finished the project the first week of January, 1972. It was good winter's work…and I made $5,000 profit.

Chapter 16

FINANCES, TAXES AND LEGAL REPRESENTATION

Over the winter of 1972 to 1973, I went home and did some odd jobs around Vancouver. Along about tax time, I was sitting in the Totem Pole Restaurant drinking coffee, and became acquainted with a bookkeeper named Ed Coyles. I told him about my tax problem left over from 1969, when I started the flooring business. He said, "No one ever makes any money their first year in business." He also told me that you don't have to pay income taxes on your own children. I hired him to clean up the tax mess. In the end, we had enough money to stay in business, or at least we didn't owe anyone any money. Ed remained my bookkeeper until I incorporated in 1983.

He also gave me some good advice at that time and told me that the first thing I needed to do was change banks. Then he told me that when I made withdrawals and deposits, to always go inside the bank and talk with the tellers and bank managers. I took his advice, which paid off over the years.

Chapter 17

1972-'74
TALES FROM MANY TRAILS

Herman Creek Trail—'72
Entiat Trail—'72
Washington Pass Overlook Trail—'72
Snow Grass Trail—'72-'73
Ten Small Trail Bridges—'73

Herman Creek Trail (Kessler-Enlow Joint Venture)

On May 25, we were awarded the Herman Creek Trail Contract #406, for the US Forest Service, just outside Cascade Locks, Oregon. This was a trail reconstruction job, which began about five miles from the trail head. Our crew, Jim, Sharon, and their son David Enlow, two others, our pack animals and I arrived at the trail head on June 1st. We loaded my horse Sonny and Jim's five donkeys with tools and camp supplies. About noon we arrived at the shelter, the mid-point of the mile-long project. We set up camp and started working. Jim's job was to buck the logs for the turnpike and puncheon sections, and fabricate the cedar puncheon planks (heavy slabs with at least one smooth surface). Sharon's job was to take care of camp and do the cooking. My job was to do the stone work and clearing for the rest of the project, including blasting the ditches.

The third morning into the job, Sharon announced that she was going to Carson to visit her sister. That left Jim to do the cooking. A couple of days later she came back with a bag of doughnuts and a fifth of McNaughton's. That night after dinner, we had a few drinks. Jim and Sharon slept in the shelter; the rest of the crew slept in tents across a small ice-water creek, which we crossed on a plank. Actually, we had quite a few drinks. When I crossed the creek to go to bed, I fell over backwards. Splash. I crawled into bed soaking wet. I didn't dry out for two days!

In the meantime, Jim's donkeys came down with a virus. A day or two later, Sonny also contracted it. I threw a blanket over him and he stood in one place for two or three days. When our ten-day run was over, we took all the animals home. When we returned to the job, we packed all our groceries on our backs.

This time in, we also had Billy Mansfield with us. His brother George had coerced me into hiring him. Jim and sons went back to work on the puncheon. Sharon, Billy and I started cutting brush on the other end. Billy couldn't hit the brush hard enough to knock the water off. That night (Monday), Billy wanted to know when we were going home. I told him, "Friday." Later on, George Mansfield called me and asked, "What's the deal with Billy?" I simply told him that he didn't want to work.

"Big Bad Bog" bridge.

The upper end of the job was what the COR Howard "Rondy" Rondathaler called "The Big Bad Bog." Ditches would be required to drain the bog. The ditches were to be made by pushing a stick of 20% ditching powder into the soft organic soil on twelve-inch centers. There was to be a ditch on each side of the proposed puncheon turnpike trail. I set off the charge. It blew crap everywhere. The ditches were six or seven feet deep, and ten or twelve feet wide on top, exposing a few boulders the size of a Volkswagen. Oops. How was I gonna get out of *this* one?

A short time later, Rondy showed up. I was rehearsing my alibi when Rondy exclaimed, "This is exactly what I wanted." He looked at our other work and liked it.

On June 23, Rondy gave us final acceptance while at the trail head. This was unusual. Normally, this wasn't done in the field. I was there, along with Jim and Sharon Enlow. Rondy was so pleased with how we expedited the work that he didn't want to slow us down from going to our next project. It was very rare that a project was bid, built and accepted as complete in less than 30 days. Jim and I shared a good profit, and in the meantime, Sharon had begun to get quite friendly with me.

The next week, Jim helped me waterproof some decks on an apartment complex in Vancouver. The deck product we were using was a neoprene—Hypalon manufactured by Gaco Western Corporation. He and Sharon parked their trailer in my driveway for a few days. I might say Millie didn't like that very much.

One morning after Jim left for the job site, just as I was going out the door (Millie had just finished getting the kids off to school, and had just left for her job at Bemis Bag Co.) Sharon came to the door. All she had on was her bathrobe. I shooed her out and headed for work. I had never fooled around with any of my employees' wives, or friends' wives.

A few hours later I had to come back to the shop to pick up some tools. When I got to 39th Street and Fruit Valley Road, there was Sharon. I picked her up and took her to the job site. She helped Jim the rest of the day. The next day they left for their home in Centralia.

Entiat Trail Reconstruction

In early July, I started the Entiat Trail Reconstruction Project. This job was in the Wenatchee National Forest, near Ardenvoir, Washington. A forest fire two years prior had damaged the trails. We started work on the lower trail. (The other trails were still covered with snow.) My six-man crew included my brother David and myself. To get to this trail, we had to walk a log lying across a raging river.

On about the third day, two of the crew got to the trail ahead of the rest of us. They had been instructed to go to where we left off the day before. For some reason, they went clear to the end of the trail. When I arrived at the work site, they were nowhere to be seen. I went back to the trail head in search of them. As there was no sign of them, I called the sheriff. He brought a search-and-rescue team to the trail head. I explained to the sheriff that I was afraid the guys may have fallen into the river.

About that time, a curl of smoke appeared on the horizon. The two missing hands took it upon themselves to proceed to the trail head. They met the rest of the crew and they all came out. This was a great relief—*and* a great embarrassment for me, but the sheriff was pleased with the outcome. He proclaimed that he wished all searches would turn out this way.

We finished this trail a few days later. My son Doug showed up to do the Chelan summit portion of the contract. I headed for the Snow Grass Trail.

The western trail head of the Chelan Trail was a short distance from the trail we had just completed. Doug took the six-man crew, Sonny and a guy named Doug Leonetti, and started. As they worked their way in, Sonny carried the camp supplies.

After a few days, Doug had to go to town to get more food. His plan was to take the pickup and trailer to the east trail head and pack the supplies in on his back, but there was another problem: Leonetti's pants had disintegrated. This meant that Doug had to go into Wenatchee (a 2-hours round trip) to buy him a new pair. Because of this, Doug got back to the trail head a couple of hours later than he planned.

He started hiking in to meet the crew when all of a sudden he met a bear. Doug scrambled up a tree, pack and all; after about an hour, the bear left, and Doug continued walking until dark. (We had learned early on not to walk when it was too dark to see.) He slept, uninterrupted, until dawn, and then hiked in to meet the rest of the crew.

He and the crew finished this job about August 10, 1972.

▪ ▪ ▪

Washington Pass Overlook
(Another Kessler-Enlow Joint Venture)

We started this job the first week of July, 1972. The crew was Jim and Sharon Enlow, their son David and myself.

Jim moved his travel trailer to the parking lot at the trail head. This was our on-site office. Also, Jim and Sharon slept in it. Sharon's duty was to cook for the crew. David had his own tent, as did I.

The job started out well. We had the clearing and grubbing done the first week and were ready for the base gravel for the trail. I told Jim that we had to find a source of gravel, which probably had to come from Twisp, a long way from the job site.

Jim replied, "I will find some."

I did not want to leave the job as I had plenty of rock drilling to do, but Jim and Sharon took off in the pickup about 9:00 am and were gone most of the day. (Sharon was very good looking and had a way about her.) They returned about 3:00.

At about the same time, a Superintendent for the new North Cascade Highway project, showed up. He, Jim and Sharon were talking. You could see the Superintendent kind of liked Sharon. A few minutes later two dump trucks with base rock showed up and unloaded at the trail head. As the trucks were leaving, the head inspector for the highway project showed up. He asked the Superintendent what was going on.

The Superintendent replied, "You don't care, do you? It's for the benefit of all to get the trail completed for the highway's grand opening."

The Inspector agreed.

Jim, Sharon and I agreed to take the Superintendent to dinner. The dinner never happened, but we ended up with several hundred dollars' worth of gravel, just the right amount for our trail. The crew wheelbarrowed it in the next day and Sharon ran the roller to compact it.

We were ready for paving, but the specs for the job required that we install a quarter inch by four inch steel plate at the edge of paving. The plate was to follow the lines and grades of the trail. I told the inspector that this was an impossible specification and that I had to get on with the paving. He told me that if I paved without the steel, I would have to tear it out. It was mandated that the trail had to be completed for the opening of the new North Cascade Highway. I had no choice but to take the risk and paved without the steel.

It was Friday and we decided to go to dinner in Winthrop that evening. We ate, danced and drank. That's backwards. We drank, danced and ate. All of the sudden it was closing time and we headed for the pickup. It was nowhere to be seen. Nor was Jim's son David. While we staggered around trying to figure out what to do, the local policeman asked if he could help us—and wound up driving us the thirty-some miles back to camp. David and the pickup were there. You know, that's just pure luck. I admired David's pluck.

Pedestrian railing at Washington Pass Overlook.

Liberty Bell.

When we bid this job, there was a line item for landscape rehabilitation consisting of 15 square yards. But the actual landscape rehabilitation was not described in the specifications, so we gambled and bid $15 per square yard, for a total of $225. This turned out to be for bark dust alongside the trail, a much greater quantity totaling about 150 sq. yards and valued at $2,200, which we installed on Saturday. We left, as the grand opening was to be on Monday.

We returned a week later, only to find there was no trace of the bark dust. It had been trampled on by about 6,000 people. Jim bamboozled the inspector out of another $2,200 worth of bark dust, and we made about $4,000 on the landscape rehabilitation.

A machinist friend, Bill Couty, and I spent the next two weeks finishing up the hand rail, completing the job on October 11, 1972. We ended up giving the government a $900 credit for educating them about the impossibility of using steel edging for a paved trail.

■ ■ ■

Snow Grass Trail

August 1st, 1972, Kessler and Wille started work on the Snow Grass Trail, next to Chambers Lake, about 20 miles south of Packwood, Washington, but we were shut down immediately because of fire danger. We were able to get started again when the shutdown was lifted on August 8th. The first mile of this trail was through rocky terrain. We used portable gasoline-powered drills called Cobras. They weighed about 50 pounds each. I hired two locals from Randle to do the drilling and blasting. One was Ron McCain, a logger; the other was a dairyman named Roger, eager to make some extra money. They were both very good workers. Ron went on to become a trail contractor, and later on became my partner on a US Forest Service contract at Thorn Bay, Alaska.

The job went well. A very important part of building a trail is conserving tread material such as dirt and small gravel. Once we completed the drilling and shooting, it was time to do the tread work.

I left the job for a few hours, and while I was gone, an inspector (although not authorized to do so) told Roger that all that dirt needed to be cleaned off the trail. By the time I got back, Roger had thrown 90% of the soil over the side. It took us a week to replace it.

We finished that section in mid-September, and I moved a different crew to the five-mile section, which was about six miles by trail from Walupt Lake. On Sunday night we hiked into the job site under a full moon with our eight-man crew and Sonny, carrying the tools we needed to get the work started, and enough food for breakfast and lunch the next day.

The following day, the packer and six mules arrived with the rest of our supplies. This included two tents, which we set up that evening. We made very good progress the first day, and enjoyed a good dinner of canned beef and asparagus. Late in the afternoon, it began to get very cold, so we went to bed, four in each tent.

About midnight I heard a howl from the tent nearby. The other tent had collapsed under the weight of snow. In the morning there was about a foot of snow. We grabbed our sleeping bags and headed out. It was very difficult going. Sonny had an especially bad time, but we managed to get to the trailhead.

A week went by before the snow melted. We went back in with four men. A few days later it snowed again— and that time, we were done for the season. Our tents had collapsed and covered all of our food supplies.

The next summer we got a call from the Forest Service saying that some hikers were seen with our canned roast beef a few miles south and wanted to know what they should do. I told them to enjoy the roast beef.

The next season, in 1973, we returned to the Snow Grass Trail head to complete some work in the parking lot. We established our base camp there.

A couple of days into the job, Sharon Enlow and her daughter showed up at camp right at quitting time. Surprise! I had to drive to Packwood to get fuel for the drills. They were still there when I got back. Doug and I set up our tents on straw. It was pretty cozy for a trail camp.

After dark, Doug, in anticipation of what might happen, moved his sleeping bag to one of the pickups. However, Doug loaned Sharon's daughter a sleeping bag, and she went to sleep in the back seat of Sharon's car, waking up none the wiser. Not knowing that Doug had left the tent, Sharon and I made use of the front seat of the other pickup.

I decided to hire a cook to do the Pacific Crest Trail section of the contract. A young lady called me at home one night and said she heard I was in need of a cook. I told her the conditions and what would be expected.

She decided she wanted the job and said, "I have a dog. I also have a sister who would like to come along and help me." Her sister had a dog too.

At that time I didn't like having dogs on the job, but I needed a cook. Right away. So I said okay, but that her sister would have to help us when she wasn't helping cook. The next day they met us at the trailhead and we hiked in with three dogs instead of two.

The work went very well. The sister came out to help me load holes with dynamite, and the food was good, well garnished with dog hair.

Because it took more open days to construct the job than there were open days in the 1972 season, the Forest Service awarded us $2,000 for an extra mobilization. We made a good profit and got to enjoy the Goat Rocks' beautiful scenery.

▪ ▪ ▪

Ten Small Trail Bridges

In 1973, the year of the oil embargo, we only did two small jobs. One was helicoptering ten small trail bridges onto Beacon Rock, about 35 miles east of Vancouver, up the Columbia River Gorge on the Washington side. The other was a trail bridge that we pre-fabricated in our yard in Vancouver.

The staging area for the Beacon Rock project was on a private dairy about a half mile upstream from Beacon Rock State Park. We had to do some cutting and burning there in order to assemble the bridges. This was a surprise to the dairy owner, as we hadn't gotten permission to stage the bridges on his land. However, he was in favor of the project and allowed us to proceed as long as we were careful not to leave any slag or scraps of metal behind that his cows might eat. We flew the bridges in with Columbia Helicopter's Soleil using a 100 foot load line. Columbia's pilots were specially trained for doing long line work and always kept the chopper directly over the load. The job went very well.

Shortly thereafter, Columbia acquired two Boeing Vertol's from New York. Columbia Helicopter, owned by Wes Lematta of Vancouver, Washington, went on to become the world's premiere heavy-lift helicopter company.

From the air, Beacon Rock bridges.

Crooked Creek Trail Bridge

Installing the Crooked Creek Trail Bridge.

The nearest road to the bridge site was just a mile away on private land, about four miles up the Wenaha River near Troy, Oregon. The owner was a retired state patrolman who did not like the Forest Service. Therefore it was necessary for us to set up our helicopter staging area about two miles away, on Forest Service land. Our intent was to pre-assemble the bridge sections and fly them to the bridge site.

While assembling, we had to trim some metal, but discovered we had no burning torch with us. As I was leaving the staging area to get a torch, I met the hostile land owner. He said, "I have a torch and I'll come down and do the work for you." While doing this, he spilled out his pent-up anger toward the Forest Service, but he told us we could cross his land any time we wanted. This was a bonus because the trail from his property to the bridge site, though steep, was only one mile. We had already flown the timbers for the bridge footings to the job site and set up a tent for the crew.

There was a log jam in the creek at the site that had to be removed. We had been told that if we wrapped primer cord around the logs that we could blast them apart. We tried it, but didn't even knock the bark off. This meant that we had to spend four or five days with chainsaw and ax cutting them apart. This was difficult to do when the logs were in the water. We finished the clearing.

The weather at the end of the first week in camp it was very hot. The crew decided to hike to Troy, get a good dinner at the restaurant, and spend Friday night in the motel. On the steep one mile hike out, my friend Rocky Delagasse became overheated. He asked me to help him, but I was overheated myself. I told him just to take a couple of steps at a time and then rest. It was slow going for him, but we made it.

At this time, several wildfires were burning in the area and the restaurant was busy serving meals to the fire crews. A troop of Girl Scouts had rafted down the Grande Ronde River and came in for a drink of cold water.

Most of our crew drank beer and ice water. Rocky and I drank whiskey. The next morning I decided to take Rocky to Lewiston, Idaho and put him on a plane home. Rocky had heart trouble, and I didn't want him to croak on our job.

I was also searching the local airports for a helicopter. As it turned out, there was only one helicopter in the area large enough to lift the bridge. It was on contract to the US Forest Service. It was based about ten miles from the bridge site. I had hoped they would release it for a few hours to fly my bridge. The Forest Service said no – I would have to wait until the end of the season. I had no option but to wait.

On Sunday, I returned to the trail head and looked down at camp. I could only see one person moving, and he wasn't moving very fast. I walked on down to camp and found out the entire crew was sick from drinking the restaurant's water. I learned later that day that forty firefighters, the girl scouts and my crew had all become sick. A couple of firefighters had to be hospitalized.

Early Bird Café, Troy, Oregon—1973—
Population 19; 16 were named Wilson.

Rocky and I were the only ones who didn't get sick. We only drank whiskey. The restaurant was shut down. Their well was too close to the septic tank. The Wilsons protested vigorously. They said they've been drinking the water all along and they didn't get sick, but they weren't allowed to reopen until they dug a new well.

We went ahead and finished the timber footings for the bridge about mid-August. At the end of fire season, the helicopter landed at the staging area and we made our plans to fly the bridge in. The helicopter only had a 50-foot load line. (Such a short line creates a tremendous amount of prop wash for the people on the ground trying to guide the bridge.)

The helicopter lifted the load off of the ground and flew to the bridge site, but instead of setting the bridge on the footings, the pilot set it on the gravel bar. I didn't know why. We had no radios.

After about ten minutes, he lifted the bridge up again and we set it on the footings. The problem had been that the chopper was overloaded and had to burn off some fuel in order to make the lift. He barely made it. We were lucky.

The chopper flew away and we never saw him again.

Helicopter setting bridge section.

After that incident, we made sure that we had at least a 100-foot line on any lifting we did, and preferably, a 150 foot line. Lesson learned.

CHAPTER 18

1974
A VERY BUSY YEAR

1. **Diablo Lake Overlook Pedestrian Safety Railing**
   US Dept. of the Interior National Park Service
   Contract No. CX-9000-4-9006
   Contract Amount: $28,990
   Awarded Jan. 8, 1974
   Final Contract Amount: $36,397

2. **Three Trail Bridges –**
   Bid # R6-74-70
   Bid Amount: $88,442
   Awarded May 16, 1974
   • West Fork Lema Creek
   • East Fork Lema Creek
   • Wapatus River

3. **Reconstruction of Pacific Crest Trail—#2000**
   Bid # R6-74-84
   Bid Amount: $28,000
   Awarded May 20, 1974

The first contract was for constructing a pedestrian safety railing at the parking lot overlooking Diablo Lake. This work was on the North Cascade Highway. The parking lot and foundation for the railing, including the anchor bolts, were constructed in the summer of 1973.

It was important to verify that the anchor bolts had been placed so that the curved sections of the 2″ pipe railing could be bent to the proper curvature.

I called Don Marx's surveying firm located in Gresham, Oregon. Don had been my boss and mentor when I worked for BPA, and later on, when he was doing contract surveys for BPA in Roseburg and Forest Grove, Oregon.

Don sent a crew to Diablo to start the bolt-as-built survey. I was to arrive the next day. About mid-day I received a call informing me that they were at Nehalem, and that there was a slide between there and the job site. As there was no way to tell when the slide would be cleared, I told them to go back to Gresham. This was a costly adventure.

I decided to buy a transit and do the as-built myself. I called the Keuffel & Esser dealer in Portland to find out if they had a transit. They said yes, they had one in stock. I said, "I'll be right over."

When they showed it to me, it looked familiar. I realized that it was the same one I had used for the three years while working for Bechtel Corporation on the Swift Creek Dam. I paid $400 for the transit, and also bought a survey rod.

On Feb. 14, Rocky de Lagasse and I headed for Diablo to do the as-built. Just past the Marble Mount wayside, there was a landslide. The highway crew thought they might have it cleared by dark. We turned around and spent the night in Burlington. After dinner, Rocky and I were sitting in the lounge having a drink and minding our own business, when suddenly a lady grabbed my hand and pulled me onto the dance floor. While dancing, she told me that her husband had passed away a couple of years ago and that she was having headaches. After a couple of dances, she told me that her doctor had told her that she needed to find someone to have sex with. She took me home with her for a very interesting night. At breakfast, she smiled and thanked me for curing her headache. I smiled, and replied, "You were wise in following your doctor's orders."

Feb. 15 and 16, Rocky and I completed the as-builts and returned to Vancouver.

Railing.

Don Winterholler, welding foreman.

The 2,000 lineal feet of 2″ cor-ten pipe for this project was supplied by the government. Our contract indicated that we were to take delivery on this pipe on Feb. 14, at the government warehouse in Seattle. I called the warehouse to confirm. They didn't know anything about it. I called Denver. They said the pipe would arrive the week of Feb. 25. I notified Albina Pipe Bending to pick it up and haul it to their plant in Portland.

Albina called and told me they had picked it up, but there was only 1,400 feet of pipe—600 feet short. I called the COR, David O'Kane, who contacted all the involved parties, and it was unclear if or when any more two-inch pipe was going to be produced.

This was a dilemma. Albina had already started bending the pipe. De Lagasse had already started fabricating the base plates. The Park Service talked about substituting 3″ pipe for the upper railing. Not a good idea.

The plans called for two-inch round bars at the splice-points and railings. I suggested to O'Kane that we substitute two-inch bars for the tangent sections on the lower part of the railing. (It must be noted that at this time, steel was in short supply.) I told them that there was enough of this 2″ bar available for what we needed. I also explained that it could be sold or disappear at any time. Naturally, the government had to fuss and fume to come to a consensus. I called O'Kane and said, "We have to act now." He agreed.

I ordered the bar. It took until April 26 (two months) to finalize a change order for $7,407. Final inspection was held six days later, May 2, 1974.

Removing railing for repair.

This was a classic example of the government benefiting from the contractor's ingenuity. The Park Service personnel cooperated, and the work was completed to everyone's satisfaction well before the beginning of the tourist season. It was great working with O'Kane. The job was an example of what people can do when they work together.

■ ■ ■

Three Trail Bridges

On May 16th of 1974, we were awarded a job to install three bridges on the Pacific Crest Trail. This was bid #R6-74-70, meaning that the job was the 70th contract awarded in Region 6, which includes all National Forests in Oregon and Washington in the year 1974. This job was in the Wenatchee National Forest, a few miles north of Roslyn, Washington.

Hughes 500 that flew our camps in.

Vertol flying first stringer to Lema Creek.

East Fork Lema Creek Bridge.

We began field work on the West Fork Lema Creek Bridge and the East Fork of the Lema Creek Bridge on August 5.

The main span of each bridge was 50 feet. Each span was constructed of three pressure-treated, glue-laminated Douglas fir stringers, 12 inches wide and four feet tall, weighing 8,000 lbs.

All three bridges had crib piers constructed of 12″x12″ treated timbers of varying lengths.

All the above material was ordered from J.H. Baxter on May 16, with an anticipated delivery date of Aug. 5.

The plan was for two camps, one at Lema Creek and the other at Wapatus. I instructed Randy Johnson to include identical supplies for each camp: a tent, food, and tools; including a roll of fuse, and enough blasting caps and dynamite for each bridge site.

In mid-July, we flew our tent and supplies to the Lema Creek site. I hiked the five miles from the helicopter staging area into the Lema Creek Bridge sites. As this was rough country, there was no place for a helicopter to land. John McLaughlin stayed at the helicopter staging area and rigged the loads. Columbia Helicopter's Hughes 500 flew the material to Lema Creek, and I unloaded them. The next day, John and a local hiked in and set up the tent.

We went back to Vancouver and fabricated the steel details and built the forms for the East Lema Creek Bridge footings, and started gathering up all the tools and materials that would be needed for the project.

A few days later, four men and I hiked in, along with two girls and their two dogs. They had been our camp cooks two years earlier in the Goat Rocks. We started excavating for the crib footing for the West Lema Creek Bridge. The very first day, the cooks complained about the site being damp and cold. I told them to hike on down the trail and find a warmer spot when they weren't cooking. After the third day, I got tired of listening to them squawk and had Doug take them home. That made me the Camp Cook again! (We didn't miss the dog hair!)

The digging was challenging and required considerable blasting, but the crew was determined. We set off a shot and sent a boulder through the side of our tent and out the top.

The design had the footing a little too close to the creek and we had to excavate in the water. For that reason, we were unable to excavate the last two feet. The COR allowed us to delete four pieces of timber, and reduced the pay item accordingly. We started building the cribs with the 12x12s we had flown in earlier.

In the meantime, I dispatched Harlan Keefer and his brother Dean to do the excavating for the Wapatus Trail Bridge. After one week, I decided to check on them and hiked in the twelve miles to the bridge site. Just as I arrived, they were getting ready to leave. I asked if they were done and they said no. They had run out of fuse. I said, "Do you have any fuse left?"

They said yes. I said, "OK, we'll cut the fuse a little shorter and run a little faster."

We still didn't have enough to make the last shot. If Randy had put a full roll of fuse in each camp as I directed, we would have been done. We hiked the twelve miles back out to the trailhead, where the Keefers told me they didn't want to work anymore.

When I got back to the motel that night, I was trying to figure out what to do next, as I was now short-handed, when suddenly, there was a knock on the door. It was Tedero Sandoval, nicknamed "The Mex." He was looking for a job. He explained to me that he'd been working for a trail contractor who was doing a contract on the same trail a few miles from us. Their tent had burned down, and they had to abandon the job. I said, "You're hired, and you can go to work with me in the morning."

Early the next morning, the lady who ran the motel told me, "A young man stopped by yesterday. He wants you to call him. He's looking for a job. I know he's a good worker, as he is the caretaker for our church youth camp."

I called him and hired him, sight unseen. He said he knew where the Lema Creek Trailhead was, and would hike in the next day. Both were super good workers. How lucky can ya get? What are the odds?

As it turned out, it took me four days to go to Vancouver, get more fuse, and hike the twelve miles back in to make the last blast. This was a high price to pay for one roll of fuse. (And of course, we gave Randy plenty of flack.)

On the hike out, I met a Forest Service pack train going my direction. It was led by our inspector. I said, "Hey, pull that big horse over next to that stump." I climbed to the top of the pack on the Morgan and rode the last four miles back to the trail head. (The Morgan didn't know the difference.)

In the meantime, Doug and his crew installed the cribs at Lema Creek.

They were very complicated and challenged Doug's excellent puzzle-solving skills. The work was difficult, but went very well, and better than I expected.

I said, "It's time for some R & R," and we headed for the nearest bar. It was September 10 and Doug's 21st birthday. I was feeling kind of smart-alecky and in a mood to celebrate. The bar maid asked Doug for his ID. I said, "Don't worry about that. I'll vouch for him. I've known him longer than anyone else."

She said, "I'm not serving any of you drinks until he proves his age."

This argument went on for about ten minutes. Doug finally showed his ID. She said, "OK Doug, what will you have?"

Doug said, "A Pepsi."

That was Doug's way of getting back at me for being ornery. We finished the celebration and headed for the motel in Cle Elum.

In the morning, we went back to Vancouver and helped round up the rest of the material for the project.

About the first of October, the trucks hauling the 50-foot glue-lam stringers and all the miscellaneous metal arrived at the helicopter staging area. Doug and the crew pre-assembled the pier for the Wapatus Bridge site and installed the necessary metal onto the glue-lams.

On October 9, the Hughes 500 helicopter arrived and flew tools and miscellaneous metal components to all three bridge sites. The next morning, Columbia's Vertol arrived, piloted by Don Patterson, and co-pilot Mr. Gardnier. Don conducted the mandatory safety meeting and instructed us in the use of hand signals and two-way radios. Don was a charismatic person and we dealt with him many times over the years. It must be noted that two-way radios never did work on this project or any future projects that we did with Columbia or any other helicopter company, but it really doesn't matter once an accomplished pilot sees what needs to be done, so there's no need to talk.

The Hughes 500 dropped me and two men off near the Lema Creek site, and two men at the Wapatus site. It was time to fly in the stringers. Doug had figured out the flying sequence, starting with Lema Creek.

The Vertol, using a 100-ft-long load line, hooked on to the first 50-ft stringer. Just as Don was ready to set the stringer, it began to rotate. He lowered it down and bumped it against a tree to stop the rotation. He then gently lifted it up and precisely set it in place. We barely touched it to move it into position. Don headed back to the staging area, made a slight adjustment to the load line, and picked up the next load. As time would tell, he was the best heavy-lift pilot we ever used.

From then on, everything went perfectly. I was able to eye-ball the bridge parts into exact position, and only minor adjustments were required after the loads were placed.

Vertol flying short bridge span to Wapatus.

We worked from dawn to dark for the next two weeks, installing the decking and the handrails. The handrails were native poles that were attached to turned, treated posts, a difficult task at best.

Once we had the rails on, the Forest Service informed me that we had to take them down so that ice would not break them during the winter. The only reason there were handrails at all was because regulations required handrails on all bridges where the deck was over eight feet above the stream bed. We took them down. They were never used again.

We were all done except for filling the crib at the West Lema Creek Bridge. This was a three-man job, and there was only room for three men to work. We had to move the fill from a borrow-area 100 feet up the trail from the crib. "The Mex" and I had sore legs and could not run a wheelbarrow, but we could load it. Once loaded, Bob would run it down the trail and dump it into the crib. The fill required 100 yards or about ten dump truck-loads.

It took us almost three days to fill the crib. We finished about two o'clock in the afternoon and started walking out. It began to snow. Once we got back to town, we called Jay Russell, our USFS COR, and asked for final inspection. It took him about a week to get there. When he finished the final, he called me. I asked him how everything looked, and he retorted, "Everything looks good when it's coated with half a foot of snow." He went on to say, "I see you put that piece of belting right in plain sight so that you didn't want me to think that you were getting away with something."

The elastomeric-bearing pad that was specified blew off one of the timbers while flying it in, so we substituted a piece of belting.

I asked him why they used three stringers when two was overkill. He replied, "When the spray from the creek freezes on the bridge, it tends to tip it over. The designer decided to put in a third stringer as insurance. It is much cheaper and less embarrassing to over-design than have to explain a failure."

One week while we were working on the Wapatus Bridge, Sonny (my horse) hauled in some supplies. When Randy loaded the pack bags, he put the gasoline cans on top of the food, which included four loaves of bread. The gasoline leaked and soaked the bread. There was very little foliage at the site, so the only thing Sonny got to eat that week was the four loaves of gasoline-soaked bread, but he did many future jobs with enthusiasm.

▪ ▪ ▪

Pacific Crest Trail

Lloyd, 1974.

On May 20, 1974, we were awarded a job for Reconstruction of the Pacific Crest Trail. This project was scheduled to be completed during the 1974 work season. That year there was a very heavy snow pack. This meant we were unable to start work until June 20th.

This job was in four sections: Three near Trout Lake; the fourth was a five-mile section at higher elevation on the slopes of Mt. Adams.

We mobilized our camp at the trail head of the lowest section. This included a 22′ travel trailer and Sonny the horse. The first section was about a mile long, and we completed it in about a week. We moved our trailer to the next trail head. During the move, Sonny disappeared. We had no idea where he went. We spent all the rest of the day looking for him, to no avail. The next day, a hiker told us he had seen Sonny at a campground three or four miles to the west. We hooked up the horse trailer and headed to the campground. There was Sonny, being fed hay and oats. The lady feeding him chastised me for neglecting him. We loaded Sonny and left.

We had been working for thirteen days straight and the next day was the Fourth of July, a Wednesday. Millie said, "Doesn't make sense to go home for one day and then come back."

I argued that the only other time I worked on the Fourth of July was during the War. I lost the argument, and we worked straight through until we finished the three lower sections on July 20th.

The Forest Service should have finalized these three sections at this time, but had some excuse not to.

On July 24th, we established our camp at the trail head of the upper section, and started working our way in. Our crew consisted of eight people: which included the four Andruss brothers; two teachers from Trout Lake; my son Doug and myself. The four brothers slept in a tent; Doug and I in the trailer; the two teachers commuted. Doug and I did the cooking and served the crew's meals inside the trailer. It took us about a week to finish the first three miles. We took a couple of days off.

Upon returning, I hired a packer to move our camp gear and supplies to the upper end of the trail. We set up camp and began working the upper two miles, which was very difficult new construction requiring removal of many boulders and stumps.

Millie decided to do the cooking. She was an excellent cook, and all the crew members exclaimed that she cooked the best food they had ever eaten.

Each morning after breakfast, the crew headed up the trail. In the meantime, I would saddle Sonny and load him with any tools or explosives that we needed for that day's work. I would then ride out past the trail crew to the part where I was doing the clearing, drilling or blasting.

The work progressed fairly well. One night after dinner, there was a lot of tee-heeing and hee-hawing in the crew's tents. The next morning as I rode past the crew, they were working furiously. I proceeded up the trail and started drilling. The drill broke and I rode back to camp to get a part. When I got to where the crew was working, they'd made very little progress. I was not happy. When we were done for the day, one of the brothers said he didn't want to work anymore. I said, "Good. You can go."

Two more brothers and one other guy spoke up and said, "We're leaving too."

I told the four of them to "get a-goin'." One brother, the best worker, stayed.

Millie spoke up, "Lloyd, they have to eat first." They had dinner and left. By the next morning I had figured out they had been smoking marijuana and they were simply hung over and unable to perform.

The next day our production doubled.

We went home for a couple of days. When I opened the mail, there was a work order the COR had written, with 18 items regarding the last section of new trail. We had been doing the clearing on this section, had felled the trees and dug out under them so we could place dynamite. We had also drilled the boulders to be removed. The work order read "Remove stump. Remove boulder," some eighteen times. The COR sent a copy to the Contracting Officer, which implies that the contractor is under-performing. This leaves the wrong impression in a contracting officer's mind. I was not happy.

After about ten days, we finished the work and told the inspector that we wanted a final inspection. He said, "You haven't done the finish work yet."

I said, "I know, we'll do that tomorrow so you can be there to inspect it."

The next day, along with the inspector, we polished the whole trail and requested a final inspection. As it usually takes a couple of weeks to get a final inspection, we moved to the Three Trail Bridges job sites, which were a few miles north of Roslyn, Washington, and started work.

As noted above, we expected to be notified of final inspection. No notice came.

As we learned by letter months later, the COR did not notify the contracting officer that we had requested a final inspection. What he did do was compose a 300-item punch list of deficiencies that we had to correct before final inspection. This letter arrived in November, long after the winter's snows started.

The following summer, I was notified several times by the Contracting Officer that the punch list work needed to be done. I knew there was nothing wrong with the work, so I put it off to the very end of the work season. In the meantime, the COR had moved on. I made a deal with the new COR that they could choose any one mile-long section of trail, and if they found any deficiencies, I would re-work the entire job; and if they did NOT find any deficiencies in that mile, they would sign off.

Luckily, they picked the first mile of the upper section, which happened to be the easiest of the whole job. We found a couple of loose rocks at the culvert head walls that was probably caused by deer breaking through the snow. They signed off in good humor, and let me know without coming right out and saying it, that the COR who wrote the punch list was not very bright.

This was a very important year since it was the first time we were able to bond over $100,000. We also proved to the bonding company that we could do this work in far less time than the contracts allotted. In spite of change orders, inclement weather, and sometimes bungling government interference, this enabled us to bond larger and larger projects in the future.

Chapter 19

1975
OZETTE RIVER TRAIL BRIDGE
Department of Transportation
Olympic National Park, Washington
Contract amount: $100,651

On April 29, we had the preconstruction conference for the Ozette River Trail Bridge project. The project was for construction of a concrete girder foot bridge, 6 feet wide by 154 feet long, across the Ozette River in the Olympic National Park, about 10 miles south of Clallum Bay in Washington State. This bridge replaced a rotten logging road bridge that was being used for foot traffic.

The Ozette River Trail was meant to take visitors out to an archeological dig site where a Makah Indian settlement was buried underneath a landslide several hundred years ago. Many petroglyphs and other artifacts were uncovered there.

This job required building a work platform to support the drilling rig that was to be used to drill 42 inch holes for the concrete pilings. We cut off the existing piling at waterline and utilized them to construct the platform. Once the concrete piling were poured, we utilized the platform to support the falsework for the bridge. We used 10" x 10" Douglas fir timbers salvaged from a railroad bridge that had recently been dismantled.

These timbers were heavy and hard to use. It took a lot of labor and time to erect this falsework. We should have used Safway Scaffolding. We could have completed in a few days with Safway what took a few weeks with the timbers. We'd wasted a lot of time and money. From this I learned it was always better to use the proper equipment to do the job, no matter the cost. It always paid off in the long run.

This was a unit price contract, meaning that each item of work had its own price. However, buried in the specifications was a requirement for concrete form liners that would give the finished concrete the appearance of crushed rock. The cost of these liners was $12,000, which we had not included in our bid.

By the time we completed the job, we had $15,000 less money in the bank than when we started, so we learned to read the specifications much more thoroughly in the future.

Despite our loss, the end product was an exceptionally good looking, award-winning bridge. It had required sophisticated work and the use of heavy equipment, something we had become adept at doing.

Here are photos taken on that project:

Ozette River Bridge under construction. Trailhead to the Makah Indian archeological dig.

This shows the 42-inch auger used to drill the hole for the poured-in-place concrete bridge pilings. The drill is on top of the work platform (in reality a temporary bridge).

The crew is taking a good long look to make sure they've filled the steel sleeve with enough concrete before the crane pulls the steel out. These pilings were set on a precise batter.

The sides and deck of the bridge are being formed for concrete. The rebar is bent to stub into the lid. The bridge is hollow inside.

A span of falsework reflected in the water below.

Finished bridge.

CHAPTER 20

1976-'77
ADVENTURES IN WATERPROOFING

City of Portland Parking Facility
Federal Building, Spokane
Washington Park Reservoir, Portland

Parking facility decking treatment

In November of 1976, we bid a project for the City of Portland to put deck coating, a waterproofing treatment, on a city parking facility. This job required sand blasting the traffic deck and applying Gaco Western elastomeric deck material. This is a waterproof material applied both to decks and roofs. Our work hours were from 6:00 pm to 6:00 am because there was little traffic in the parking structure at this time of night. We mobilized and were ready to sandblast.

However, there was a fancy sports car parked in our work area despite the notices posted in the area that said "no parking." We wrapped the car in plastic and began our sandblasting operation. Sandblasting is a messy business. At 10:00 pm, the owner of the sports car showed up and was irate. We dusted off his car and sent him on his way.

We finished sandblasting and applied our first coat of elastomer, or prime coat. The next night we had just completed the second coat when two skate boarders came flying down the ramp and all the way across our freshly coated deck. They kept on going. We put our golf shoes on and re-rolled the deck. The next day we finished.

We had done this same type work at the Federal building in Spokane, and went on to do more at the Federal building in Salt Lake City, the post office in Portland, City Hall in Vancouver, the fish hatchery at Lost Creek Dam near Shady Cove, Oregon, and many other places. These jobs were very profitable.

Federal Building

In April of 1976, we were awarded a contract by the U.S. General Services Administration in the amount of $44,237 for installing 20,000 square feet of Gaco elastic membrane to seal the basement garage floor of the Federal Building in Spokane, Washington. The work consisted of cleaning by grinding and sanding the concrete floor. The crew was one subcontractor, my son and I.

The subcontractor's only duty was to core four holes for the basement drains. When the prep work was done, we started installing the two-component prime coat. Specifications called for this material to be rolled on, but for some reason, rolling would not work. I decided to trowel the material into place. (This material is very expensive and has a work-time of less than an hour.) At that moment, the COR, Mr. Sakaguchi, showed up and said if I didn't roll it, he wouldn't accept the job.

I explained to him that rolling was just one method, and that the most important thing was to get the proper millage. The U.S. Government contracts allow the contractor to use his own methods to reach the specified end result. I told him that it would take two days for the prime coat to dry, and that I would have the Gaco representative on site on Monday to verify that I had the proper millage. The COR left without saying anything. I got down on my hands and knees and troweled the entire 20,000 square feet in one shift. (Doug said to me, "I didn't believe ANYONE could do that!")

On Monday, Pat White, the Gaco Rep, showed up and after much rhetoric, got Mr. Sakaguchi to accept the work. He made sure that I had to fill out enough paperwork to pay for my "crime." We went ahead and completed the job to everyone's satisfaction, in spite of the inspector's interference. And the job was profitable.

■ ■ ■

Washington Park Reservoir
Original Contract Amount: $211,382
Final Amount: $246,929

We started work on the Washington Park Reservoir Rehabilitation project for the City of Portland in May, 1977. The demolition work consisted of removing deteriorated concrete liner, parapet walls and stairways, then forming and re-pouring concrete. Next was rolling the liquid urethane coating on the dam section (no pun intended). Then we placed a Hypalon liner over the entire inside surface of the 2 ½ acre reservoir. (Hypalon is trademark for chlorosulfonated polyethylene (CSPE) *synthetic rubber* (CSM) noted for its resistance to chemicals, temperature extremes, and ultraviolet light.)

To keep the job interesting, there was an addendum to the original specifications informing us that due to the potential water shortage, the city could shut us down on five days' notice, allowing the city to put the reservoir back into service.

Washington Park Reservoir under rehabilitation.

Access to this project was severely limited. The half-mile trail around the reservoir was only six feet wide. Only the dam section was accessible by truck. Our trail experience became invaluable to this project, as did our trail-building equipment, which by now included a four foot wide front end loader. The roll cage top and front bucket could be used to haul lumber and forms. The front bucket was used to haul demolition material and for pouring concrete. In addition to the front loader, we had rock drills and concrete splitters, not new, but few contractors knew about them. Using the drills and splitters, we were able to break up the concrete wall and remove it with the front loader. This made the reservoir trail wide enough to accommodate a 580 Case backhoe, which we used to remove the deteriorated sections of the concrete slab.

Most of the deteriorated concrete was in the top ten feet of the reservoir. For access and safety reasons, we built a plank scaffold with hand railing around the inside of the reservoir. During the concrete removal operation, eight dump truck-loads of concrete wound up in the bottom of the reservoir. We used the front loader to load the concrete into skips that were hoisted out and into dump trucks.

Removing deteriorated concrete.

Our plank scaffolding helped us access the most deteriorated concrete.

VIPs overseeing concrete removal.

Using a chain saw and tongs to remove chunks of concrete.

Our front loader did this work in one day. Most of the other contractors were going to use Bobcats and figured it would take four to five days. Once the demolition was done, we used the front loader to place the concrete. On one section, we had decided to pump the concrete. The pump truck arrived and set up in the street. The concrete truck backed up to load the pump. Just as he started pumping, I looked in the direction of the pump and saw a fancy Mercedes spinning around in the middle of the street. It spun two or three times but didn't hit anything and kept on going. Immediately we began running to flag anyone else down but one or two more cars went spinning through the oil that was leaking out of the pump. We sent both the pump and the concrete truck home.

Ingenuity and our front loader got the concrete where it needed to be.

The next day we decided to try it with a crane and concrete bucket. We got off to a fair start. We unloaded a couple of yards and then the crane broke, so we moved the truck to the only other access point, which was near the control house. We poured the concrete into five gallon buckets, lifted them over the fence by hand, and set them in a wheelbarrow. Then we rolled them along the scaffold, lifted them out of the wheelbarrow and poured them into the new slab. The ingenuity here was brute strength and determination. We unloaded that truck and were ready for the next one. When the driver went to move, he snapped the drive line. This was a four-wheel-drive truck. I told the driver to tie up the drive shaft and move the truck out of the way. He said that his company procedure was to send out a mechanic to do that. I said that my procedure was to make way for the next truck. He fumed, fussed and explained that he was a senior driver, blah, blah, blah. I told him, "Move the truck or I'll push it over the side." He finally got the hell out of the way. We poured the whole truck load by lifting buckets over the fence.

Problematic concrete pump truck at center right.

This completed the concrete portion of the project. It was time to begin clean up in preparation for installing the Hypalon liner in the reservoir section and the liquid urethane coating on the face of the dam.

Installing the Hypalon liner.

We began by dragging the huge sheets up the 1.5:1 reservoir slope. This required eight men, including one on the loader. Ropes were run through pulleys at the top of the slope and connected back to the loader. As it pulled, the men fluttered the sheet to get air under it to break the friction. At the top of the slope, the sheets were attached to the concrete liner with anchor bolts. The seams were then welded.

Welding seams in the liner, very carefully.

Once the sides of the reservoir were done, we repeated the operation on the floor. After the liners were welded everything was air tested for leaks. As we had been very careful, we found no leaks. We then proceeded to apply the water proofing to the vertical sections of the dam, which required a white water based primer. Once the primer cured, we coated the entire surface with a black high-density liquid urethane waterproofing.

The reps, Dick Nelson from the Burke Rubber Co., which manufactured the Hypalon liner and Pat White from Gaco Western, the urethane manufacturer, had a very good rapport with the water department's engineers, Fred Whitfield, and Dale Pestes. The close cooperation of all of the parties ensured that the job was completed to the highest standards.

CHAPTER 21

1978
SANTA YNEZ RECREATION IMPROVEMENTS
U.S. Department of Agriculture
Los Padres National Forest
Near Santa Barbara, California
US Forest Service

The US Forest Service awarded us a contract to build one new campground and remodel four others adjacent to the Santa Ynez River and near the town of Santa Ynez (about 30 miles NE as the crow flies from the town of Santa Barbara, California). The job included installation of five miles of waterline with 300 pounds working pressure, removal of two existing steel tanks, and building a low-water crossing (fjord). The job included six new masonry block comfort stations, some trails, a road, a concrete bridge, two miles of road resurfacing with chip seal, and installation of special Pullman-style toilets like those used in passenger trains.

Fjord (low water crossing) under construction.

Fjord completed.

This job began and ended with toilets. The make and model numbers were on the plans, but there was no address or phone number for the manufacturer, the sole supplier. After I'd requested this information many times from the Forest Service, they finally came up with a telephone number, which I called. After many attempts, someone finally answered the phone. I was told that these items were out of stock and would not go into production for at least three months. At the end of three months, I called again and was told that they wouldn't go into manufacturing mode for another few months. After about six or eight months of that nonsense, it became obvious to me that they didn't plan on ever manufacturing again. I informed the Forest Service, who replied to me that we should "wait a little longer."

The job lasted one year, and I kept notifying the Forest Service about the problem. Two weeks before final inspection, the COR said, "Let's try waiting one more week." Of course the toilets didn't show up! After a mere year of misery, which will be described briefly below, we had the final inspection. The Forest Service wanted me to give them a price to install a different type of toilet. This came after I had completely demobilized. I said, "No, thank you." I learned my lesson about taking on work after the contract is complete: I basically assume all of the risk all over again.

In order to bid this job, I joint-ventured with Bob Davis of Park Construction, Inc. from Vancouver, Washington. Bob had been an iron-worker most of his life, but had bid the Sacajawea Park job in Longview, Washington. He was the only bidder, had very high prices, and a lot of change orders at very high prices. He subbed out all of the work. He had subcontractors who knew what they were doing. He got lucky and wound up making a bunch of money.

As our joint venture was on federal land, a California Contractor's License was not required, nor was I required to pay California sales tax on materials other than road materials. However, California suppliers would not sell any material unless one pays the tax. For this reason, we bought all of our pipe and fittings from Familian in Portland, Oregon, loaded it into forty-foot vans and shipped it to the job site. This turned out to be a not-so-great idea. When we needed an extra part or fitting or whatever, we had to buy it locally, pay the tax, and as often as not, could not get the same brand we were using. Paying the tax and buying from local suppliers would have been much cheaper,

For environmental reasons and otherwise, the pipe manufacturer had changed the formula for plastic pipe. This created hard spots in the pipe. After we'd put in five miles of pipeline, we could not get certain sections of pipe to test. When we tested a section of pipe, one joint would fail. We'd repair that joint and re-test. That meant cutting out a coupling and replacing with two couplings and a short piece of pipe. This went on for about a week. Bob was having a fit, blaming everything and everybody, including me.

One morning I told Doug to go along the pipeline, cut out every coupling and dump them all next to Bob's trailer. Bob was a tightwad, and had moved his trailer and wife onto the job site. We also used it for a job office. His son Jerry, and son-in-law also had their trailers on site. After hours, they climbed up the bank and cut the tanks into pieces small enough to drag down to the road, where they could be loaded onto a scrapper's truck. (I had originally planned to move the tanks with a helicopters and load them directly onto the truck. It would have taken about two hours and they would have been gone!)

We called the pipe manufacturer's representative to the job. He determined that it was necessary to double prime each part prior to gluing.

Construction was booming in this area. There was little skilled help available and no equipment operators. Equipment was also in short supply. Bob owned a Long backhoe that he had purchased from a friend of mine… cheap! It was just a little bit better than worthless. Jerry didn't claim to be an operator, but he operated the best he could. Jerry also had a pretty good idea of how the work should proceed and soon became at odds with his dad.

Due to the soil conditions, we should have used a track-mounted excavator but there were none available. I wanted to bring in a subcontractor who had all of the equipment we needed from Vancouver: excavator, loader, grader, and compactors, to do the pipeline and roadwork. If we'd had this equipment, we would have completed the pipeline and roads in two or three months. Instead it took us nearly a year. We did subcontract some of the pipeline work. The problem here was that the subs tended to skip the hard spots. I learned long ago that the prime contractor has to watch the subs just as close, or closer than he watches his own crews. Bob, like a lot of other contractors, let the subs do anything they want. If they didn't get the work done, they didn't get paid. The only problem with this is that if the job doesn't get done, the prime still has to pay all bills plus the sub-contractor for the work he didn't complete. Bonding companies don't like losses. I like them even less.

PARK CONST. CORP.
GENERAL CONTRACTORS
14204 N.E. 29th Avenue
Vancouver, Washington 98665
Phone (206) 695-5073

Sept. 15, 1978

Mr. Lloyd Kessler
7206 N. W. 25th Ave.
Vancouver, Washington

The reputation of Park Construction Company is at stake. I must preserve that reputation. The meeting with the Forest Service this past week and some of the comments made have criticised the company of the following.

1. Poor management
2. Lack of communications
3. Poor workmanship
4. Disention within the ranks

Jerry and I have discussed where the company stands. We would be ill advised if we did not make you aware of our feelings on this matter. Before we signed the contract for this job it was agreed that we should have only one boss. At your suggestion I was to be supervisor over the entire job with the final say. We are all aware that this has not been the case. I have been trying to come to a realistic solution and find that I have the following options open to me any one of which would make a difference on the criticisim.

1. First is to require all orders for agreements for equipment material and man power to go through the office for my signature or the signature of any two of the three of us.

2. To express my opinions to our bonding agent.

3. To ask if you would take a two week vacation or until I could find out exactly where the company stands.

I have real concerns about the criticisims as they effect the reputation of our company. I also am concerned that we had to borrow money at this time. I feel that if we had been able to operate with a closer relationship this might have been avoided. Personally I would like to use the first option of haveing all material, labor and equipment agreements carry my signature or two signatures out of the three of us. Also that I will be active supervisor through the office not on the end of a shovel. If you have any other suggestins I am willing to listen.

Bob Davis

Bob Davis (Pres.)

Recieved Sept 16 1978

Sept. 17, 1978

To Bob Davis, President

To reply to your letter of Sept. 15, 1978, concerning the reputation of Park Corporation. I am only concerned with the performance of Park Construction and Lloyd H. Kessler Joint Venture. At the meeting on Sept. 14th with the USFS, certain commitments were made in regard to office help, scheduling, performance and payroll. I intend to see the "Joint Venture" performs as I promised at that meeting. Mr. Wilson, CO for the USFS, and Al Mansfield, representing the Fireman's Fund, were at the meeting. They expect us to perform as promised.

If by Oct. 20, 1978, we have not performed, default is imminent. I will expect that you and Jerry Davis will be cooperative with me in this commitment, and that you will accept any recommendations of the contracting officer and the bonding company.

Lloyd Kessler

Jerry, bustin' his ass.

We also built a 50-foot long bridge, which required considerable carpenter work to form the footings. Carpenters were also in short supply, but as luck would have it, Millie's cousin Diane, who lived in Santa Barbara, was married to an architect, Stan Riffle. Stan had two brothers who framed houses. I hired them to do the work. They got off to a good start. About an hour into the job, one of them sawed his extension cord in two. About twenty minutes later the other brother sawed his extension cord in two. Somehow they both survived and managed to get the forms built. We poured the concrete. I told them I had other carpenter work for them to do, but they said the job was too rough for them. One of them went back to framing and the other started building surf boards.

Setting the pre-cast planks for the bridge.

After letting the concrete piers cure for 28 days, we set the pre-cast planks and installed the hand rails. In the meantime, we had been constructing the comfort stations.

Comfort stations under construction.

Foundation slab poured for comfort station.

Masons stacking comfort station block. The best workers are happy workers.

Completed parking lot/station.

One of our bid items was fabricating picnic tables from ten-inch pipe (well casing), supplied on site by the government. I decided to buy the pipe in Vancouver and fabricate it in our well-equipped shop. This was much cheaper than doing it in the field with portable equipment, and paying prevailing wages.

We exchanged the pipe supplied by the USFS when we arrived on site to install the tables. When the project was complete, we hauled the exchanged pipe to our yard in Vancouver. A year and a half later, this pipe was used as columns for our new 50 x 100-foot shop.

Labor Day, 1978, the comfort stations were ready for roofs. This required beveling some heavy redwood timbers. We had shut down for the holiday. The day after Labor Day, it poured down rain and it was too wet to do anything but bevel the beams, so I sent everyone home except for three carpenters. I instructed them to bevel the beams. They moaned and groaned and said it was too dangerous to work in the rain. I fired them. They squawked to the California Department of Safety and Health (DOSH). Three weeks passed. DOSH ordered me to pay them three weeks' pay.

Two of the workers accepted the pay, the other one said, "This is B.S.—I will not accept the pay." I sent him a check anyway with a note explaining that if he didn't accept the pay, I'd be in more trouble. He replied that he'd work for me anytime. Unfortunately, all the carpentry work was complete.

We were required to make some welds on the comfort stations. One day as we were welding, DOSH showed up and wrote me a ticket because I didn't have a fence around the portable welding machine. I asked why I needed a fence. They explained that somebody could walk up to the welder and burn their ass on the exhaust stack. I built the fence and in my entire career, this is the only time I ever saw a fence built around a welding machine. The fine was only $1,100, but my ass really got burned.

The pipeline specs required sand bedding around the pipe. There was a lot of sand on site, but the Forest Service specs called for washed sand. I asked the COR what difference it made, but he said, "Because that's what the spec requires." I wound up buying sand in Solvang and hauling it the 60 miles to the site.

The job site sand would meet bedding spec anywhere, so I got a little smarter and dredged the sand out of the river on weekends. It was washed!

At the peak of the job, we had about 40 men working. Due to delays in the pipeline construction, payment was slow in coming. The well was running dry, so I laid off half the crew. The best thing about this is that production doubled. During this time Bob (the crew called him Buzzard Bob) liked to stand behind a tree and watch the guys work. All this did was slow them down. When Bob wasn't watching the guys, he was busy arguing with the inspectors. Finally, Jerry Davis told Bob that he needed to take a vacation—and sent him home to Vancouver. He was still on vacation when the job ended six months later. He decided it was time to retire for good.

We made a six-month job last a year—for very little profit. I promised myself I would never again get in a position where I did not have complete control. Foolishly, I broke this promise more than once.

CHAPTER 22

DOGS ON THE JOB

The whole dog-gone thing started when I was working at Santa Ynez. I never really liked it when Jerry Davis let his dog "Rough" roam the job site.

I had never even thought about taking a dog onto a job site. In my mind, it was a distraction, and unsafe. Rough was a good dog, but we had to be careful not to run over him. He seemed to lie in precarious places.

One day I hired a guy to help with a big vault toilet that we had to tear down, pump out, and get rid of all the crap (literally). He had a dog—a German shepherd mix. Nice, friendly enough.

This guy sat on the edge of the toilet vault, with the aroma below, eating his lunch. His dog sat about 30 feet away.

I told the guy that I didn't want dogs on the job site, but he told me that he didn't have anywhere to leave him.

I said, "Well, figure something out."

However, he kept appearing. By that time, I was getting irritated with the guy anyway because he wasn't much use. I told him, "You can't bring the dog to work anymore."

"So, I quit," he said.

"OK, I'll just write you out a lack-of-work slip." I never saw him again.

■ ■ ■

Brutus

Somewhere along the way, however, my heart changed. His name was Brutus, and he was owned by Fred Meier. He was to become our First Job Dog.

Brutus

At the Yakima Tieton job in 1981, Brutus and I were walking through a narrow tunnel in the canal. Somehow, a deer had gotten into the canal. It was a buck with a large rack. There was barely enough room for two people to pass in the tunnel, but here came the buck, charging toward us. Brutus took off and ran down the tunnel about 50-60 feet ahead of me, grabbed the deer by the throat and killed it. Whew.

The reason Brutus was in the canal with me is because Fred and the crew were working on the trail above the canal. The trail ran all the way back to Trout Lodge, where we were staying. Brutus had fallen in love with Rawley's dog Dipstick, who lived directly across Highway 12 from the Lodge. If Brutus was topside of the canal, he would sneak back to Trout Lodge to play with Dipstick. That meant that I would spend a couple of hours and a long drive to fetch him back.

Never-the-less, he saved my life and Job Dogs were welcomed on our projects from then on. Who was really responsible for saving my life—Brutus or Dipstick?

What are the odds?

■ ■ ■

Grover

One day in 1980, while my workers were building our new shop, a dog wandered into the yard. After the crew had gone home for the day, the dog was still here. The next morning, I asked who owned the dog. No one answered.

In the meantime, my Grandson Collin was playing in the sandbox and the dog curled up next to him. They became good buddies, and Collin got to name her. He said, "I've always wanted a dog named Rover, but that's a boy dog's name, so we will name her Girl Rover. Oh yeah—we'll call her GROVER!"

Grover

She was 3 years old. She claimed to be an Australian Kelpie, but was a dark chocolate Lab color. Kelpies weigh in at 30 lbs., but Grover weighed 60. We were never sure just what breed she was, but she could run a rabbit down and devour it, guts, fur and all, before she would come to complete stop!

One day she took off really fast and tore the ligaments in her leg. I took her to Dr. Slocum in Eugene. He sawed the leg in two, put bone marrow into the saw cut, and fastened a metal plate to her leg. She was walking within three or four days. It cost me $1,300 for her operation. I got lots of criticism for spending that much on the dog. That was more money than I'd spent to bring my four kids into the world!

She stuck around for about ten years. She stayed in more "no-pets motels" and flew in more helicopters during *her* short life than most people do in their entire lifetime! She seldom barked, but did that only if someone appeared who wasn't supposed to be there.

One day Fred, our engineer, and I were driving home from Denny, CA. We were pulling our horse trailer containing our tools. We went into a motel to register, but the proprietor did not like animals, and did not allow dogs. I told the manager that we would leave the dog in the pickup. He reluctantly rented us the room on condition that no dogs went inside.

The room must have been 400 sq. feet. It was huge. We went to dinner, and afterwards we snuck Grover into the room. She did a belly-drag, and then managed to formulate an enriched circle around the entire room's carpet, scooting on her butt. We had a good laugh.

Sometime later we stayed in a Truckee, CA, motel where no pets were allowed, AND where the proprietor also hated animals. At that time, Grover, Kenny's dog Brutus, and Rosie were with us. To get the dogs in, one person went into the motel hallway and stood in front of the security camera's view. While they did that, the other guys shoved the dogs through the window and took them to their respective rooms.

This routine became a joke—mostly because Kenny was on good terms with the receptionist.

▪ ▪ ▪

Rosie

When working on the Ora Vega project in 1991, we sent one of our workers on an errand. He hurried to the pickup, and jumped in without looking around. He backed up and rolled over Rosie's leg. She had been napping by the back of the truck.

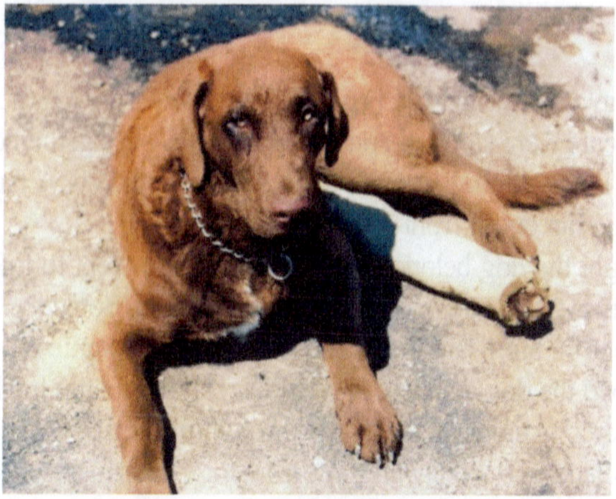

Rosie

She was a true Water Dog. No matter where we went, she'd find water.

When we were doing Coleman Fish Hatchery, she came down with salmon poisoning. We took her to the vet, who kept her overnight. The next morning, we were getting ready to go home at noon on Friday. As the crew was still working, I went to the vet to pick Rosie up. When I arrived, she ran and flopped right between my legs. She was very happy to see me, and made a full recovery.

Rosie was good company but had one quirk (she was Kenny's dog): For no apparent reason, and no matter whether in the middle of the day or at night, she'd go into an open area, stick her head in the air, and howl for five or ten minutes. Must have been the ancient wolf in her.

One time when we were near Entiat, we pulled into a restaurant for breakfast with Rosie in back of the pickup. She started doing one of her howls. The people in the restaurant said that she must be talking to the wolves that howled last night. We said nothing to dissuade them, and continued eating.

Sometime later, Kenny left her with a friend at his service station. When he went to pick her up, his friend told him that some yahoos in a Jeep drove into the yard and deliberately ran over her. She was dead. It broke our hearts.

■ ■ ■

Monica

One day as I turned off Fruit Valley Road onto Whitney Road, a couple of cars were stopped and several people were gathered around a dog lying in the ditch. I stopped to see what I could do. A lady told me that the dog ran out in front of her and she hit it.

I thought the dog belonged to my neighbor. I went to find him, He wasn't home, so I came back and told the woman. Someone had called animal control, but I said it was the last thing they wanted to deal with, so I scooped the dog up and took it to Dr. David Slocum in Hazel Dell.

We weren't sure that she'd live through night. Dr. Slocum said, "I am scheduled to go to Hawaii tomorrow for a veterinary convention. If necessary, I'll stay here and take care of her."

I said, "No. Go. You need a rest."

They kept her in the clinic over the weekend. Bright and early Monday morning the caregivers called to say "Come get your dog! She's tries to bite us any time we get near her."

"I'll be right there," I said.

The dog wasn't friendly to me either, but I brought her home, threw a couple of bundles of straw on the shop floor, and laid her on them. I left the outer shop door open.

I never did see her go out, but every 2 or 3 days she'd go outside to relieve herself. She was so weak that I'd have to put a blanket under her and drag her back into the shop. It took 4-6 weeks for her to recover.

She got her name during the days of the Clinton Administration. At that time, Linda Tripp and Monica Lewinski were doing battle in the media. Doug came into shop one morning while the rest of the crew was getting ready for work. Noticing that the dog was bright-eyed and feeling good, he said. "Ya know, she's got eyes just like Monica

Lewinsky." From that day on, she was known as Monica, friendly to everyone.

Monica

Unlike most water dogs, she didn't particularly like the water, even though she was a Chesapeake mix with curlier fur than most. And as for a guard dog's duties, if you acted normal, she would open the door for you.

She was about 3 when she showed up—and we have no idea where she came from. During our El Dorado job in 1988, Monica got to ride back and forth to work in the helicopter, right along with me.

■ ■ ■

Kenny's dog Brutus

While Kenny was driving east on 88th St. (Vancouver) during a thunder storm, he saw a dead-grass-colored Chesapeake running down the street. He stopped, opened the door, and "Brutus" jumped in. They immediately were adopted by each other. When he rode in the back of a pickup and recognized some place we pulled into, he had the odd habit of spinning around in circles. As he did that, the slobber flew all over the bed of the pickup, making a helluva mess. Every single time. He spun many circles.

One day when we were doing a job for the Forest Service near Lake Wenatchee, he began spinning and slobbering. The inspector, who we did not like—and called "Dumb-dumb"—asked Doug what was wrong with that dog.

Doug said, "I don't know. He's been acting like that ever since he got bit by that raccoon a couple of weeks ago." Silence. The inspector kept his distance from then on.

One time, while on the Truckee, CA job, we stayed at the Boomtown Motel, just across the state line toward Reno. Our rooms were on the third floor. When the desk clerks were looking down, one of us would hold the elevator door open and we'd rush the dogs into the elevator and go to our respective rooms.

We stayed there for a week. Brutus was a pretty good dog once he'd had his after-dinner, evening walk. We didn't have to worry about him until morning. However, things are not always perfect when animals act like animals, and this one time Brutus suddenly had to get up in the middle of night, so Kenny let him out into the hall. Brutus crapped there, but quick-on-the-draw-Kenny brought a pile of toilet paper and laid it next to Brutus' pile.

We checked out early the next morning. The motel clerk thought some drunk left a pile in the hall. It was difficult to contain our smirks. We were lucky once more, and Brutus stayed with us for quite a few *more* years.

■ ■ ■

Kuila (pronounced Kee-la, short for Tequila)

My grandson Owen (Doug's son) got him when he was a puppy. I don't remember from where. He kept him for only a couple of years and then gave him to Doug. When we were doing the Longmire job, Monica and Kuila cost us a $1,000 ticket. Kuila spotted a female National Park Ranger across the river, and like a lot of females, she started yapping. As dogs are not allowed in National Parks, the ranger came over and wrote us a ticket! I thought, "What's another $1000?" It was worth it.

Kuila on duty at the Vista House.

Kuila is retired now at age 14. Her main pleasure is napping and harassing the mail carrier.

▪ ▪ ▪

As I said, it wasn't until I met Fred that I began to appreciate dogs on the job. I learned this from a small crew while working away from home:

1. Many of my crew had no one to care for their dogs when they were away.
2. Dogs had a calming effort on the crew
3. The crew was much happier when the dogs were around.
4. Pets matter

That was enough for me. Although I don't have a dog of my own now, Kenny carries on the tradition of Job Dogs wherever possible, for all the same reasons.

CHAPTER 23

1979
BIG SUR TRAIL
U.S. Forest Service
Ventana Wilderness Area
Los Padres National Forest, California

In late 1978, we were awarded a job to reconstruct the Big Sur Trail in the Ventana Wilderness Area near Big Sur, California. The goal of this project was to correct the damage from a devastating forest fire in the area two years before. It had damaged many of the trails and required two miles of new trail construction.

We loaded our two pickups with all the tools and camp gear necessary to do this project, and the crew (minus me) departed on Tuesday at 6 a.m. for Big Sur. At nine I received a call from the Forest Service saying there was a state-wide fire shut-down. I had no way of contacting my crew, so I called the Oregon State Patrol and told them that my pickups should be nearing Medford soon, and would they please stop them and have the crew call me. The siren stopped them in their tracks, and my call-back prompted them to turn around and return home.

We had just been awarded the Splinters Cabin Trail Bridge contract and needed a shop in which to fabricate the metal-work, so Wednesday morning we designed and started building a 50′ x 80′ shop using the pipe we brought home from the Santa Ynez job. By the following Tuesday we had the trusses up and the roof on.

The next day, the crew headed to Big Sur to begin reconstruction of the Terrace Creek Trail. The trail head was about a half hour's drive from Big Sur. While working this trail, we stayed at the motel in Big Sur.

We started with a four-man crew and were using two McCullough chain saws. Foreman Randy Johnson decided to show off his logging abilities and felled a tree onto the other saw and smashed it. This meant that I had to drive to Salinas, the nearest saw dealer, about a three-hour round trip. I bought a new Stihl chain saw, and by the time I got back to Big Sur, the crew was done for the day.

The next morning we started clearing more trail. The new Stihl worked well for twenty minutes—until the muffler fell off. I bolted it back on. It fell off again. I told the cutter to "Keep cutting, no matter what." I again drove to Salinas to get another saw. When I got back, there was a horrible noise. The muffler had fallen off, but the cutter had kept cutting, just like I told him to do. I handed him the new saw. It wasn't twenty minutes before the muffler fell off!

I told the crew to struggle along and do the best they could with the remaining McCullough saw. I took the new saws back to the dealer, got on the phone and called the distributor to see if we could find out what the problem was. This took a couple of days. It was finally determined that the only way to keep the mufflers on was to use Loctite (an adhesive/sealant) on the threads.

In the meantime, I'd sent Randy back to Vancouver to begin metal fabrication for the Splinters Cabin Trail Bridge. Doug Kessler, who had much trail experience, was our trail foreman. Due to the muffler problem, it took three or four days longer than planned to finish this trail.

We then moved our operation to the Big Sur trailhead at Cold Springs, where there was a corral we could leave the horses in at night. During the day, we'd load old Sonny the Horse with the tools and gasoline needed for the day's work. After work, Sonny stayed in the corral and we stayed in the motel in Big Sur.

Sonny's hotel at Big Sur trailhead next to the '66 Chevy that would not start.

Milt, Bill and Lloyd.

After four days of work, it was taking too long to hike in and out. We loaded up the horses with tents and supplies and set up a complete camp at Mocho campground. The crew worked out of this camp for two days.

In the meantime, I had gone to town for more supplies. While I was gone, the crew moved the entire camp to Rainbow campground. This camp was at the junction of the two main trails that we would work. For this reason, we camped there for about three weeks.

While I was in Big Sur, I mentioned to the restaurant owner that I was looking for a camp cook. It just so happened that a young woman from Shelton, Washington, was passing through. She came into the restaurant looking for work. I told her that she would have to hike in, and that we would normally work 10 days and then come out for two. She said, "It sounds good to me. I'm a good cook. I'll take the job. I'll make a list of the food and supplies I want."

She drove a pickup with a canopy. I gave her directions to the trail head and told her to hike into camp and take over the cooking. Jill's dad was a logger and had raised her like a boy. She was completely able to take care of herself in the woods. I told her I was going to Monterey for the groceries and would be back to camp the next day by noon.

I got back to camp the next day at noon, as promised. The crew and packer had done a good job of setting up the camp. Jill had my lunch ready. Sonny and I ate, and then headed down the trail, sawing logs, brush and danger trees.

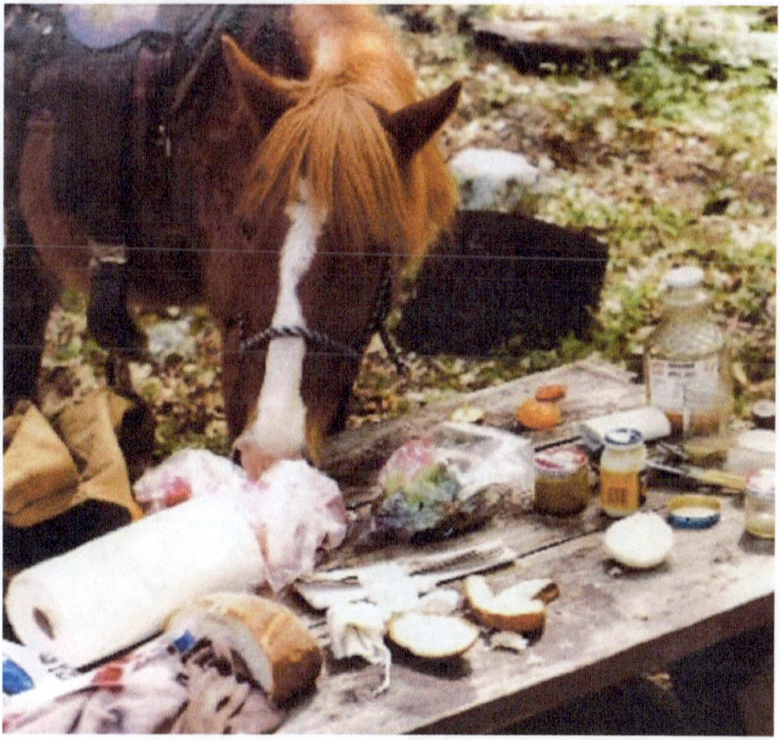

Sonny, munching lunch.

Lloyd, axe and chainsaw.

When the crews returned from work, we experienced Jill's first recipe. The food tasted good, even though it was sea foam green. We didn't pay much attention to the color at this time.

It was late fall and the camp was set up next to the Big Sur River. It was convenient, but very damp and cold. We made up our minds that we would put future camps on high ground, and pack the water a little farther.

Tent on high ground.

During this ten-day cycle, the work proceeded very well, so we headed out for a little R & R. As it was late fall, there was very little forage for Sonny. He was weak and had lost a lot of weight, so I decided to take him to Nason's (a nearby ranch) to fatten up. We stopped at Big Sur and tied Sonny to the restaurant porch.

While having our before-dinner drinks, a lady ran into the bar and shouted, "Bartender, bartender, there's a horse tied up outside!"

He looked up at her and asked her where she was from. She said, "New York."

The bartender replied, "This must be your first time out West."

The lady left.

After dinner, we loaded Sonny into the trailer and headed for the motel at Carmel. When we pulled into the motel, Sonny fell down in the trailer, and I couldn't get him up. Since we were all tired and grungy from ten days on the trail, I took my shower and checked on Sonny.

He was up and happily munching on the motel's lawn. In the morning I told the proprietor, who replied, "Sonny's welcome to munch on the lawn anytime you guys stay here." Sonny took him up on his offer a couple more times.

On one section of the Big Sur trail, the contracts required us to remove about a hundred danger trees. The Forest Service was responsible for marking these trees ahead of the reconstruction work. About a week before we were ready to do this work, our inspector, "Ranger Dick" rode into camp.

Brian, Lloyd, Ranger Dick & his horse.

I asked him to mark the danger trees. He said he would, on his way back to the ranger station; he rode off in that direction.

I hired a timber faller from Washington, equipped him with the proper saw and tools, and sent him to fall the danger trees while I went into town overnight for supplies. When I arrived back in camp about noon the next day, there was my faller, bullshitting with the camp cook. I asked him why he was in camp. He said he cut all the trees that were marked. I asked him how many he had cut. His reply: "About a dozen." Ranger Dick was 88 trees short.

Since he wasn't interested in doing any work other than falling trees, I sent him back to Washington.

We kept reconstructing the trail. In about a week, Ranger Dick showed up again. I asked him to please mark the danger trees. He said he would, but he didn't have any paint. I told him, "Don't worry. I've got plenty of paint." So he again agreed to mark the trees on his way out.

By this time, our crews were working many miles away, and it was time to move the camp. The Forest Service recommended that I hire Fred Nason, a Native American, who lived on the far end of the project, to move camp to the Black Cone Trail, a distance of about five miles. (One of the trails we were working on was on his property.) When the crew left for work that morning, I had them take their sleeping bags and enough food for that day and the next morning's breakfast. The packer was scheduled to arrive at about ten a.m. At noon, he galloped into camp, waving a bottle of Jack Daniels. He was smashed. There was also a good looking woman with him. She was sober.

I left Daryl to help with the packing. Daryl and the girl started loading the horses. Fred Jr. took a nap. I hiked back to the trailhead and drove the pickup around to the next trailhead. By the time I reached the new campsite, it was dark. We ate our dinners and slept on the cold ground.

The next morning I hiked back, looking for the pack string. About half way back, I found them. The camp gear and supplies were strewn all over the trail; Daryl and the young woman were packing the horses. Fred Jr. was asleep. We got the horses loaded, tied Fred Jr. onto his horse, and headed for the Black Cone camp.

During the night, Daryl and the young woman bedded down on the camp supplies. To keep warm, she snuggled right up to Daryl. Daryl thought she was the packer's wife. She was actually Nason's 18-year-old sister, Elizabeth, and was not promiscuous. She was an excellent horsewoman and a crack shot with both rifle and pistol.

Upon arrival at Black Cone, we set up camp. The pack string went home to the Nason ranch, a distance of about three miles.

It was now early November and the crew asked me if they could work the next nineteen days straight so they could be home for Thanksgiving and take the following seven days off. I agreed.

When the time came to leave, I loaded the whole crew into my pickup and took them back to the Cold Spring Campground where we had left our vehicles.

Our 1966 Chevy Pickup would not start. It was already hooked to the horse trailer, but was not getting fuel. I decided to hook my Ranchero to it and tow it far enough down the road where we could coast on down to Big Sur.

The problem was that there was a dip in the road. I told Doug, "I'm gonna tow you across the dip. Be sure not to touch the brake."

We started across the dip, and Doug hit the brakes anyway, which resulted in snapping the drive shaft in the Ranchero. Now we only had one vehicle that would run—a Plymouth 4-door sedan. All six of us climbed in and headed down the road.

We barely got started when the driver hit a rock in the road—and that knocked a hole in the gas tank. *(It must be noted that when a crew is in the woods for nineteen days, they not only get grungy, they get rummy! The only thing they're thinking about is getting HOME!)*

The first part of the road was fairly level, but the last part was very steep, with bluffs on either side. This car had both power steering and power brakes. As we started down the steep section, I told him to keep the speed down to around five mph, slow enough so that he could stop the car with his emergency brake. He didn't listen. I knew we'd be running out of gas soon and have no brakes at all. I finally ordered him to stop. Everyone got out except the driver. He drove on.

About a half mile down the road, he stopped and parked. We caught up to him and walked the four miles into Big Sur.

I hired a Local to take them to the Monterey airport in time to make their flight to San Francisco and Portland. To the dubious benefit of the other passengers on the plane, they were all wearing the same clothes they'd been wearing for the last nineteen days!

I spent the night in Big Sur. The next morning I got a Local to take me up the hill to retrieve the vehicles. I then headed for the airport and home.

I was scheduled to arrive in Portland about 8 p.m., but the Portland airport was fogged in. The pilot went around twice and headed for Seattle. Once we landed, the Portland passengers were advised to board a bus that would take us to the Portland airport. Most of us sat on the bus for about three hours. One by one, some of the passengers left and decided to stay in a hotel. Finally, the bus departed for Portland.

When we reached Portland it was very foggy, and obviously, the bus driver was confused. I took over the navigation and we finally arrived at 5 am. (Because of situations like this, I never gave my ETA to Millie.) I waited at the airport a couple of hours until the fog moderated, and then called her to come and get me.

The whole family feasted on turkey that afternoon.

During the Thanksgiving layover, I took delivery on a new 1980 Ford F-250 pickup truck, equipped with a five-speed manual transmission. Sometime before the beginning of the Santa Ynez project, Randy Johnson purchased for me a 1972 Ford pickup with an automatic transmission, but it was very poor at trailer-pulling. When I pulled the horse trailer down steep roads at Big Sur, I had to rely completely upon the brakes. There was no way to make this pickup slow down under compression. Every time I pulled the trailer down the hill, I burned up a set of brakes. All previous pickups we used on trail work had standard transmissions. As a result, I pressed the old '66 Chevy pickup into service for this job. It was the one that wouldn't start when we were leaving for Thanksgiving.

After the Christmas break, we moved back to the job. One of the first things we did was to hire more people because some of the workers didn't return—for various reasons.

When one of the new hands arrived at camp, his boots were falling apart, so we duct-taped them onto his feet and ankles. He said, "How am I gonna get them off?"

"You won't get them off. You don't need to worry about that until after you leave the project."

We finished this section of trail and packed up. We always burned our garbage, but the guy with the bad boots piped up and said, "I'm hauling my garbage out. I have a compost bin in the back of my Volkswagen bus."

I didn't care what he did as long as he got out of my sight. I learned later that he walked into Elizabeth's house unannounced, in the middle of the night. She grabbed her pistol and ushered him out.

Another incident happened in a difficult section of the trail. We threw a lot of dirt and rock into the creek. There was no other place to put it. The Game Dept. complained that we were messing up their fish run. They wanted to meet with me, but I put them off. As it turned out, heavy rains came and washed the material away. Their concerns washed away with it.

■ ■ ■

Our company's first new pickup—Ford F250 5-speed manual transmission; approaching Cold Springs at Big Sur Trailhead

When we returned from the Thanksgiving holiday, we finished the Black Cone trail section, broke camp, and moved it the three miles to the Nason ranch to start work on the trail that crossed Nason's property. For this portion of the work, we set up our camp on the road leading into Nason's, and used our travel trailer for cooking and eating. Jill was still the cook.

Brian Surbert and Ringo—Black Cone Wilderness in background.

Ringo, Daryl, Brian and white horse.

It took about four days to finish this trail, and it was now time to start the two miles of new construction, which was in a different part of the project. The problem was that the streams were high and we couldn't get across them with the horses. As a result, I decided to fly the camp in by helicopter from the village of Carmel Valley. From the staging area, we had to fly right over the top of the Carmel Ranger Station.

Once the camp was in, we started the new construction. The plans showed this work being on a flat ledge. However, there was no ledge. This required us to do far more excavation than we bid. It took us ten days of drilling and blasting to do the hard part, leaving about a mile left to do before we went home for Christmas. This remaining mile was fairly easy work, only requiring removal of an occasional boulder.

After the Christmas holidays, Daryl, Hank, two horses, and I began finishing the remaining work. At noon on the second day, the sheriff and his deputy rode up. The sheriff was the very picture of the old-time movie sheriffs—complete with Stetson, boots and gun. His deputy was a dud.

The Sheriff asked me if I had any explosives with me. I said, "Yes."

He said, "Where did you buy the explosives?"

I said, "Kelso, Washington."

The sheriff said, "I know. I already called there."

He went on to explain that another trail builder, Idaho Trail Builders, had gone home for the holidays and left dynamite in their tent. The bears had gotten into the tent and scattered food and dynamite all over the trail. A couple of hikers had reported it to the USFS, and The Forest Service had asked the sheriff to check on my operation. He went on to explain that there were a lot of "crazies" around, and if they found out I had explosives, they would take it away from me. He also mentioned that local thieves were using fifth-wheel trailers to steal cattle, and selling meat to McDonald's.

All I did was listen.

He also explained that I was legal to use explosives in part of the Ventana Forest, but not this part. He then said, "Can I see the explosives? How much do you have? Where is it?"

I said, "It's on the horse."

I took the box out of the saddle bag and set it on the ground. The deputy looked into the box. He claimed, "I'll SAY you've got a lot!"

He asked the sheriff, "Do you want me to take a picture of that?"

The sheriff gave him a pained look, but said, "Okay."

The fifty-pound box was shiny white, and had about twenty pounds left in it. The deputy put the gel explosive back in the box, and I set it in the bright sun, knowing that the glare would keep the camera from recording the serial numbers on the box.

The sheriff asked me how much more work we had to do. I told him, "Two or three days."

He told me to go ahead and finish the work, and as soon as I was done, to come and talk to him at his office. He said, "I'll figure out what to do then." He also said, "Promise me you will not take any explosives out of the forest." (Which meant that I was to blow up anything that I had left over.)

We finished the trail, and I had four sticks of gel left, and a 100-foot roll of primer cord. Keeping my promise, I blew up the explosives. The only problem was that I had put the primer cord on top of the gel, and when the blast went off it blew the bright orange primer cord up onto a sixty-foot tree. I quickly sawed Uncle Sam's tree down, and gathered up the primer cord, which I stuck into a deep hole in a basalt rock pile. The primer cord is probably still there!

I went to Salinas to see the sheriff, as I promised. On the way, I called for final inspection, and called my lawyer. The sheriff greeted me in a friendly manner. I noticed he was moving slowly. He explained to me that when he was riding out from my job, he came to a little creek and his horse bolted, throwing him off. He said he almost fell over the bluff. I said, "You're probably mad at me."

He said, "Why should I be mad at YOU?" And he went on to say, "I try never to blame other people for my mistakes." He told me, "Have your lawyer call me and we'll work out some kind of a deal."

When I called for the final inspection, the Forest Service let me know that I had a ticket for using a helicopter in the Ventana Wilderness Area. I turned it over to my lawyer.

Harry Wilson, the Contracting Officer, decided to do the final inspection himself. He enjoyed the chance to get out in the woods for a working vacation. Upon completing the final, which I did not attend, he mailed me the punch list, but to my dismay, he wanted more danger trees cut in the area that Ranger Dick was supposed to mark, but did not. Daryl and I packed in, removed the danger trees, and fixed the damage they caused to the trail tread. It took us three days.

The punch list also included ten feet of heavy construction on the Black Cone Trail, which was on the opposite end of the project. Technically, it made spec, but the crew had done a crappy job. It required some drilling and blasting, and took three days for Daryl and me to complete.

■ ■ ■

As mentioned earlier, we had used a helicopter in the wilderness area, and as a result, I got a ticket. My attorney set up a date with the Federal Court at Fort Ord. That morning at 11:30, I called my attorney and he said, "You're supposed to be in court at 1:00 this afternoon. Where are you?"

I said, "I'm about ninety miles away. Call the court and tell them I'll be about a half hour late." I barreled up the highway and arrived at court at 1:30.

It was unseasonably cold that day. The court was held in the base auditorium: no heat. The judge was an elderly man, near retirement. He had a very friendly attitude and an authoritative voice. He was wearing a dark blue cardigan, like people did in those days.

I apologized to judge for keeping him waiting.

He said, "You better go out and get your jacket."

"You folks have been waiting too long." I said, "Let's start."

He said, "No, go get your jacket."

He asked the prosecutor from the USFS to state his case. He was a little Mexican guy sitting on a hard bench with a leather jacket on, trembling from the cold.

Judge asked him to state his case.

He grunted, "Uhm. Uhm."

Judge led him, saying "Flying helicopter in wilderness area?"

The prosecutor again said, "Uhm, uhm."

The judge asked, "Was the helicopter disturbing the wildlife?"

The guy said, "Uhm. Uhm. Disturbing wildlife."

It's interesting to note that all the while we were doing the trail work, we didn't see any sign of wildlife. Not even a raven.

He asked me, "Was there a deadline on the job?"

I said, "Yes."

He asked me why I used the helicopter. I said, "Because the streams were too high for the horse to cross." I also explained to him that the same day we flew our camp in, the same helicopter company had rescued some Boy Scouts who had been camping at Pico Blanco.

He said, "I'm fining you $1,000 for disturbing wildlife, and suspending all but $200. Go pay the clerk. If that's too much, have the clerk talk to me."

I calmly walked over to the clerk, handed her $200 cash and left. I didn't want to take the chance of anybody changing his mind. $200 was a pittance to have the camp flown in.

■ ■ ■

Tree in foreground where extra-heavy trail excavation was thrown over side and into the creek.

The night we finished, Hank, Daryl and I stopped at a small bar in Chautauqua where the Locals hung out (mostly widows and divorcees). It was raining, and the Locals were all inside having a drink. We were leaning against the wall having a drink when a masonry contractor, a big guy about 45 years old and 250 lbs., started giving us crap. We were in our trail clothes and wearing our cowboy hats.

He was half drunk and mean, and was enjoying goosing women at the bar. He now decided he'd have more fun screwing with us, and threatened to beat us up. Daryl told him to back off. He didn't listen, and became more threatening.

Hank opened his coat, and showed the bully his Colt .45 as he pulled the hammer back. CLICK. Hank said, "You wanna hear the next sound?" No one else saw what happened. The guy turned pale and walked away. We finished our drinks and left.

A couple of weeks later, Hank got drunk and rode his white horse up to the Chautauqua bar. The problem was that he was naked. When the sheriff arrived, Hank galloped away and fell off his horse. I heard later that he told the sheriff, "Lloyd is going to blow up the bridge." He was so drunk that the sheriff didn't pay any attention to him.

Final Meeting

After the final inspection was completed, the Contracting Officer, Harry Wilson, along with the inspector, Ranger Dick, set up a meeting at the Monterey airport. Harry had also been our CO on the Santa Ynez job. The first thing he said was, "I want to compliment you on the excellent work you did on the new trail."

I said, "Thank you, but I think you should pay me for the extra excavation."

He seemed surprised, so I explained to him that the plans showed the trail on a flat ledge. He asked for an explanation. I looked over at Ranger Dick and asked him if he had seen a flat ledge. He said, "No."

Harry asked "What were the extra costs?"

And right then said, "Let's take a break and have lunch." He suggested that I try the calamari. (I had never heard of calamari, but that's what I ordered. It was superb. Though I've ordered it many times since, I've never had any that tasted as good.)

After lunch, we negotiated the change order for the extra work, and finalized the job. Harry retired a short time later and went into the trail-building business. He soon learned how tough it was, and that you could not delegate the work to a supervisor and expect it to be done. He lost money and gave up contracting altogether.

■ ■ ■

During the breaks in the Big Sur project, I returned to Santa Ynez to do warranty work. While there, I stayed in a motel in Santa Barbara for about three weeks. I ate my dinner at Harry's Bar and Restaurant, which was a popular place where many of the "Santa Barbarians" ate. The food was good and the drinks were excellent. Harry poured them himself. I ate and drank there many times during the year I worked at Santa Ynez.

The waiters and waitresses work mainly for tips. One blond waitress had waited on me many times. One night, as she was cashing out for the day, I asked if I could buy her a drink. She replied, "I never drink here. I have too many friends and relatives that eat and drink here. I don't want to give them any ideas."

I jokingly said, "Come to my motel and we'll have a drink."

She replied, “I’ll be there as soon as I finish checking out.”

She drove a very distinctive, though older, white Cadillac. She said, “I’ll park in the back.”

I left, and she arrived a few minutes later. I asked her what she would like to drink. She hugged me and said, “I don’t have time to drink. Let’s get started.”

It was fast and good. And then she jumped up, laughed, and said, “My oldest daughter still lives with me and I don’t want her to get suspicious. My ex-husband, who has remarried, lives next door. And we’re still good friends.”

Never mind these details. This still happened a couple more times during the next couple of weeks while I completed the project.

Chapter 24

1979
SPLINTERS CABIN TRAIL BRIDGE
(Built in 1980)
US Forest Service
Pacific Crest Trail
San Bernadino National Forest, California
Solicitation No. R5-27-79-66
Bid amount: $167,088.

During the winter months of 1979 and '80, Randy Johnson, our shop foreman, fabricated the steel arches and other components. His crew also built the concrete forms and procured the reinforcing steel. All this work was done in our new shop. Randy was very good at procuring and expediting, but did have a "bean-counter's" attitude, and was always looking for a "deal" on tools and equipment.

Checking out an arch.

Concrete forms.

May 16, 1980—All these components were loaded onto trucks and transported to the helicopter staging area that was adjacent to Splinters Cabin, a privately owned residence. The cabin was about 600 feet cross country from the bridge site. We used an Aerospatiale Lama helicopter to fly the materials to the bridge site.

Flying forms.

On May 19, Our five-man crew, which consisted of Doug Kessler, Brian Surbert, Daryl Elliot, Randy J. and me, precisely surveyed and laid out the bridge foundations and determined that everything fit the plans, so we began excavating for the footings.

As we were not allowed to use explosives, this was very difficult and tedious work. The process was: drill holes in the rock, insert the rock splitter, and break the boulders into smaller pieces. We used the same procedure for solid rock.

Split rock.

Man-handling rock out of excavation area.

This procedure worked well, but we could not get all the way down to grade in one of the solid rock areas, I asked the COR if we could use explosives to blast out the last two feet of solid rock. He went into a long-winded diatribe of conditions I would have to meet, etc. It would have taken me a month to get proper permission.

Early one Sunday morning, we heard the sound of thunder. Somehow, the two feet of hard rock had been miraculously shattered.

We moved a total of 91 cubic yards of rock this way, the equivalent of nine dump truck loads.

During this period, Randy, Brian and I stayed in our travel trailer, which was parked right next to Splinters Cabin. Randy had his own pickup camper. We cooked our breakfast and lunch in camp. In the evenings we drove the three miles to town for dinner, and because our boots were so aromatic, we left them under the trailer. One night when we came home from dinner, our boots had been stolen, leaving the three of us to stumble around in our tennis shoes, while three new pairs of Westco boots were flown in from Portland.

Every time we left, another tool was stolen from our tool trailer, the last being a chain saw. We loaded all our tools into my pickup, and Brian and I moved into a motel in Lake Arrowhead. One night we decided to drive up to the Rim of the World restaurant to have dinner. We took Randy's camper and my Ranchero. When we finished dinner, it was so foggy that we couldn't see to drive home, so the three of us spent the night in Randy's camper.

At the site, one of the footings required drilling ten-foot-deep holes in solid rock for special "Williams" anchors, so I built a special scaffold to support my Cobra drill. Drill steel comes in two-foot lengths. As there were two holes to drill, I drilled two feet in one hole and then two feet in the other hole. The Cobra drill couldn't blow enough air down the hole to blow out the cuttings, so I drilled a few inches, raised the drill and washed the hole out with water. After I was down eight feet, I changed to the ten-foot steel. At the 8 ½-foot depth, the drill broke out of the rock into dirt, which, of course, is impossible to drill.

The problem then was that the ten-foot anchors could not be used in the manner in which they were designed, which required testing with a hydraulic jack. I discussed the problem with the COR, who told me that I'd have to get them re-designed. This would probably have taken a month. I gambled. I cut them off, grouted them in using normal trade practice, placed the forms over them and proceeded to fly in the concrete with the Lama. (Nothing was ever questioned.)

Formed piers—upper right background bridge arches and scaffolding.

Helicopter is controlling the concrete bucket.

The COR seemed to have abandoned the job, but he did send out a young lady as an inspector. She told us that she was in training and didn't know anything, so any help we could give her, she would appreciate. She was quite attractive and very pleasant.

One Friday she said to me, "I'll buy you and Brian's dinner if you will meet me at the country-western dance hall tonight." It sounded like a good deal to me. We had a few drinks, ate dinner and danced. I danced pretty close to her on one dance, and afterwards she said, "I really liked that dance." After a while, she said, "Will you take me to my trailer? US Forest Service-furnished."

I said yes, and *I* paid for our dinner! When we got to the trailer, she said her roommate (female) was gone for a few days. By this time, it was after midnight and we had to work the next morning. We talked a bit and I decided to myself that I didn't want to put Brian, my son-in-law, in a position where he might have to defend my actions.

We left and went back to the motel. I felt bad about this, and felt obliged to make it up to her after final inspection!

The next couple of days we spent setting up the scaffolding "false work."

This scaffolding was set up prior to flying in the arch.

Flying the first arch section.

When mobilizing, I instructed Randy to buy two Rigid® pipe wrenches, which were going to be needed to bolt the bridge together. As we started bolting, the wrenches did not work. Why? They were the same color as the Rigid's®, but they were cheap, and manufactured in Spain. (Randy could not resist a bargain!) I threw them into the deepest part of the creek, and said, "Randy, shag your ass to San Bernadino and buy two Rigid® wrenches and hurry back. Don't stop for wood, water or coal!" He did.

The one mistake I made was throwing the wrenches into the creek because Randy spent more time trying to figure out how to retrieve them than he did working! As far as I know, the wrenches are still there.

Lloyd overseeing the splitter.

Total flying time for setting the bridge was about two hours. Installing the hand railing and decking, and completing the bridge took another two weeks.

Finished bridge.

After final inspection I fulfilled my obligation to the young lady inspector. This job was fun, challenging and very profitable.

Chapter 25

1980
NORTH DRYDEN FLUME REPLACEMENT
Icicle Irrigation District
Dryden, Washington
Contract Amount: $345,554

This job was bid Aug. 13, 1980. The engineer was Dick Happala, of CH2M-Hill, at their Yakima office. This was the first of three projects we did that Dick designed. The purpose of this contract was to replace the dilapidated wooden flume that had been wiped out by a landslide, and replace it with steel pipe by March, the beginning of the irrigation season.

Portion of wooden flume to be replaced with metal pipeline—contractor also used this flume to access the work.

This work was in a road-less area, so the engineer designed the pipeline so that it could be air-lifted with a Lama helicopter that could lift up to 2,200 lbs. The chopper was based at Cascade Helicopter in Cashmere, Washington.

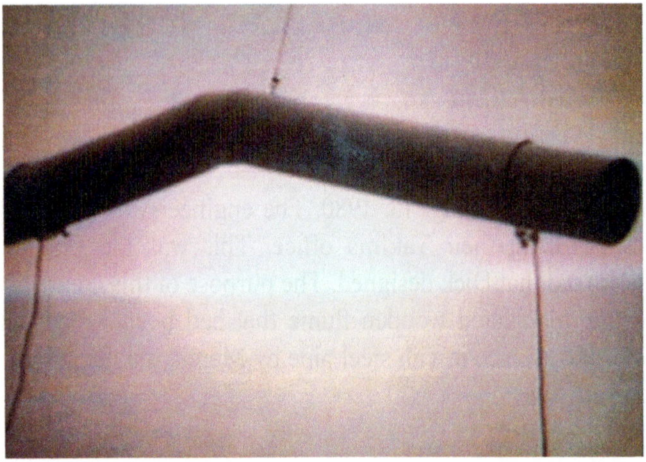

Lama flies a 30-foot section of 30-inch, spiral-weld pipe. The load line is visible at top center.

At the peak of construction, our crew of fourteen included Doug Kessler, Brian Surbert, Daryl Elliot, Fred Meier, and myself. Randy Johnson fabricated the pipeline supports in our shop. This was a very difficult job, as every support was a different length, varying from two feet to twenty-five feet. This required making field measurements and sending them to the engineer, who in turn adjusted the dimensions so that the supports would fit the ground. To everyone's surprise but mine, the supports fit perfectly.

This job started with a bang!

After the blast.

The anchors for the supports required drilling a hole into the rock and inserting an expansion anchor rod. Once the anchors were in, they were to be tested hydraulically to a pre-determined pressure.

When foreman Daryl and I were doing the first test, the pump gauge was not indicating pressure, so we kept adding more pressure. My instincts told me to stop. Daryl had his head over the rod when I told him, “Hold it.” He moved his head back. At that instant, the rod shot forty feet into the air. If it had happened an instant sooner, I would have needed a new foreman.

It was obvious that these anchors were not going to hold in the soft sandstone. Therefore, the engineer decided to use concrete footings. It took two weeks to design them. This required some blasting and extensive hand excavation, as some of these footings were five feet deep. This work took thirty days to accomplish. Over all, the extra work required 45 days, resulting in a $50,000 change order, and causing us to overrun the deadline by seven days. It also forced us to buy an extra $7,000 worth of Railroad insurance because the flume ran directly above the Burlington-Northern railroad tracks.

The day we were finishing, it started to snow. By noon we were no longer able to work, which meant that we had to come back two weeks later to finish. The worst part of this was that the contract said we had to have any slide removal done upon completion. It took us two hours to finish the work we couldn’t do the day we got shut down by the snow, and four days to remove the slides.

A November 4, 1981 article in the *Daily Journal of Commerce* wrote:

The custom-designed supports allow for irregular rock formations and varying grades of steepness on the face of the cliff. Concrete footings with rock anchors enabled the fabricated steel supports to be put into place by the helicopter, then bolted down insuring a solid foundation for the pipeline

Kessler Construction handled all metal fabrication for the supports and concrete work for the support bases.

Kessler shop foreman Randy Johnson indicates job complications resulted not only from different-sized supports, but also from differ-

ent types of supports. Light-duty metal heavy-duty metal and concrete supports were used at various locations along the line.

During installation, the pipe was lowered onto these supports by helicopter and put in play by Kessler crewmen. The crew maintained the original grade of the wooden flume using survey levels, following the engineer's specifications.

Kessler is well-known for helicopter work as well as performing in other difficult construction situations.

Forming concrete supports.

Work in progress—Doug is perched upon the pipe.

This is a sign that no one can see. It rests high in a tree with no access.

This is yet another example of how important it is to complete a job in the original time frame. The high-cost of coming back the next season chews up the profits. Luckily, we realized a good profit from this project.

CHAPTER 26

1981
YAKIMA TIETON CANAL COVERS
US Department of Reclamation
Trout Lodge, Washington
Original Contract Amount: $871,373.
With changes: $899,981.

The US Department of Agriculture awarded us the contract for installation of light and heavy canal covers in the Yakima Tieton Irrigation District, outside of Tieton, Washington. As a result of the eruption of Mt. St. Helens in May of 1980, ash washed down into the canal, so the federal government paid for this project with disaster relief money.

The initial work included excavation for the gabion basket foundations that were designed to support the canal covers. In many areas, the concrete walls of the canal were not strong enough to support the weight of the covers once they became loaded with debris. These were the areas where the light covers were used. In most cases, timbers were laid on top of the gabion baskets and the covers were bolted to them. Some parts of the canal had concrete that was strong enough to support the heavy covers, and in these areas, they were installed directly on top of the canal walls.

Gabion baskets, and timber supports for the covers

While the foundation work was going on, the canal covers were being manufactured by Armco Steel Corporation, and the pressure treated timbers by Idaho Pacific Timber Corp. These materials were scheduled to arrive March 1st. The timber arrived on time, but the covers were a few days late and missed our pay-estimate cutoff date.

At this time, interest rates were 18%. If I didn't pay Armco by the 10th of the month, they would charge me interest even though they were the ones who caused the payment to be late. The bill was $480,000. Once I received my payment from the Soil Conservation Service, I called Armco and asked if I would still get my discount. They said no, so I put the money in the bank for a month at 18%. At the end of 30 days, I took my discount, which Armco graciously accepted. This left me with a $4,800 bonus, the only time I ever made any money with money.

Galen—sorting the materials into 2,000 pound bundles.

The six semi truckloads of covers arrived at daylight. By noon, we had them unloaded and sorted into 2,000 pound bundles. After lunch, using Cascade Helicopter's Lama, we started flying them out to the various work sites along the canal. This took a couple of days. Early the second day, the pilot, who was kind of a hot dog, took off and let the load swing wide. Unknown to me at the time, he had been using a rope load line, even though I had specified a 100 foot steel cable. This wild swing put so much pressure on the line that it broke, scattering a load of light covers across the landscape.

Cascade Helicopter's Lama with the pilot, Carpenter Fred Meier, Inspector Chuck Palmer and my Foreman Daryl Elliot.

I immediately called Cascade's owner and bitched about the load line. He replied that they'd been using that line for six years and never had any trouble with it. I said that's not what I'm worried about. Since I had ordered a steel line, that's what I expected to get. He said that it would take him a couple of weeks to get another line. I told him that I'd get one tomorrow and send him the bill. He reluctantly agreed.

In the meantime the inspector, Chuck Palmer, arrived and started giving me and the pilot hell. He should have been happy no one was hurt and no damage had been done. While he was scolding us, I had a white-knuckled grip on the pickup so I wouldn't smack him. The pilot was doing the same. He should have dropped the matter then but instead, commanded me to write a letter to the Irrigation District explaining what had happened. I didn't know it then, but he would cause me considerable grief on a future job.

The Crew

Our nine-man crew, which eventually grew to fifteen, began installing the covers and timbers onto the gabion basket foundations. Five were local loggers, and they were grateful for the construction work since there wasn't much logging going on in 1981. Not only that, but they were getting paid twice as much.

This tool (hay hook) had a very high benefit-to-cost ratio.

These smiling faces were damn happy for the work.

Daryl and LHK, damn happy for the work too!

Installing covers on support timbers and gabion.

There were three canal tunnels on this project. They were so narrow that there was barely room for two men to pass each other. As there were no trails or roads, it was necessary to walk through these tunnels to get from one part of the project to the next. One day, Fred's dog Brutus and I were walking through one of the tunnels when Brutus killed a deer. (See Chapter 22 for details.)

Brutus, life-saving dog, and honorary "First LHK Job Dog."

Inside the covered canal.

We were able to haul our generator and heavy tools with the canal buggy. Daryl and his crew of seven began installing covers at the east end of the project. Randy and Joe began the light covers at the west end of the project. In the design stage, the engineer did not realize that the steel cross tie canal reinforcers were above cover grade. A change order was issued to cut off and lower the reinforcement. Randy was an excellent burner and a good welder. Randy determined that if he welded three of the light covers together and bolted them to the top of the canal, it would eliminate the need for the steel reinforcers. The CH2M Hill engineer, Dick Happala concurred.

Daryl Elliot in the canal buggy.

During this operation, Randy tack welded the nuts but did not put washers on the bolts. It took him and Joe three days to fix the problem. The same amount of time it took him to do the work in the first place. He was trying to save the price of the washers.

The job went very well for the most part because we had the proper tools and manpower.

During the job Daryl, Fred, Gaylen and I stayed in the old Trout Lodge Service Station, which was owned by the Summit Restaurant, which was right next door. It was our good fortune to be able to rent the Lodge as the next closest place was 50 miles away over icy roads in Yakima. Randy Johnson parked his camper next to the Lodge. It was also our good fortune that most of the loggers that we hired lived locally. Most nights after work, they would stop by the Lodge for a beer or four. Rooming with your employees forces you into becoming their mother. It ain't much fun.

The boys were on their second beer one night when I returned from Yakima with supplies. Fred had decided to bring his girlfriend, who lived in Yakima, to the Lodge for the night. That was bad enough, but there was another girl with her. The energy in the room was negative and getting worse fast. I told Fred to take the girls home. He said the roads were slippery and he could have an accident. I told him that it couldn't be nearly as bad as the one that was about to happen here. He made it back the next morning in time for work.

Trout Lodge—a converted service station.

There were a large number of rattlesnakes on this job. Randy was terrified of the snakes and it was slowing down his production, so I offered a bounty of $2 for each snake caught. The next day the crew showed up with 50 snakes. I welched on the deal, and instead offered to put the snake money into an end-of-job party.

Randy is happy to see the snakes.

...and THIS is the party the snakes funded!

We started field work on this project on February 16th, 1981, and completed the job on May 1st, 1981, way ahead of schedule—thanks to our jolly crew. With change orders, we completed $899,981 worth of work in 74 days. We made a nifty profit and had a lot of fun.

Chapter 27

1982-'83
THORNE BAY, ALASKA, MAINTENANCE AND OFFICE BUILDINGS
U.S. Department of Agriculture (USDA)
Tongas National Forest
HQ: Juneau, Alaska

In the spring of 1982, the Forest Service called for bids on this project. They had contracted with a private engineering firm to design it. There were five bidders. When the bids were opened, they were all far over the engineer's estimate, as well as the Forest Service's budget.

The Contracting Officer, Dick Kent, operated as he pleased, but not necessarily according to government contracting rules. He ordered the engineer to revise the plans and cut out as much as he could in an attempt to get within budget, and asked the five bidders to negotiate the job.

At this time, Ron McCain was in Kent's office doing final paperwork on a very profitable trail job that Ron had just completed. Ron and Dick had become good friends. Dick said to Ron, "As this is a negotiated job, you have a right to give me a price on it."

Ron mentioned to me that he had decided to put a price on the job. He got a couple of friends to help him to do the take-off and pricing, and had the advantage of knowing the original bidders' prices.

It took a month to put the bid together. As it turned out, Ron was low. His price was about two million dollars and required a twenty percent performance bond. Ron did not have nearly that much bonding capacity. He came to me and asked if I would bond it.

I said, "I'm not interested,", but he kept after me. I reviewed his numbers, and they looked very good. It was decided that if I helped bond it, we would joint-venture the job as Kessler and McCain and share equally in the profits. It was agreed that I was to have final say on all decisions.

I called my agent, Mansfield and Co. and they were able to get the bond; the USFS awarded us the job. We started ordering the long lead-time items, such as the office building modules and steel trusses for the maintenance building, along with a myriad of other items.

In late July we were notified that the site grading was done, and were issued the order to begin the field work.

On July 29, John Wheatley, our Carpenter Foreman; Fred Hyke, my Engineer; Ron McCain, and I, caught the Alaska Airline 9 a.m. flight to Ketchikan. Once there, John and Ron started rounding up lumber and other materials for the building footings. Fred and I spent the afternoon reviewing the plans and figuring the surveys for the building locations. The plan was for Fred and me to fly to Thorne Bay the next morning and start the layout. John and Ron were going to stay in Ketchikan and make sure the building materials got loaded onto the freight/ferry boat.

After dinner that night, we decided to go to the local topless bar and celebrate our new job. We drank a considerable amount. As it turned out, the joint was topless AND bottomless! After a performance, one of the girls came over and flopped into my lap. She said, "I like you. I'm coming to your room after I get off work."

About this time, Fred said, "Lloyd, we've got to go. We have to take the early morning flight to Thorne Bay."

We went to our room. About one o'clock the girl knocked on the door. Fred didn't let her in.

The next morning Fred and I flew to Thorne Bay with the intent of laying out the maintenance building. The problem was that there were fifty-thousand yards of crushed rock on the building site. This was rock that the site contractor, Seley, Inc., had contracted to place on Forest Service roads. (They did not get this rock off site until October 1st.) Fred and I started laying out the office building, as this was the only place on the entire site that wasn't covered with rock.

The day was very hot and we were both suffering from last night's celebration. We did well until noon, and then decided to get some lunch at the local restaurant. It just so happened that the town's power plant had gone down early that morning and there was no electricity for the refrigerator. Also, the town's water reservoir had gone dry. The only thing to drink was warm pop. And there was no food.

Hungry and thirsty, Fred and I went back to finish the layout. The temperature was over 90 degrees. There are twenty hours of daylight at this time of year. It gets hot early—and stays late.

At 5:30, feeling miserable, we went to the logging camp mess hall for dinner, washed it down with lots of cold milk and water, and felt good for a few minutes. Both of us then paid the price for pigging out on cold milk. We were almost as miserable after dinner as we were before dinner.

In the morning we negotiated with Seley's operator to excavate the office building footings. His name was Bob Clearwater, an excellent operator. His twelve-year-old son was watching, so we let him run the survey rod. By noon the excavation was nearly complete, and as luck would have it, Ron McCain and John Wheatley pulled into the dock with the forming material.

We began forming the footings as we continued with the excavation. Just as we were finishing, the Forest Service inspector showed up. The first thing he said was, "You can't let that kid hold the rod. He's not 18 years old." Then he said, "I thought you were going to do the maintenance building first."

I replied, "You should walk over to the site and look at it."

He said, "Which direction is that?"

I pointed down the path. He went, looked, and when he came back, he said, "I don't see any problem. There's plenty of room for a building over there."

I took him by the hand and went back and explained to him that the building site was under that pile of crushed rock. He didn't say much, got on the float plane and flew back to Ketchikan.

That was the first and last time I ever saw that inspector. I'm not sure I ever knew his name.

By the end of the third day, we had the forms set. The next morning, our fourth day on the job, we poured the concrete. It was August 4th. I remember it well because it's my Dad's birthday. We hopped on the next float plane out, and were home in Vancouver in time for dinner.

Our entire bid for the project was based on working two shifts in order to take advantage of the twenty hours of daylight. Our plan was to have the building foundations ready by the time the steel trusses and other materials for the maintenance building arrived. We had scheduled thirty days for fabrication and shipping.

Our plan was that when the maintenance building shell was completed, we would take delivery on the modules for the office building, which had a much longer lead time. We wanted to have the project complete by November 1, 1983.

We didn't know when we'd be able to get back on site. We had no way of knowing when Seley was going to complete their work, but we were finally able to restart on October 1st.

The delay caused many problems. The major one was that the Forest Service would not pay for materials until they were on site. Also, the modular manufacturer required that he be paid 80% before the materials left his shop. As there was nearly $400,000 in materials, this put us in a serious bind.

This forced me to go to my bank (NW Bank) for a $400,000 loan. My attorney and I had already started a delay-claim, and he was instrumental in the loan process. There were some papers that required both McCain and my signatures. Neither one of us could leave the job, so I instructed my attorney to put the papers in the mail at the Portland Main Post Office by 7 a.m. This way, they would be on the Alaska Airlines morning flight scheduled to arrive in Ketchikan at 10 a.m. From there, it would be put on the mail float plane that arrived in Thorne Bay by noon each day.

However, my attorney didn't listen. He sent the paper by FedEx instead. As there was no FedEx station in Ketchikan, they went on to Anchorage.

We needed the papers signed NOW! I called Mike Roberts at Northwest Bank and explained the situation. The next day he caught the morning flight to Ketchikan and arrived in Thorne Bay at noon. We signed the papers, Mike looked over the job, and was home in Vancouver for dinner that night. The papers that were sent by FedEx showed up in the mail fourteen days later.

During August and September, Randy, McCain and I spent most of our time following up on the orders we had placed—making sure the office modules were being built according to plan. If the contract had gone according to schedule, we would have had the maintenance building up and would have been ready for the office building modules.

We began excavating for the maintenance building footings, and at the same time started setting forms. My engineer Fred Hyke and I kept the carpenters on line and grade. John Wheatley, a house-builder and the Carpenter Foreman, was amazed. He didn't have to screw around with his tape and the plans to do a layout. In fact, we told him the only thing he needed was his hammer! We set forms for half the footings the first day, and poured concrete the next morning. The second day, we repeated, and finished the concrete footings the third day.

Once the footings were completed, we began forming and pouring the building's floor slabs. This took about two weeks, by which time the steel trusses and other building materials arrived, along with the office building modules. We used our Lull fork lift to unload everything except the modules. It took the rented crane two days to unload and stack them on the office building foundation.

Office building foundation.

Stacking office building modules.

Completed office building.

Once the office was stacked, we moved the crane to the maintenance building and erected the steel trusses. Once they were up, we then used it to load the roof sheathing.

The plan showed the roof sheathing as half-inch plywood spanning four feet. When I first saw the plans, I recognized that this was a recipe for disaster. No way could a man walk on half-inch plywood sheathing and not fall through. For safety reasons, I ordered special plywood from Vancouver Plywood. It was ¾-inch tongue and groove, 4 feet wide and 24 feet long.

Wheatley began installing the plywood on the roof. Shortly after he started, I walked up and saw that he had cut one of the sheets in half. I said, "What the hell did you do THAT for?"

He said, "That's the way we always do it when we're roofing a house."

I said, "We're roofing a building. Just start at one end and go to the other."

He said, "What about the two feet at the end?"

I told him, "Cut two feet off the extra sheets."

End of argument.

It took just two days to sheathe the entire roof.

Sheathing the roof.

John Wheatley and Ron Capps sheathing roof with ¾-inch x 4-foot x 24-foot plywood.

The roofing material specified was standing-seam metal roofing, manufactured by Clip Rib Corporation. The specifications called for screwing down a row of clips and laying a sheet of roofing; a second row of clips were attached, and so on. This is a slow and tedious process.

Fred and I figured out that we could screw the clips to a 1 x 4 and precisely attach the 1 x 4s to the sheathing. We spent several days doing this in our spare time.

In the meantime, Fred and I did a precise layout on the roof, and Wheatley and crew installed the 1 x 4s.

Clip Rib's manufacturer's rep showed up and we started the installation. Even though we had notified him in advance of what we were going to do, he was somewhat skeptical. Our four-man crew started laying the roofing down, and completed the 40 x 160-foot section of roofing that very day. The rep was amazed…and the following day we did the other 160-foot section! He told me that he estimated it would take eight to ten days just for the roofing.

He called me a couple of times afterward, and said he had told other people about the job that my crew and I had done. (That felt good.)

Once the roof was on, it was time to install the ridge cap. I climbed up the ladder to see how it was going. Wheatley and Ron Capps had just finished the roof, so when Capps saw my head peek over the edge of the roof, he started doing a dance—a move which caused him to slip and fall on his ass. I yelled, "Enough of THAT!"

Once the roofing was on, we had a dry and level floor upon which to work. It was now time to start installing the mansard sections. Wheatley wanted to frame them in place, one section at a time. I said, "Hey, John. We're not doing them that way. We're gonna pre-fab them and set them in place with the Lull."

Pre-fabricating mansard sections.

He said, "How are we gonna nail them to the siding sheathing?"

I told him, "We are not going to nail them; we're going to bolt them."

Wheatley said, "Where are we gonna get the bolts?"

"Out of those bags that are laying right there on the floor!"

If we had built these sections John's way, it would have taken three men one day to install a section. We built a jig and it only took three men two hours to build a section, and install the Clip Rib roofing. We worked two three-man crews and built ten sections per day. In two days we built twenty sections, enough to do both sides of the 160-foot long building. It only took two days to install them.

This was the direct result of Fred and my layout experience and mass-producing abilities.

Finished Maintenance building.

The building was completely weathered in the week before Thanksgiving. We decided to go home, as we did not have enough daylight to do outside work. We had about twenty men on the payroll at the time. We decided to use one of the local charter boats to ferry the men to the Ketchikan airport since it was much cheaper than flying them.

We did send three men ahead on the float plane to do some business in Ketchikan; one of them was Ron Capps. When our boat arrived at the Ketchikan airport dock, all twenty of us began unloading our baggage. The tide was out, so the ramp was very steep. Ron ran down the ramp, loaded a heavy duffle on each shoulder, and galloped up the ramp to the airport. He made several trips, which I videoed.

When we re-started in October, Ron McCain hired an office manager who had been a bank manager. His duties were to do the payroll and make sure we were in compliance with all of Alaska's regulations—in particular, Workman's Comp.

At the first of the year, the office manager was preparing the year-end statements when I asked him if he was clear with Alaska's Workman's Comp. He looked kinda dumb, so I asked what our policy number for Comp was. He said he would look it up. It turned out that Alaska doesn't have Worker's Comp. It's up to the contractor to buy his own.

I choked. We'd worked all this time without insurance.

I told McCain, "We don't need him anymore. I will take care of the office from here on."

Many months after the project was over, I got a call from the Washington State Workman's Comp. representative. They were concerned because Ron Copps had been prescribed too many pain-killing drugs from the Longview hospital.

I explained to the rep that I had no idea about what was going on, but he told me: "Ron put in a claim for an injured back due to the fall he took on the maintenance building roof." He also explained that Capps had been drawing Workman's Comp.

I then explained to him that McCain had kept me posted on Ron, and that he was building pole barns. That's hard to do with an injured back.

The rep said, "Let me review this, and I will call you back."

A few days later he called, and I told him about my video of him arriving in Ketchikan, he said, "Between you and me, I'm going to show you having Washington State Workman's Comp while you were working at Thorne Bay."

I didn't like the idea of Capps getting away with something, but the rep said, "If you let me use Washington State, it will save both you and me a lot of trouble."

I came to my senses and said, "Thank you."

I got lucky again: Capps had to repay the State compensation.

What are the odds?

During the winter, I had two residents of Thorne Bay, Leonard Barnes and one other, install insulation in the maintenance building. Leonard also ran a boat repair business; his wife Charlotte ran the Thorne Bay Post Office. Leonard was a very good worker, and had no fear of heights. This was a plus, as the ceiling of the building was 34 feet above the concrete slab. It took Leonard about a month to complete this insulation.

In the spring of 1983, we returned to finish the project. During the course of the winter we spent a lot of time reviewing the plans and figuring our strategy. There were a number of problems that needed to be addressed. They included the power line, the auxiliary generator, the electrical panel and others. Although the plans called for the power poles to be set in solid rock, there was no road access to them.

I thought, "Why not go underground?" There was a natural ravine between the maintenance building and the City of Thorne Bay's power plant. We proposed this to the USFS and they agreed. It was also agreed that we could use a Winco generator instead of a Caterpillar. Everybody wanted Cat. It was also agreed that the electrical panel was way over-designed, and that we could use a much less expensive one. We negotiated a no-cost change order that saved us close to $100,000.

From the very beginning of the job, Vondell Balls, the COR, insisted that everything be done exactly according to the book. One of the classics was the office building. It had numerous vertical ¾-inch rods tying the two-story building to its wooden foundation. These rods had to be precisely located in order to connect to the foundation. I tried to tell Vondell that some of them should be left out, but he said, "Put them in according to plan."

I did as he ordered. Some of them came right through the open spaces of some of the offices. Installing these rods was a tedious and costly operation. Vondell showed up and said to me, "That's ridiculous—putting those through the office like that. You should have known better."

I replied, "I did know better. I tried to explain it to you."

He said, "Take them out."

I said, "I will, as soon as you write a change order for the extra cost."

This pissed him off, but he had no choice. Our relationship was becoming more adversarial each day.

One Thursday, Ron McCain informed Vondell that we were going to do the underground power line Saturday and Sunday. These were scheduled work days. Vondell told McCain, "You can start Friday. I have to be in Ketchikan Saturday and Sunday for a meeting."

He was thinking that we'd have to dig a trench and place bedding, and he probably knew in his own mind that we wouldn't have it done by the time Monday rolled around. I also had to attend the Ketchikan meeting.

When I returned Sunday afternoon, Ron had the underground line in and completely back-filled. The trench was very steep, so Ron had laid filter fabric in the bottom, which acted as a chute, and dumped sand into the top end of the chute, which then slid to the bottom, filling the trench. In one place the line went right under the roots of a large stump.

When Vondell showed up Monday morning, he couldn't believe his eyes, and couldn't figure out how we got past the stump. He asked McCain for an explanation. Ron said, "Everything is according to plan and specifications."

Vondell had the authority to make McCain dig it up, but he knew that if indeed it WAS to plan and specification, he would have to pay us. He grumbled and walked away. Ron smiled. We were having fun.

During the winter, Randy diligently pursued procuring all the materials for completing the inside of the building. This included heating systems, generators, plumbing, and a myriad of other items. The heating system specifications were poorly written, and we had to virtually re-engineer them. Randy called me from Vancouver to tell me that he was still having trouble with Barbara Coleman. He was very busy, but I told him to stay with it anyway.

One day he mentioned it once too often and really ticked me off. I told him, "Why don't you just tell her to go to hell and we'll deal with someone else?"

Randy replied, "It's not a "she"; it's the name of the manufacturer that supplies the heating and air conditioning equipment."

I got educated, and Randy got the job done.

Upon our return to the job, we brought in several specialty personnel, which included Rick Adams, for tile and counter tops; Tom Gantz, the plumber; and an experienced sheet rocker. All the other work we did with our regular crew.

We were still boarding the crew in the logging camp facilities, and John Wheatley was always late for breakfast. This agitated the cook. John was also late getting to the job, so I told him that he needed to start at the same time as the rest of the crew.

He said, "I start late, but I always work longer."

My deal with Tom Gantz was that he could work all the hours he wanted. He liked to start as early as possible and work until it was time for dinner. It irritated Tom that John was always delaying him and the rest of the crew from getting to the work site on time; I had also noticed that when the crew quit for the evening, John dropped his hammer at the same time as everyone else.

Tom was very smart—and very productive. He worked by himself mostly, but once in a while he would ask for a laborer to help him. One day, when the project was just about completed, one of the contractors from Ketchikan who had bid the project, dropped in to see how we were doing. He asked how big a crew we had doing the plumbing.

I answered with a question: "How many men did YOU plan on doing this work?"

He said, "Four men, for four months."

He asked again how many men I had. I pointed toward Tom and said, "There's the entire crew."

The guy didn't believe me, shook his head, and left.

Staying at the logging camp was costing us about $50 per day per man, and it was starting to shut down. McCain had struck up a friendship with the camp manager, Cliff McCartney, who had helped us in many ways, renting or loaning us equipment. McCain talked him into renting us one of the company's large trailer houses for our crew to stay in. Though I knew better, McCain had decided the crew would do their own cooking. This lasted three days. Then I hired one of the camp's cooks.

She and her husband also owned a little store named "The Bare Necessities." After about a week, her husband was transferred to the mainland, and she had to run the store all by herself. She simply didn't have time to cook and clean up the messes my sloppy employees made!

So then I made a deal with the local restaurant. They agreed to open early and serve breakfast. This worked well and the crew could eat dinner anytime they wanted.

My office was a block away from the restaurant, so I often went there for lunch. Charlotte Barnes, the postmaster, got into the habit of bringing my mail to the restaurant. The guys chided me a lot about this.

The work inside the maintenance building was going very well. As I was the only office personnel, I had to work two or three hours after dinner every night to keep up.

The rest of the crew spent their evenings in the trailer playing poker. Leonard Barnes always got into the game. As they soaked up lots of beer, the guys teased him about Charlotte bringing me the mail.

They could figure out how to get the beer on the float plane and to the trailer at my expense, but they couldn't figure out how to get the cans from the table to the trash can! This made the housekeeper mad, so she quit. (We did hire another one.)

One night, when the poker game was going on, Charlotte came to my office to give me a massage. It was very relaxing. This became a habit, and Leonard got more teasing.

Leonard and I had become good friends, and he and Charlotte invited me over for dinner on occasion. One Friday night, Leonard said to me, "I need your help. I have to go to Juneau for eight or ten days. Would you mind driving Charlotte over to Craig this weekend? She wants to visit her girlfriend."

I said, "She can drive."

He said, "I don't want her to wreck my pickup."

So I agreed. Saturday afternoon we took off. It's about an hour and a half's drive from Thorne Bay to Craig on gravel roads. We got there about four o'clock. It was hotter than hell in the house. I went outside. I think they smoked a few joints in there. After about an hour, Charlotte said, "Let's go have dinner."

We left and went to the local restaurant that was on the second floor. There was a good view of the town from the dining room window, where four or five overweight Indian men sat at the bar. We had dinner and spent the night at the motel. The next morning we went back to Thorne Bay. I had office work that had to be done in prep for Monday, after all.

About two years before we started the Thorne Bay project, McCain married a woman with three teenage daughters. McCain had also bought a beautiful home in Kalama, Washington, along with a Lincoln Mark IV and a Cessna 185. (The 185 is mentioned earlier in this book.) He had large monthly payments, which we will talk about later on.

The work on Thorne Bay was progressing nicely, but Ron got tired of living in the trailer with the crew. His new wife Tammy had been hearing rumors, and decided she wanted to come and stay with Ron at Thorne Bay, so they rented a trailer for themselves. This was about two months before we finished the project.

About two weeks before finishing, all the crew from Washington left, including Ron and his wife. I stayed to wrap things up with the help of our two local employees.

About two days before I was ready to come home, I got a call from Millie. She told me that Tammy had called, and she was coming to our house the next morning at nine o'clock to tell her about Charlotte and me.

I called Tammy and told her not to go if she didn't want a broken neck. The next morning Millie called me and said, "You must have got to Tammy. She didn't show and she didn't call."

I told Millie, "I'll be home in a couple of days." This was June, 1983.

Millie met me at the airport. Grover was with her. Millie said, "At least SOMEONE is happy to see you!" The atmosphere was a bit icy. After dinner, I planned on sleeping on the couch. She said, "You might as well come to bed." It was warm and cozy under the covers, but she did remind me a couple of times over the years, more or less.

A few months later when I was in Louisiana, Millie wrote to me, "Thorne Bay makes my heart ache."

▪ ▪ ▪

It was then July of 1983, and my attorneys continued working on the delay claim. In February, we were finally able to set up a meeting with the contracting officer, Dick Kent—"we" being Ron McCain, our attorneys, and I. The meeting started at 9 a.m. in the conference room, and went fairly well. Our main goal was to convince the CO that we were entitled to a delay claim. The claim, we figured, would be worth at least $400,000. When the attorneys intuitively felt that Kent was ready to negotiate, they suggested we take a break. We stepped into their office, but McCain and Kent remained seated at the conference table.

After about 15 minutes, the attorneys and I walked back to the conference table; I walked in front. McCain said, "Lloyd, we've made a deal. We settled for $150,000."

As McCain was my partner, he had that right in Kent's eyes, BUT he left me without the right to make a "final decision" as outlined in our agreement. I had no recourse. Ron explained to me that he had to make payments and couldn't afford to wait for several months until all the red tape was taken care of. The fact was that it wouldn't take any longer to do the red tape for $150,000 than it would for $400,000. I didn't say anything. It took a couple of months.

In the meantime, Ron had to sell his house and the Mark IV at a loss. He moved back to his father's place in Randle, and told me later on, "Lloyd, I should have let you guys finish the negotiations. I gave away $300,000."

Sometime later, Ron and Tammy divorced.

By now, I should have learned the dangers within partnerships.

CHAPTER 28

1983
TREE COOLERS
US Forest Service

In July 1982, we bid on Tree Coolers for the US Forest Service at 15 different locations in Idaho and Montana, in this rotation:

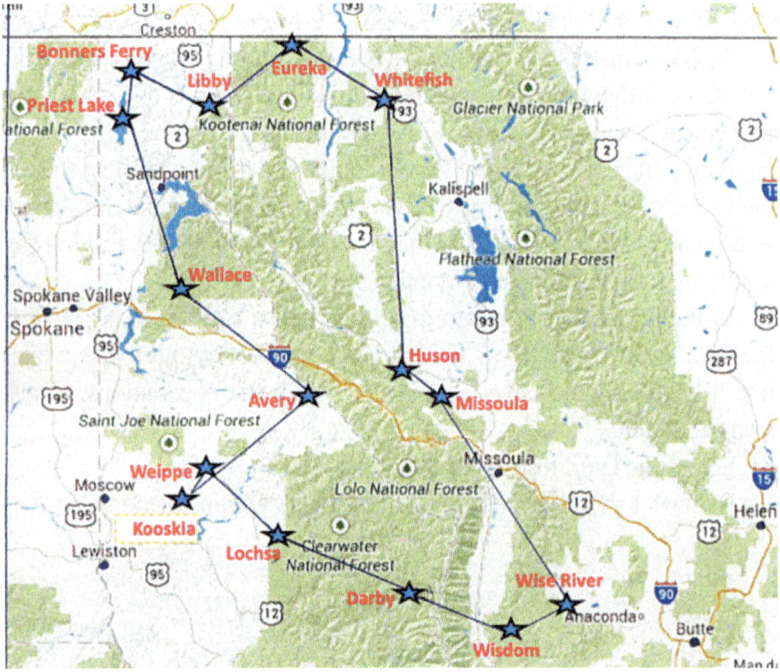

Tree cooler locations in Idaho and Montana.

This project required large refrigeration units for storage of seedling conifers to keep them at 31° until planted. The government put the bid out with two options. Option one was for stand-alone refrigeration units. Option two was for refrigeration units built on a concrete slab, with a shed to protect them. It was the general opinion that the Forest Service wanted the sheds. I bid the job putting a high price on the refrigeration unit and a very low price on the sheds. If I was low overall, I would get the job. I also felt that it would be a lot easier to assemble the refrigeration units under a shelter, particularly due to the fact that most of this work was going to be done during the winter, and the completion date was April 15th, the beginning of the planting season.

At the bid opening, the other bidders were chuckling at my high price on the coolers. Suddenly, one of the bidders piped up, "I know what that son-of-a-bitch is doing! He's giving the Forest Service the sheds for the same price as the coolers." I was low bidder on fifteen out of the sixteen units. The person who bid low on the one remaining unit told the government that he'd just as soon not do the job.

Once awarded the contract, we immediately ordered the refrigeration units, a long lead-time item. We began the on-site work. The sequence was to grade the site (the Forest Service specs said that the sites were already graded, but in order to expedite the job, we graded the sites ourselves.) We then poured the floor slab. The next morning we poured the section of the slab that required insulation under where the refrigeration unit would sit. The first pour required sixteen cubic yards of concrete. The second pour required eight cubic yards. This operation took about a day and a half. Once the second slab was poured, we'd move on to the next site.

My plan was to do the work in three rounds: Round #1—install all fifteen slabs; Round #2—build fifteen shelters; Round #3—install fifteen refrigeration units.

We had to do a fourth round because the refrigeration hula skirts (the split vertical plastic curtains you sometimes find in store coolers) did not show up until after the refrigeration units were installed. This caused numerous problems, which of course delayed final inspection.

The fun part of the job was that we got to stay in the same motels and eat at the same restaurants four different times in the friendly towns of Idaho and the super friendly towns of Montana (except Eureka).

The first round went very well until we got to Avery, Idaho. This site was a little different. The Forest Service had removed a section of an existing building. Their plan was that once we installed the slab and the cooler, they were going to rebuild. When we arrived at the site, the on-site inspector showed us where they had relocated their new water line and assured us that it was okay to dig for the slab. It was noon. I had concrete ordered for the next morning at 8:00 am. The first dip with the backhoe created a geyser. The water went 30 feet in the air and completely saturated the subgrade. Once we finally got the water turned off, we had to dry up the subgrade. After three hours I decided that we weren't going to be ready for concrete as scheduled, so I went to the US Forest Service office to call the batch plant—but the phone lines were down. That meant that I had to drive the 47 miles to St. Marie's to cancel the pour. I took off, but about three miles outside of town there was a slide, the same one that had taken out the telephone lines. There was nothing to do but go back and help get the slab subgrade ready.

When we arrived that morning I had rented motel rooms but didn't look at them. We worked until dark and were cold and wet, so we went directly to the restaurant for drinks and dinner. After dinner we had more drinks and finally headed to the motel about midnight. Only one problem, the beds only came with springs, no mattress or blankets. We put on all of our heavy clothes and had a "great night's sleep".

At 6:00 am, I again headed for St. Marie's. The slide still hadn't been cleared, but after a half hour or so, the road finally opened and I headed to the batch plant. About a mile before I got there, here came the concrete trucks. I turned around and barreled back to Avery to help the crew get the slab ready.

A half hour later, the trucks showed up. I told the lead driver what the problem was. He said he'd park in the shade and turn the drum as slowly as possible and add a drop of water from time to time. It was now 9:00 am. It should also be noted that the batch plant had scheduled to shut down for the winter once this pour was completed. This added a little urgency.

We started the pour at 1:00 pm with the blessing of our COR. The concrete had been in the truck for six hours. The COR said, "I'm not going to take any concrete test cylinders."

I said, "Let's take them anyway. I'm curious."

He said, "Okay, but I'm not going to record them." I had them tested and they made the break (specifications).

We moved on to Wallace where we completed round one and went home to Vancouver to rest and stock up. (It must be noted that Randy Johnson had planned and made sure that we had all the materials we needed.) One of the problems we were having is that all of our tools kept getting buried in the beds of our pickups. I had instructed Randy to go to the local horse trailer manufacturer on Fruit Valley Road and order a trailer to keep our tools in. I told him that I wanted to see it before we bought it. Randy, as usual, was trying to get a deal. The trailer he picked out was UPS brown. I wanted something that was highly visible —like our pickups—so I said no.

However, while we were both at the manufacturer's, I spotted a fancy fifth-wheel three horse trailer that was all gussied up and headed to the Cow Palace in San Francisco for a show. They said I could not have it, but I said, "Are you guys in the business of selling trailers or putting on shows?"

They sold it to me.

We started Round #2 by building shelters at Weippe, Idaho, moved to Kooskia and then on to Lochsa, where things got interesting. This was a large shelter and took over two days to build. The first day went well. We ate our dinner at the Lochsa Lodge and Restaurant.

The next morning when Fred Hyke and I went to breakfast, the restaurant was not open, and Kenny was nowhere to be seen. As it turned out, he spent the night with the red-headed cook. He did show up for work on time, but we got no breakfast or coffee.

When we started work on the shelter, the young lady who lived in the nearby trailer came out on her deck calling for her dog, "Packy! Packy!" What was more interesting was that all she had on was a negligee. But Fred wouldn't let us look and made us go to work instead!

We finished the day's work and headed for the Lodge (the cook was there) and had a few drinks. It was a Wednesday night and all of the locals came in to socialize. Packy's owner told me that her husband was the trail man for the Forest Service, and he was going to be gone all week. I just left it at that.

Sometime after dinner, the cook's boyfriend drove into the parking lot. He was unhappy that he couldn't find her the night before. He had a .357 magnum pistol, and as he was getting out of his car, it went off and blew a hole through his transmission. He got a good look at Kenny and decided to leave.

We finished the next day and headed for Darby, Montana, where we put the shelter up in one day, except for the roofing, which was three-tab shingles. The next morning, a Sunday, we continued installing the three-tabs, even though it was obvious that we sorely lacked the skill and mentality for this work. About ten o'clock I told the crew, "I'm going to the bar and watch football. You guys can do anything you want." They followed me. I contacted a local roofer, who agreed to finish the roofing.

The next morning we headed for Wisdom, Montana, and started building a shelter about three miles from town. The temperature was near zero, slowing the work. That evening we had drinks and dinner at the restaurant in town, after which we headed across the street to The Antlers Inn, best known as the place where the Big Hole girls get together with the Bitter Root boys. We sat a table with a local man and his eighteen year-old daughter. This was her first time drinking in a bar and she was celebrating. I flirted with her and asked if she wanted to go to Las Vegas. She said yes. I didn't think this was a very good idea, and neither did her dad. At any rate, we all got loaded.

Kenny and my rooms were on the second floor of the motel. Kenny was so drunk he fell up the outdoor stairs, and the next morning at breakfast, we were both holding our heads. About half way through breakfast, I looked over at one of the other booths and spotted a familiar-looking woman. It took me a while to make sure I knew her. I walked over and started to ask her name. She said, "Hi Lloyd." I suddenly realized it was Sharon, who had been long-divorced from my old partner Jim Enlow.

She said, "I wasn't going to say anything to you." But we talked a bit. She had just driven from Salmon, Idaho, where she had been visiting her daughter, and was on her way home to Billings, Montana, about 400 miles away. This was two days before Thanksgiving.

I asked her if she wanted to go see what we were working on. She said yes, and we drove out to the job site. It was thirty below zero. We talked for a few minutes, exchanged a few hugs and decided neither one of us wanted to celebrate Thanksgiving with a hangover. Besides, I had to work. I drove her back to her car, and we said goodbye. I got reports on her from her brother-in-law from time to time, but I never saw her again.

Fred Hyke in the bucket, Kenny Piper on the Swinger.
Temperature: 30 below.

Crane lifts shed roof into place.

We finished the shelter that day and moved our equipment to the Forest Service compound in Wise River and went home for Thanksgiving—about a 700-mile drive.

The following Sunday we drove back to Wise River and got there in time for dinner. We asked the bartender when the entertainment would begin. He said that there was a bus load of virgin nurses coming in from Butte about nine o'clock, so we waited until nine—but no one showed. We asked the bartender where they were, but he said, "How would I know what they're doing?" Foiled again.

We finished that shelter and moved on to Missoula and Huson.

When Randy Johnson dispatched Jeff Strong to Wise River, he made out a map and gave Jeff explicit instructions on how to get there. I always told Randy that when he sent somebody on the road, to mark out the route on a state roadmap, which he did, drawing the line from Vancouver to Spokane, from Spokane to Lewiston, from Lewiston to Darby and from Darby to Wisdom and on to Wise River.

The correct route should have been approximately 700 miles from Vancouver to Wise River, but due to Randy's explicit instructions, Jeffrey drove an extra 230 miles, making him only a day late getting to the job.

While working at Huson, we stayed in the motel next to Fred's Restaurant Bar and Lounge, at the intersection of Highway 90 and Highway 93. Fred's was also a topless bar. The one fully-clothed waitress was a good looker. She took orders from the whole restaurant and relayed them to the kitchen—straight from memory.

One day, our Cessna 185 pilot, Marvin Alfred, flew in some parts and spent the evening at Fred's. Marvin had been a preacher. He did not drink but he sat with us and watched the entertainment.

It was time for the crew to head for bed. After the restaurant closed, the waitress went to Kenny's room. She told him, "You know that guy that was sitting with you? He came back and sat in the front row until closing time."

Armed with that information, we continued on to Whitefish and Eureka. At this time, our crew consisted of Fred Hyke, Kenny Piper, Jeff Strong and myself. As mentioned above, Jeff had come on the crew when we were at Wise River. He and Kenny had gone to high school together. Jeff was also a smart-mouth, which didn't help Kenny much.

At the motel in Eureka, our rooms were on the second floor. The restaurant and motel were separated by a parking lot, and as the days were short and the nights were long, we spent a lot of time in the bar. When Kenny and Jeff weren't chasing fat girls, they liked to play pranks, especially on Fred.

The weather was snowy and cold, in the low teens. Late one night when Fred and I went to our room, the door was open and the heat was turned off. We survived, but Fred wasn't happy.

The next morning, on the way to the job, Jeffrey (this is what we called him when we were mad at him, which was nearly all the time) parked his van the wrong way—right in front of the police station. The police weren't pleased, and were even less so when Jeffrey smart-mouthed them. They wrote him a ticket and told him, "You're not going anywhere until this ticket is paid." Jeffrey asked them when he could do that. They told him not until nine o'clock.

In sympathy and pragmatic understanding of the situation, I intervened and explained to the police that we had a four man crew and it took all four of us to make things work. I promised I would come in and pay his ticket. They said, "Okay, but we never want to see him in our town again." That meant we had to drive back to Whitefish that night to eat and sleep.

The next morning we started erecting the building at Eureka. Jeffrey was setting up the crane, but not fast enough to suit me. He said, "I've got to place this outrigger pad." I told him not to worry about it as the ground was frozen two feet deep and we didn't need the pad. We had already set one roof section and were setting the next one. We were working at the very outside reach and weight limits of the crane.

Kenny was running the swinger, and Fred was in the bucket installing some bolts when the crane began to slowly roll over. Kenny let Fred down fast and backed out of the way.

Fortunately, there was a contractor's yard about a block away, and in the yard was a loader that had been shut down for the winter. I talked to the owner, who said it would take him a couple of hours to get it started and warmed up, and then he'd help us lift the crane.

Once the crane was upright, we checked it out. All that was broken were two turn signal lights and a mirror. There was a slight tweak in the boom, but the rental yard never noticed it.

Lloyd's reward for getting in a hurry.

We moved on to Libby and started roofing the shelter. We did not quite finish the roof before dark, and during the night it snowed about three inches.

The next morning Kenny began finishing the roof. The building was next to a steep slope downhill. Kenny slipped, slid off the roof and sailed about forty feet through the air, landing on his back just a couple of feet from where I happened to be standing, which was right next to the Forest Service office. He was not moving, so I stepped inside the office and called emergency services. The medics arrived in about five or six minutes, and by this time, Kenny was breathing again. All that was wrong was that the wind had been knocked out of him. He climbed back on the roof, we finished by noon, and travelled on to Bonner's Ferry.

From there we moved to Priest Lake. The shelters there were much larger and housed four coolers. What we noticed first was that there was plastic over the concrete slabs that we had poured two months earlier when the temperature was 51°F. When we removed the plastic, we noticed some spalling—chips of concrete caused by the surface water freezing. This is when I first discovered that after we had finished the concrete pour, the inspector, who was based at this one site, had made the finishers cover the pour with plastic. Our procedure had been not to cover the concrete, and let it cure as fast as possible to get the water out, the only part that freezes. It had worked well on all the other sites. At this site, when the temperature dropped to minus 30°F, the water froze, causing the surface to spall.

The COR asked me to buy some special concrete patch and give it to the inspector who had ordered us to cover the pour. That way the inspector could fix the damage he had caused. We couldn't have asked for a better COR.

As these were very large units here, we hired Fred Meier, who had worked with us at North Dryden Flume, to help. Fred was a finish carpenter and used a finish carpenter's hammer. This irritated me, so I stole his hammer and hid it in the tool trailer. When he whined that he lost his hammer, I said, "Here, you can use my 16 oz. hammer." He whined and cried, but at least he could drive a nail!

We had been working twelve days straight, so Fred Hyke and I flew home in the Cessna 185 for some R & R. Kenny and Jeff decided to stay at Priest Lake.

Sunday afternoon Fred and I returned, and when we went into the restaurant for dinner, the proprietor said, "Lloyd, I'd like to talk to you in the back room for a moment." He told me that Kenny and Jeff had gotten into an argument with one of his customers and brandished their guns.

The proprietor said he didn't want them staying there any longer. I gulped and said we'd only be here a day or two at the most and promised that I'd keep them under control. He reluctantly agreed. He didn't want to lose the bucks (Pun intended.).

What happened Saturday night at the Priest River Inn; The band was playing and the Locals were celebrating. Kenny was sitting at the bar talking to a very good looking bartender named Megan. Jeffrey was at a table trying to make out with a fat girl. When the time came for the bartender's break, she and Kenny slipped out the side door and headed for the front seat of my pickup, which Kenny had been driving. After a time, the gal's boyfriend started wondering where she was. He and his buddies started searching for her. Just as she and Kenny were getting out of the pickup, one of the boyfriend's buddies spotted them and attacked Kenny. Kenny flattened him and three others, but was becoming overwhelmed. By then, a whole crowd was watching. Kenny pulled his gun and fired two shots into the ground.

The crowd dispersed, the band kept playing, Megan kept pouring drinks, and Kenny and Jeff jumped into the pickup and got the hell out of there!

(I didn't hear the whole tale until this year.)

■ ■ ■

We then started Round #3. Our deal with the refrigeration manufacturer's representative, Milt Merrick, was that he would send his expert installation team to assemble the refrigeration unit at Kooskia, the origin of our circuit. Our team was there to watch and learn. His guys fumbled around for about a day and a half, and finally got the unit complete—and went home to Arizona.

It appeared that his out-of-town experts had only experienced about a day and a half of training themselves. The main test required was for a man to stand inside when the door was closed and not be able to see any daylight. The Merrick crew did not make the test. I was too dumb to make the test at this time and we moved on to Weippe. We easily set the unit up in half a day, and did the test.

It passed, so we moved on to Lochsa. This unit was much larger, but we were able to finish it up in less than a day, and continue on to Darby and through our rotation to Priest Lake.

From Priest River we moved to Wallace to complete the shelter that we were unable to complete earlier due to snow and ice. Once the shelter was complete, we were ready to install the final refrigeration unit. As we worked, I turned to Fred Meier and said, "Hey Fred, kick that snow off the floor over there." He did—and there was his finish hammer. We all laughed. "You can go back to tap, tap, tap."

At noon two days later, we finished the refrigeration and were loading up to go home, when one of the personnel from the on-site Forest Service office came out and told me I had an important phone call. When I went inside, the office manager told me that I'd received a message from home that my father had died.

My brother had called a month earlier and told me that my dad wasn't feeling well. I said I'd come down, but he told me it wasn't that bad. My plan had been to visit him the moment I finished with the tree coolers, but I had missed my chance. My heart was broken. All I knew was that I had lost my Dad.

▪ ▪ ▪

Because some of the mechanical cooling parts and the hula skirts did not arrive until long after the refrigeration units, we had to make a fourth round to all the cooler sites. Milt Brown was to supply two mechanics, and we were to supply a helper for this portion of the work. As Kenny had his own pickup, I sent him to help. They started this round at Wallace, and then moved to Weippe.

Fred Hyke and I had been home in Vancouver doing some other work, but we were scheduled to meet Kenny at Kooskia on Sunday night. We had expected the Kooskia unit to be completed by the time we arrived. It was the middle of winter and very icy. I had instructed Kenny to take the main road from Weippe to Kooskia.

Fred and I had stopped at Kamiah and were gassing up when Kenny pulled into the station. He didn't see us at first. When he did, he drove off, but came back in a few minutes. When he left Weippe, he was so proud of his four-wheel-drive that he took a shortcut and had the refrigeration crew follow him. About two miles out of town he slid into a ditch—and the refrigeration crew slid in after him. Just trying to save ten miles cost us two days in production, which put us behind schedule.

I never did learn the whole truth.

In order to speed up and catch up, Fred and I, along with Kenny, helped the Merrick crew finish the refrigeration. Just as we finished, the hula skirts finally showed up.

Fred Hyke and I installed the hula skirts and called for final inspection, once again beginning at Kooskia. The first thing the inspection team noticed was light shining through the refrigerator door. I winced and promised I would get it fixed. All the units our crew installed passed inspection. Fred and I went back to Kooskia and used all our leak-fixing experience to stop the light from shining through. The Forest Service was happy and to this day, I don't know if the door ever leaked light again.

The job was done on time and we made a good profit.

Chapter 29

1984
LOUISIANA PILE DIKES
Army Corps of Engineers
Venice, Louisiana

In 1984, we filed W-2's in seven different states. Louisiana was one of them.

Months earlier, Bob Rice, a long-time acquaintance from Vancouver, called me and said he knew about a pile driving job that I might be interested in. My curiosity was aroused as I was always looking for another job. He asked to meet me at the Gaslite Bar and told me he would introduce me to a guy who knew all about it. It turned out to be Bob Colgrove, who worked for Peter Kiewit, one of the largest employee-owned contractors in the nation. The job was installing pile dikes on the last twenty miles of the Mississippi River in Louisiana.

The dikes are driven about a quarter of a mile apart, the purpose being to speed the flow in the center of the river. The idea is to keep the sediments from settling in the shipping channel. The Corps of Engineers normally use treated wood piling. For this job they had decided to use triangular shaped concrete piling. This was the first time concrete was used for this type of application.

Colgrove and I looked over the plans and specifications for the job. Bob had also studied the soil reports. These reports showed mud, which makes it easy to drive pile. (It should be noted that at this time, the pile driving companies in the New Orleans area were busy with several years backlog.) He and I took off the quantities and figured out the cost per foot of driving a piling. There were three different sizes of concrete piling: 12 inch, 18 inch and 24 inch, and the piling varied in length from thirty to seventy two feet. There was also wood piling at the channel end of the dikes that were from thirty to ninety feet long.

Completed pile dike.

Partly-completed pile dike.

The reason Bob Colgrove knew about this job is because his son, Mike, was working on a pile driving job in Florida for Hobbs Construction. Hobbs was based in Panama City and was looking for a pile driving subcontractor to do the pile dike portion of the Mississippi River job.

We presented our numbers to Hobbs and they decided to give us the job. This required a subcontractor's bond, so I went to my bonding agent, who agreed to write the bond. However, there was a problem. When we were figuring the job, Colgrove thought it was on the west side of the river. My agent pointed out that the job was in fact, on the east side of the river, and that the bonding company does not underwrite any work east of the Mississippi River. I (foolishly) gave Hobbs a personal letter of credit for $100,000 in lieu of a bond.

We began mobilization, renting a spotter and pile driving hammers from PACO, a Tacoma, Washington firm. They had been a rental yard, and when the pile driving boom ended around 1980, they began buying pile driving equipment for a dime on the dollar from the many pile driving companies around the country that had gone out of business. They in turn, rented or sold this equipment to contractors like me.

I dispatched Bob Rice to New Orleans to locate and rent a Vicon Manitowoc 3900 crane with three drums. He took one of our orange and white pickups with life vests, hard hats and other safety equipment that we would need, and headed for New Orleans, stopping in Sacramento to visit his brother, who owned a trucking company. When he got halfway through Texas, he called us and told us he was out of money. This didn't please me. I'd given him plenty of cash to make the trip.

I told Randy, our office manager, who said, "You should tell him to come back home." I thought if I sent him money and told him to come home, I wasn't sure what he would do. If I gave him just enough money to get to New Orleans, at least I would get my pickup there.

Sometime later on Randy found out that Bob had stopped at a topless bar on the Texas-Mexico border and outfitted all the strippers with our hard hats. He saved one hat, and continued on to New Orleans. Once there he drove to an equipment rental yard in Metairie to rent the crane we needed. He was plastered and got in an argument with the owner, who didn't want to cause me any trouble, but Bob didn't give him a choice; the owner called the police and they threw Bob in the slammer. The next morning he was allowed to make one phone call.

Fortunately, Randy answered the phone and somehow managed to get Bob released, ordering him to go to the New Orleans airport and get on a plane bound for home. Instead, he drove down to Venice and negotiated a deal to sell 40,000 pounds of shrimp to the Hong Kong Restaurant in Vancouver. (Be aware that there were no shrimp available at that time of the year.)

While in Venice, Bob got in contact with our front man, Paul Gibson. Paul owned four crew boats, and we planned on hiring one to carry our crew up and down the river. Paul was the wheeler-dealer in Plaquemines Parish, Louisiana. He also owned a beautiful two-story brick home in Buras. He had a complete set of exercise equipment in his garage where the Plaquemines Parish sheriffs worked out. He was also deeply in debt. The oil wells in the local bayou had gone dry and the overall economy was poor. Paul did whatever he could to make money.

I called Paul, who informed me that Rice was in Venice making a fool of himself. I asked Paul if he could get Bob on a plane headed for home. He said yes, and had one of the deputies take Bob to the New

Orleans Airport and put him on the plane. But he didn't make it home. As we found out later, he got off the plane in Dallas.

In the meantime, I made arrangements with the dealer in Metairie to load the 3900 Manitowoc three-drum crane onto to a barge and haul it to the Venice boatyard so we could equip it with the pile driving leads. It sat there for two or three days—and no work happened. As I learned later, they considered me a Yankee and an outsider, and just didn't want to do the work. I had the rig towed to the Metaire shipyard in New Orleans. These people were low on work and very happy to help us. This was January, 1984.

We started outfitting and installing the spotter on the crane. (This is the job that Colgrove and PACO said would take about four days.) Colgrove had hired Doug Keefer to operate the crane, which sat on the conventional barge that transported it from the rental yard. We used it to set the Flexi Floats in the water and install the 12″ x 12″ wooden mats. (This was the type of barge Kiewit Company used on other projects.)

We then moved the barge and the Flexi Floats to a harbor where we walked the crane from the conventional barge onto the Flexi Float barge.

At the end of two weeks, the work was not yet complete. One crew member went back to Portland, but Keefer, Colgrove, Kenny Piper and Jim Lindberg kept working on the spotter for another three weeks. This required a lot of cutting, burning and hose fitting. Colgrove was directing the work. Once the spotter was connected, Colgrove had the crew install the pile driver leads. We discovered later that Colgrove, the expert, had installed the leads upside down, and that's why all the cutting, burning and fitting were necessary to connect them to the spotter.

While the rig was being outfitted, Kenny Piper and Paul Nordahl built a template float that properly spaced the piling to be driven. They fabricated the float at the beach in Venice.

The template float—The lighthouse in background was destroyed by Hurricane Katrina in August of 2005.

Assembling the Flexi Floats.

Finally outfitted, we moved downriver and began the first dike. I think we got 30 piles the first day. Not bad, considering…

We bought an 18-foot aluminum flatboat with a 40 hp Yamaha outboard engine for moving men and small tools around the job. On the second morning we hooked the flatboat to Gibson's crew boat, the Miss Sheila, and headed down river at 30 mph. After about three miles, the motor flew off the flatboat. The boat driver yelled, "Do you want to stop?"

I thought, "What's the use? The motor is in 50 feet of water," and told him to keep going.

A couple of minutes later, a fisherman in a very fast boat caught up to us and started waving for us to stop. He said that the motor was still hooked to our boat with the tow rope. We pulled it up and sure enough, we still had the motor. We went on to the first dike, lifted it onto the barge, and poured the water out of it. It started right up and ran just fine.

The only problem was that the steering was tweaked and the boat never again steered correctly. Mike Colgrove, who outfitted the flatboat, had failed to tighten the bolts after he attached the motor to the transom.

The next day Bob Colgrove was showing off, and rammed the boat into a submerged piling, knocking himself overboard. The crew boat driver rescued him from the "Muddy Mississippi" water. As Bob's leave with Kiewit was up, he returned to Vancouver.

Batter pile setup Template barge, leads, spotter and crane.

A couple of days later Mike tied the flatboat up between the pile driving barge and the pile barge. It wasn't two minutes later that a wave from a passing ship pushed the two barges together and crushed the flatboat, knocking a couple of holes in it. We patched the holes with Red Hand (a filler paste compound for steel) and put it back in the water. It wasn't pretty but it still floated.

Actually, we did very well the first week, averaging 50-60 piling a day. The next week was the same. And one day *we set our record of 115 piling.* In most cases, the piling dropped right into the mud, and the crane had to hold it in place for a few moments until skin friction kept it from sinking. We hired a lugger (a tugboat holding up to two thousand gallons of fuel) from Jack Bristo called the Captain Jack, named after Jack himself. This vessel was used to fuel the pile driving equipment and move the pile barges. His company served us well throughout the project.

■ ■ ■

Hobbs Construction had originally assigned Mike Colgrove to this project as their superintendent. During the time we were outfitting the pile driving rig, Mike occupied a temporary office in New Orleans. Hobbs had given Mike a draw and a credit card. During the six-week period we spent outfitting the pile driver, Mike spent all the cash and ran up a $1,500 bar bill on Hobbs' credit card, so Hobbs canned him and assigned Pete Boseman to be their superintendent.

Colgrove then hired Mike to be our pile driving superintendent. The problem was that neither Bob, Mike, nor I knew anything about pile driving. The first month or so we were driving, Mike did a lot of yelling and screaming, but he never did learn how to set up the template barge. In the meanwhile, my crewmen, Kenny Piper and Jim Lindberg, learned how to move the template and spot the piling.

We were losing and breaking small tools and chokers on a daily basis. Replacements needed to come from suppliers in New Orleans and get shipped to Venice by hotshot freight drivers. The problem was that the hotshot people required someone to be there to receive the shipment.

One day Randy was ordering chokers, complaining to the salesperson about the problem, when the salesperson said he knew a guy who was trying to start up a business delivering to Venice. He put Randy in touch with Joe Newby. Joe was happy to get the work and served us well throughout the project. (By this time, we had rented a house trailer from Sally Rouse.)

During the beginning of the job we stayed at the Venice Inn and rented an office next door. While staying there, one day I had to take a trip to the concrete pile manufacturer's plant in Bienville, Mississippi. I drove over with Pete Boseman in an effort to get the manufacturer to do a better job of placing the piling on the barge so that we didn't have to do so much work to pick them off. It was a particularly hot, humid, miserable day, and we didn't get back to the Venice Inn until about 8:00 that evening.

I went to dinner and finished eating my salad (the only really good thing about the place). I wondered where my dinner was. I had ordered it a half-hour earlier and it still hadn't come out to me. The staff hadn't even brought me the drink I ordered.

There were only two other guys in the dining room. They were sitting behind me, three or four tables away. After waiting as long as my patience could stretch, I got really angry, grabbed my salad dish and started to throw it toward the dish table. As I started my throw, I decided it wasn't a very good idea, and attempted to check it, but due to the mayonnaise on my salad saucer, it sailed over and conked one of the men on the forehead. The guy was more stunned than mad.

I immediately tried to apologize. He wasn't too upset—but we decided to settle up before they left in the morning.

We finished our dinners and the two guys went to their rooms; I went to mine. They got to thinking that it wasn't a good idea to wait until morning and called the sheriff, who immediately notified Paul Gibson.

We all met in the dining room. Paul asked the man how much he would settle for, but the guy didn't answer. Then Paul asked him if he'd settle for $100 and the guy said no. Paul then asked him if he'd settle for $200 and the guy said no. Then Paul said, "As you don't want to settle, the sheriff will make sure you are out of town by morning." Obviously, this became known as the "Flying Saucer Incident."

About this time, we started working two shifts, and hired a second crew with Mitchell Rouse as Foreman and crane operator. Sometime later, we moved out of the Venice Inn and moved into a large mobile house in Buras that we rented from Sally (Mitchell's wife).

Crane on board the Flexi Float work barge.

Our 18-foot flatboat.

By the end of the first month, it looked like we might have a money-maker in spite of all the problems during outfitting.

We were paying all of our crewmen $15 per hour, including Bob Young, the operator. One day Mike said to me, "I need more money."

I said, "The pay is the same for everyone."

A couple of days later he quit. The whole crew celebrated.

We hired a local pile-driving contractor to drive the wood piling at the channel end of the dikes. He had a small barge and used a gravity hammer. On the way downriver each morning, we dropped him and his crew off at his rig. They got on their knees and prayed, and then start driving piling. At 10:00, 12:00 and 2:00, they prayed again. When we picked them up on the way home, the owner complained about how little work he got done.

I diplomatically suggested that they should spend more time on the pile driver and less time on their knees.

Actually, the praying may have been appropriate. They were using swinging leads and the man riding the lead had to hold on with one hand while he hooked the lines with the other. They did fairly well until one day they had some hard driving. I told them to hang in there and that it would be better on the next dike. He finished that dike, but then told me he was done. I again suggested that the next dike would be easy but he said, "I'm done."

Picking piling.

Later on we came back and drove the remaining wood pile sections. The next piling—the one I had told him—about was the easiest driving on the entire project! The further downriver we went, the harder the driving became. The harder the driving, the longer the piling. The soil had changed from mud to sand. This took a great toll on our hammers and the rig and our morale, but not our determination.

Positioning piling.

Driving piling with the lighthouse in the background.

We moved in and started one of the longer dikes. One day as we were driving, the pile ran. Frank Bittencourt, the rigger, had his hand wrapped around the wire choker. He *should* have let loose of the choker. He did not—and the choker pinched off the tips of his fingers.

We packed them in ice and sent him upriver in the *Miss Sheila*. I wanted to send along someone to drive him the 90 miles to the hospital in New Orleans, but he insisted on driving himself in his own car.

The next day, Randy and I arranged to have Louisiana Workman's Comp pay for his medical care. However, he told us he didn't want Louisiana to know he was working in the state. He told me he would pay the $1,500 medical bill if I would pay him $3,700. Against my better judgment, I agreed. He was happy and I never heard another word from him or the state of Louisiana. I got lucky again.

The piling were driving hard but we were able to get 30 or more per day.

After we made a move one day, we started driving, but could not get the piling started; there was something hard below. We moved ahead and did a little better; this went on for two or three days, but we only got in about four or five piling.

We learned later that we were driving through a rock jetty that had been replaced many years before. This jetty did not show on the plans. We were to encounter it on three or four of the other dikes.

James Scarborough, the Corps of Engineers' inspector, said, "Keep track of your costs and we'll take care of it at the end of the job." Jimmy was a Cajun from the bayou with a melodious voice. Everybody liked him.

Once past the rocky areas, the piling drove harder and harder. As we later learned, the engineers had used the soil samples from the west side of the river to design the pile lengths for the east side job. As the contractor, we needed to keep driving pile to the best of our ability, as it says in our contract. Out on a remote location without the ability to contact the engineer (who didn't want to be reminded of his mistakes anyhow) we were left trying to negotiate back up the pipeline through the general contractor.

When we started, we had four pile hammers, one large, two medium and one small. It was our intent to drive the wood piling with the small one and the 12-inch concrete piling with the medium hammer. We pounded away with the medium hammer until it broke, and then started using the second one. We made little progress, so we switched to the large hammer and did a little better for a while. All these hammers and the equipment we were using met or exceeded the criteria specified for this project.

It was about the first of May and the driving was still going slowly, so I decided to start a second shift. I figured that if I could get twenty pilings per shift I could break even, and decrease the amount of time to complete the job. I hired Mitchell Rouse, a Local, to supervise the crew and run the crane. He, in turn, hired three other Locals he knew to fill out the crew. We took his crew downriver with us for a day to watch the operation, and to learn how to make the necessary moves.

The next day, he started the swing shift and was able to make two moves and drive twenty-two pilings. I was pleased. He did well the first week. The next week production dropped off considerably. The following week was even worse.

I had instructed him, no matter what, that he was to grease all the machinery at the end of each shift. This included the sheave (load) pin at the top of the leads, 115 feet above the deck. I began to notice that the fewer piles that were driven, the earlier the crew was arriving back at the dock. By the fourth week, they were only driving one or two pilings a shift. As this was financial suicide, I ended the second shift.

One evening while the second shift was going on, Paul Gibson had invited me to dinner at the restaurant in Buras. While we were finishing dinner, Paul got a call from one of his boat drivers and had to leave. I finished my dinner and walked out the door just as a car drove up with two ladies in it.

The driver hollered, "Mr. Kessler! I'm Mitchell's wife." We exchanged a few words, and she said, "Don't tell Mitchell you saw me."

I had a lot of other things on my mind, so didn't think much more about it.

It was then the first of June; Paul Gibson had experienced an upturn in his crew boat business and was having trouble finding boat drivers. Several mornings the drivers showed up late, leaving our crew waiting at the dock from one to three hours. This was costing everyone. I decided to hire a Jo-boat (a rental), slower, but at least we had control. It took us 45 minutes more travel time per day, but the crew wasn't getting paid to travel.

This worked out quite well, but I soon realized that I needed a second Jo-boat. It was mandatory that one boat be next to the work barge anytime we were working, in case of emergency. I also needed the second boat to shuttle men and supplies during the work shift. This worked well, except that the second boat was brand new, and was powered with a Caterpillar engine.

This was the first time the boat works had used a Cat engine, and, after a few trips up and down the river, the engine died, and I had to get the owners to come and repair it, which they didn't like very much. They were based far away and were expensive. The problem was that the engine compartment had not been properly vented, and the exhaust smoke clogged up the air filters. They fixed it and the boat ran okay—for a while.

We had to rent space at the local moorage in order to moor the Jo-Boats, which were equipped with radar. When I rented the second boat, the company charged me three thousand dollars to install radar. The moorage was primarily for the local fishermen who really didn't like contractors or oil people. One morning when I went to the boat, the radar was missing. I used the boat anyway, but eventually had to pay the boat company *another* three thousand dollars for a new radar.

I decided to rent a quarters barge so the crew could be closer to the work.

As usual, Randy did all the procuring and coordinating. To do the cooking, he hired a black gentleman, who insisted on having a helper, who insisted on having a dishwasher. This was a three-man kitchen crew serving an eight-man work crew. When my crew went aboard, including Dick Wills, who brought his wife Heddy along, they weren't pleased with the food. They weren't used to grits and other southern specialties. The black kitchen crew really didn't want to work anyway, so we sent them home and paid Dick's wife to take over the cooking.

To make matters worse, the air conditioner quit on the second day. In order to save money, Randy didn't insure the operation of the quarters barge, so the rental company charged me an arm and leg to come down and fix the problem.

The crew boat "Terry Lynn" waits next to the quarters barge. The crew boats were powered with twin 450 hp GMC engines. They could carry twelve passengers at speeds up to 30 mph.

In the meantime, Bob Colgrove had returned to the project, bringing Mike along with him. (I think he may have quit Kiewit and withdrawn his retirement money.) At any rate, he was going to show us *how to drive piling!*

In spite of the fact that Marine Law does not allow alcohol on these vessels, never-the-less, the beer got warmer and the tempers got hotter.

One night Bob and Mike Colgrove got drunk and got into a fight. Bob fell overboard. Kenny fished him out, and has always said that it was the biggest mistake of his life.

A few days after the quarter-barge arrived, Kenny and I returned to Vancouver to take care of some other business. I only expected to be gone a few days, so before I left, I gave the Sheepherder (Bob Bell) explicit instructions to keep the dike on line and grade. He was the only one on the crew who knew how to do this.

However, as soon as I left, both Bob and Mike Colgrove quit listening to him, and the Sheepherder was too intimidated by them to call me and let me know there was a problem.

While I was gone, I received daily reports from Bob Colgrove. Going by the reports, the crew should have been well into a second dike. The Corp's report showed them still working on the same dike. In fact, Colgrove had been cheating on the pile counts. So I called Pete Bozeman to ask him how things were going. He said he thought everything had been going well.

The only problem was, as I later learned, Pete had not been going downriver for the last three weeks. He had found more important things to do on shore—like entertain his landlady.

This created a host of problems, but the main one was cash flow. The Corp only paid us for the actual number of pilings we'd driven. To make matters worse, Hobbs refused to release the retainage.

I had been dragging my feet the last few days about going back to Louisiana. I was both physically and mentally worn out, but I *had* been able to spend the time at home recuperating and reconnecting with Millie, and I needed that. With this latest news, however, I knew I needed to get back to Louisiana to take charge.

At this same time, Bob Colgrove picked six of the crew up at the dock for a weekend off. Three of them decided to get off in Venice. He continued towards Buras, but just as they were leaving Venice he spotted a bar, which was on the opposite side of a divided highway.

He turned across the median and rolled the truck. Bob Young was sitting in the middle and the Sheepherder was sitting on the right. Upon impact, Young severely injured his elbow.

Although Colgrove was drunk, he played it cool and they all went into the bar and had a drink. The sheriff showed up and hauled Colgrove to the Port Sulfur jail (not a pleasant place). Bob Young, our key man and crane operator, went home for six weeks until his elbow healed.

The next morning, Randy used his negotiating skills to get Bob bailed out of jail, and had Gibson's wife drive Bob and Mike to the West Bank Hotel in New Orleans. I had Randy arrange to have Bob Colgrove's ticket to Portland ready at the ticket counter. Mike was Bob's responsibility.

Colgrove called me from New Orleans and said that he didn't appreciate being hauled in Mrs. Gibson's station wagon. He also said that he and Mike were going to stay in a fancy hotel near the French Quarter and spend a couple of days taking in the sights.

I said, "Fine, but I'm only paying for one night at the West Bank."

They went home the next morning.

We then hired David Rome, who lived in New Orleans to replace Young. David was a bit egotistical, but a good crane operator who quickly adapted to our operation.

Before I returned to Louisiana, I had Randy get rid of the JoBoat and quarters barge. I cut the crew down to five men, which included Dick Wills. The crew moved back to the trailer in Buras. I instructed Randy to put Dick Wills and his wife up at the Venice Inn.

After we moved back into the trailer house, Sally Rouse called me and wanted me to go with her and her friend to New Orleans. I told her I hadn't been paid for a long time and didn't have any money. She didn't want to take no for an answer and told me they would pay for everything.

I still said no; after all, Mitchell was my friend. I went to work instead.

It was now hurricane season, and I was very concerned, something I expressed to Captain Jack Bristo. He said not to worry, "If a hurricane approaches, I'll make sure all the equipment gets safely moved upriver."

This did ease my mind—and what other choice was there?

We finished the dike the Colgroves had screwed up and started the next one. The driving became harder and harder and we continued to make adjustments to the equipment. During this time we were having trouble moving the pile driving barge anchors. They got stuck deep in the sand. To solve this problem, Dick Wills had us build an A-frame winch on the front of the *Captain Jack.* With the A-frame's help, we could pull the anchors up much easier, allowing us to position the pile-driving barge much faster. We also reconfigured the Flexis Floats and added another spud. In addition, we added another air compressor in order to increase the pressures at the pile hammers.

Our crew now consisted of Kenny, Dick Wills, James Walp, David Rome, the Sheepherder, and a Local named Melvin, the only black man on our crew. All of our adjustments helped, but the driving still got harder and harder as we hammered away.

The Sammy D and the "Captain Jack" with our custom A-frame winch.

Adding another spud to the Flexis.

One morning I decided to stay on shore. When the crew got to the dock, the *Miss Sheila*, Paul's best and fastest boat had, eight 50-gallon drums of diesel on the rear deck. We found out later that the *Miss Sheila* made a trip to Colombia.

Kenny asked Reggie, the boat driver, what was going on. He said he had to take somebody offshore fishing, but took off all by himself. Reggie, born with a bad disposition, had only been driving the *Miss Sheila* for a couple of weeks, and it didn't help his temperament much when he caught Kenny drinking a beer on board. This left us with the *Terry Lynn*, a much slower boat, to haul the crew, which didn't make them happy. However, LJ, our driver, was good.

One foggy morning I was standing next to Reggie at the controls as we barreled downriver. Reggie was relying on radar, as we couldn't see past the end of the bow, when all at once the fog broke and we found ourselves only four feet from the side of a ship. Reggie slammed the controls backward and started swearing because he had been focused on the long range instead of short range and missed the readings. Thankful to be alive, we made our way on down to the rig.

We completed the dike and decided to move to the very last one, as the river was low and the waters were calm. This dike was between the lighthouse and the ocean. The concrete piling were 24-inch—and the hardest to drive. We spent several days pounding away with our largest hammer (the 010). The driving was the most difficult on the entire job. In order to obtain more driving force, Dick Wills had removed some of the pile cushions from the driving helmet. We used every trick we could think of, including cutting off the piling before we started driving it. We had all but five of the piling in when the hammer broke. We had wanted to complete this dike before hurricane season started and before the waters got rough. As the hammer was broken, I decided to move to the only dike that had 18 inch piling. This gave us time to replace the broken 010 (ought ten) hammer. We set up and started driving the 18-inch piling with the 06 (ought six) hammer.

18-inch pile dike. Some of the piling had to be cut off—see the red line at upper left.

As the piling were driving to the point of refusal, it was better to cut them off before we drove them and we didn't have to patch them.

Cutting off piling after we'd driven it to the point of refusal. Patching came next.

The driving was very difficult, and early in the shift the 06 hammer broke. We shut down for the day and sent the *Captain Jack* to New Orleans to pick up another 010 pile hammer. It arrived in time for the start of the shift the next morning. The piling were still driving very hard, in spite of Wills' increasing pressure on the hammer.

It became obvious to me that the hammer wasn't functioning right. I shut the work down. I arranged for a float plane, and had the hammer supplier send a mechanic down to fix the hammer. The mechanic explained to me that the hammer was not properly timed. Neither Wills, nor Colgrove, nor any of the other experts who had been driving piling all their lives knew how to time a hammer!!

It only took about ten minutes to adjust the timing, and we started driving again. I asked the mechanic to stick around for a while, just in case, but the hammer worked well. However, he told me that we were working with pressures far in excess of what the hammer was designed for.

Even though the piling was driving very hard, we were able to finish the 18-inch dike. The new 06 hammer arrived, but as it turned out, the only one that could drive any of the piling was the 010.

All of the concrete piling left to drive were 12-inch. However, we were out of 12-inch pile cushions, so I decided to cut the surplus 18-inch cushions down to 12-inch. I had Melvin watch me cut one down to size with an ax, watched him cut one, and left him to cut the rest of the cushions.

An hour or so later I smelled something like burning brakes and thought, "Uh oh. There's a friction smoking on the crane." I then saw a white cloud where Melvin was working. He had decided to use a die grinder instead of the ax. He was pure white from asbestos dust. The darkest part of him was his white teeth.

At this time, I was having a difficult time paying the bills. My friend Harold L. Coffman, who was a land developer from Vancouver, very mechanically inclined and with a good business sense, offered to come down and see our operation. "I'll bring Wanda and it will give us an excuse to go to the World's Fair."

They came down to the job site, where I explained the operation. Harold said, "You're doing everything you can, but you should get rid of Dick Wills. All he's doing is supervising, and you can do that. Your main problem is cash flow." This advice eased my mind, so I sent Wills on his way, and Harold and Wanda went on to the Fair.

Another incident happened on a Friday when the crew came in due to bad weather. David Rome did not head back to New Orleans. Instead, he and Kenny went out for a drink.

At about seven, Kenny came back to the trailer. The next morning we learned that David had sideswiped four cars in Buras. He was driving his wife's beautiful Ford Galaxy, and when he turned around to see what damage he had done, he sideswiped another three cars on the other side of the street. In order to get bailed out, he had to put up the title to his house. His wife wasn't pleased.

David called me on Sunday and asked if we were going to work Monday. I told him that I wasn't sure what I was going to do, and to call me later. As it turned out, the weather stayed bad and it was obvious we weren't going to be able to work Monday. When he called back I told him I was shutting the whole job down and everyone was going home for a week.

This worked well, and the two guys I was going to lay off anyway quit by themselves. The following Monday, the crew returned to work, along with Bob Young, whose elbow had finally healed. (This is the crew who toughed it out from the end of August to the last day on the project.)

We had a new boat driver the day we re-started work. We called him *Captain Hoss*. He was a good driver and a good guy. Kenny bought him a pair of Logger suspenders. He thought this was the greatest thing ever. All of the other boat drivers wanted a pair too.

We weren't about to give a pair to Reggie. Although we did try to get a pair for a couple of the other guys, they quit making them about this time. We told the other drivers, but they were still jealous of Captain Hoss.

One morning when we arrived at the dock, there was a different driver on the *Terry Lynn*. We asked him what was up and he said Captain Hoss couldn't make it. When we got down to the pile driving rig, there was Captain Hoss on the *Miss Sheila*. He had stopped for fuel before going back up river and had wound a mooring line around the prop. We used the crane and our nylon slings to lift the stern of the *Miss Sheila* out of the water in order to remove the tangled lines. Captain Hoss then headed upriver. We didn't bother to ask him where he'd been.

We had worked many days in a row and decided to take the weekend off. Most of us went to the World's Fair in New Orleans. When I got home Sunday night, I noticed that Kenny wasn't there. The next morning when it was time to go to work, he was a no-show, but he was there when we got back to the trailer that night and he told us he had been "entertaining Sally and her sister". He said he "only missed a day's pay, not a full paycheck—like in Wallace."

Kenny Piper positioning the template barge.

Our progress was slow, but we kept banging in piling. As the pressures were set up three or four times the maximums for our pile hammers, we had to change the pile cushions out at a rapid rate. Our supplier could not keep up with us, and we were on the verge of not being able to work.

When my fifteen year-old grandson Collin visited us, he noticed the pile cushions. I called home one night in November, when he said, "Hey, Grandpa, I can make those pile cushions—and I know where I can get the material."

I told him to go for it and he made most of the cushions for the rest of the job.

In November we were making fairly good progress when one day, the sheave at the top of the leads sized. It took Bob Bell and Kenny a day and a half to beat the pin out of the sheave. Our cheers abated when the spare pin would not drive in; the problem was the salt air had caused the metal to swell. I had to take it to a machine shop in New Orleans and have it machined down. That took another day and a half. The crew just hadn't been greasing the sheave as I had instructed them to do.

Man basket at the top of the leads—over 100 feet up.

When we moved down river to do the long dikes, we had just finished driving the batter piling and installing the caps on the first section of the dike when the water got rough and we had to move out.

You can't drive piling in water this rough.

We moved upstream where the water was calmer and drove wood piling. The water got rougher and rougher, so we had to shut down for a week or two. When the waters calmed, we sailed back to the concrete dike we had started. As we were sailing, Fred stayed in the pilothouse with the captain, and the rest of the crew, including me, went down to the small galley for a cup of coffee.

I heard the engines reverse, knowing that we were back at the dike, when Fred came in and said Captain Axel had rammed the dike and knocked it over. Jack Bristo canned Axel a few days later.

I didn't believe him at first. Now we had to start all over.

If I had it to do over again, I would have moved over a couple of feet and started driving more piling. But the specs required any broken concrete to be removed. I called in a diver from New Orleans to remove the concrete. It took about four days to remove the five piling.

Once we got re-started, we got as good progress as we were going to get for the rest of the job. We were using the largest 010 hammer to drive all sizes of piling. All other equipment we used exceeded contract specifications. We were expending pressures many times greater than the equipment was designed for.

About mid-November, the water was too rough to work and all of the crew except Kenny and I went home. We had three barge-loads of piling on site, and some of the barges were leaking. We kept them pumped out so they didn't sink.

We had Thanksgiving dinner at Milljack's Café in Buras. Food here was served semi-cafeteria style. The waitress/cook/whatever told us that she had worked every day in that restaurant for the last 37 years, even when Hurricane Cecelia came through in 1970.

I was thankful we had no hurricanes that year. I also remembered Jack Bristo telling me that he had ridden out Celia, but would never stay to ride out another hurricane. Ever.

Because the piling was driving slowly, we weren't getting paid much. This meant that things were tough at home. Millie sent me a letter just before Thanksgiving, with this excerpt:

"Please don't ask me to pay another bill! Have mercy on me. You know that I usually like to savor that money in the bank for a week or two...I don't have to buy cheap dog food! Good bye Alpo! Collin spent the money he earned making pile cushions on 3 shares of Intel Corp. stock (an electronics firm) and they jumped three points the next day."

During this stretch, we worked 39 days straight and then took four days off for Christmas.

On Super Bowl Sunday, when the crew came home from work, I decided to go to the bar to watch the game. I tried to get Bob Young to go with me, but he was suffering from emphysema. The game had not yet started and there was a $2,000 board with four spaces left. I called Bob and asked him if he wanted to buy one of those spaces, but he said no. I told him I was going to put his name on one. Instead, I put his name on all four. Each quarter paid $500.

As it turned out, Bob won three quarters for $1,500. I called him to tell him that he had to come over to pick up his money. It didn't take him long to get there, and the proprietor paid him off, saying, "Are you going to buy a round?"

Bob replied, "How long have we been coming in here?"

The proprietor answered that we'd been coming in for close to a year.

Bob said, "Did you ever buy us a drink?"

The proprietor looked kind of sheepish…and Bob left.

■ ■ ■

During January, we finished all of the piling except the five 24-inch piling that we had not been able to drive on the last dike. We moved in and attempted to drive the remaining piling. Just as we pulled the spuds up to make a move, a Navy ship sped up the river and threw a big wake. This caused the whole rig to shake violently, and it broke the spud cables so that we had no way to let them down. We were left hanging by a thread, and the water was getting rough.

Bob Young and the crew hammered away. I could see that the pile helmet was about to break; the one line that was holding the barge was about to break too. We only had one tugboat standing by. If the line broke, we'd surely be swept out to sea.

I yelled, "Stop everything!"

Jimmy Scarborough had been watching our operation from the tower of the tugboat. I told him that we couldn't drive that piling any farther. I told him we were done or we were going to have a disaster. He told me that if I didn't drive it, he couldn't pay me for it. I decided that was okay and asked him to tell us we were done. He told us that very thing, and we left.

The tug hooked on and we barely had enough power to get started upriver for New Orleans. Just upstream from Venice, we passed a tugboat that had sunk a couple of weeks before. Alongside it was the *Miss Sheila*, driven by Captain Robert. The salvage crew was Divine Salvage from Portland, Oregon. When the tugboat started to sink, the deckhand ran down to the engine room to get his dog. They didn't make it. We talked to the Divine guys for a few minutes and then headed on to New Orleans to disassemble the rig.

We finished this work on Fat Tuesday, and the whole crew celebrated by going to Mardi Gras, including Millie and Kenny's girlfriend Wendy. The next day Millie and I drove one company pickup home, and Kenny and Wendy drove the other one.

The biggest problem we faced on this job was one we never had any control over: The Corp of Engineers had used core samples from soil on the wrong side of the river from which to base all of their specifications for the job. Everything from the material used for the piling to the length of the piling specified, was engineered for the rich muddy soil found on the west side of the Mississippi. The entire time we had been trying to drive pile in the hard, sandy soil on the east side of the Mississippi.

It wasn't until my attorney Arnie Grey, a representative of Hobbs Construction and I were negotiating the claims for extra work that the COR finally revealed the source of our frustrations. I had asked why the piling were so long. He said, "I'll tell you why. A couple of years ago when we built new dikes on the west side of the river, the wood piles were not long enough and we had to pay the contractor to install longer ones." This gave us instant entitlement to our claims.

The engineer used this same information to design the piling on the east side. Luckily for us, the Corp of Engineers had agreed that we should be compensated for all our extra work. To the best of my knowledge, this was the first and the last time anyone had ever driven triangular shaped piling.

Due to defective specifications, the dikes began failing from the very start of construction.

With a settlement of $500,000, Arnie and I headed home to Vancouver. Our flight got grounded in Denver due to weather, so the airline upgraded us to rooms at the brand new Embassy Suites. I was jubilant, and went directly to the bar to celebrate. Arnie went to his room. I've always accused him of padding his legal bill!

I'm glad to have these photographs. This design was doomed to failure from the very beginning.

Chapter 30

1987-'88
THE LATE EIGHTIES
US Forest Service

El Dorado Canyon Trail Bridges
Near forest Hills, California

This job was bid in late 1986, and as it turned out, was plagued by design problems as well as government administration problems. Even though we were low bidder, and within the range of the USFS estimate, they took a long time to award. Once awarded, it took even longer to schedule the pre-work conference, as the USFS did not issue the order to proceed.

I finally called to find out why. They told me that the trail contractor, Harvey Bell, had not yet built the trail to the bridge site. This was a surprise to me since the bid documents clearly showed that the trail was existing. I asked the government why it had not been built, and they said that Harvey was "busy on other trail work".

I said, "We at least need to have the order to proceed on fabricating the bridges," and explained to them that the bridges had to be flown in when the weather was cool. (The only available helicopter with the capacity to lift the bridges was a Sikorsky based in Oakland.) They issued the notice to proceed.

We fabricated the steel bridge trusses, handrail posts and miscellaneous metal for the two bridges in our Vancouver shop. We hired a local firm to do all the welding inspections required by the specifications. Once the beams/trusses were fabricated, we drew the required shop drawings and sent them to the Forest Service for approval.

Of course, we already had the fabrication done, so a week after approval, we loaded the bridge materials, along with concrete forms, onto trucks and sent them to the helicopter staging area east of the town of Forest Hills, California. Our construction crew, engineer Fred Hyke, Kenny Piper, Dan Lindberg and I, met the trucks and unloaded them.

When I informed USFS that the materials were on site, they were unhappy because I did not give them the choice to inspect the components while they were at the shop. The design engineer was based in San Francisco, as was his assistant, a woman who insisted on doing everything by the book. They were unhappy because they didn't get to make a field trip to Vancouver. Once I explained the delay situation to the engineer, he understood and accepted the bridges. He was a good guy and a good engineer.

There was an unusually heavy snow pack that year. A few days before this meeting, I had hired a Local to plow the six miles of road to the trailhead. He was only able to plow the first of the six.

This was a bad situation. If we could not get the footings built while the weather was still cool, we would not be able to fly the girders in with the only available Sikorsky helicopter. This was definitely a "differing site condition" as described by the plans and specifications.

I decided to take the risk of hiring a Hughes 500 to fly the crew, forms and lumber to the bridge sites. We built a heliport right in the middle of the El Dorado River.

Dennis Pearson landing the 500 on what we called "El Dorado International Heliport"

I attempted to notify the USFS CO (Contracting Officer). For whatever reason, the office girl and others did not get the message to him. (Notifications are supposed to be done in writing.)

Communication between contractor and the USFS was very cumbersome at best, as there were no radios or telephones at the work site.

That's what a contractor is: *a risk-taker. In this case, the stakes were high, but I had to take the gamble.*

I informed the USFS what I was doing, and they responded by sending a COR to watch the work.

In order to get to the heliport, Dennis had to drop straight down and fly under the canopy. I said to Dennis, "If you want, I can take that tall tree out."

But he said, "Don't do that; it's my reference point."

We proceeded to build the concrete form on the near side of the river. That work went well, as the ground line shown on the plan was correct.

As the USFS was now on notice that we were using the Hughes 500, and that they would have some financial responsibility, they mandated that we play by their rules. This meant that we had to keep a person at the staging area with a radio at all times so that in case of emergency, Search & Rescue could be notified. Dennis Pearson's girlfriend fulfilled this role. The only effect on us was that we had to leave Grover-Dog to keep her company.

Fred and I did the layout for the pier on the far side of the river, and started excavating. We found solid footing eight feet lower than the elevation shown on the drawings. This forced us to build a much taller pier.

Oversize pier, eight feet from red line to base.

When we finished forming the downstream bridge, we moved the forming operation to the upstream bridge site.

The ground line on each end of this bridge was different than shown on the plan. We went ahead and adjusted the excavation and forms. Once the forms were set, we were ready for concrete.

Grover's ride at the upstream bridge heliport—(Grover is at center, far right)

We hired a Sikorsky helicopter that was able to lift half a cubic yard (2,000 pounds) of concrete on its 150-foot-long load line and started pouring the oversize pier on the downstream bridge. There was no scaffolding, so Kenny had to stand on top of the form to manually open and close the concrete bucket. A skilled pilot can bring the bucket in very slowly so that it does not swing back and forth.

This pilot was not skilled, and the bucket came in swinging, so Kenny had to climb onto the bucket and swing with it. The pilot finally got the bucket over the form and dumped the load. It took about an hour and a half to complete the pouring of the two piers. No one but Kenny had the strength and skill to survive that operation.

The next morning our crew was sitting in a booth at the restaurant in Auburn. As we were talking about the previous day's operation, I blabbered, "Those are the two dumbest pilots we've ever used." I didn't realize the pilots were sitting in the booth across the aisle from us and heard every word I said.

We went ahead and poured the upstream bridge that day. The operation went better, mainly because there was a place for a man to stand.

Sikorsky flying bridge to the site.

A few days later we flew the bridges in with the Sikorsky 538. The pilot was excellent.

Lloyd on the completed upstream bridge.

Lloyd and Fred Hyke on finished bridge.

The USFS was wise in standing back and letting us take the lead to solve the engineering problems on this project. They gritted their teeth about us using the Hughes 500 to ferry Grover and the crew back and forth to the bridge sites, but they "gratefully" paid the $70,000 bill.

The gamble paid off, as we completed the job in the construction window and made a good profit.

1987
Nordheimer Fish Ladder
US Forest Service
Yreka, California
Bid amount: $78,000

The purpose of this job was to get salmon, trout and steelhead above the 30-feet-high Nordheimer Falls. The sand and gravel deposits in the area above the falls was ideal for spawning. The USFS believed utilizing this spawning area would greatly improve the fish runs in the Salmon River.

Constructing the fish ladder in solid rock was difficult, and made more difficult by the fact that it was on the far side of the creek that flowed through a 40-foot-deep canyon. There was no trail, so the workers had to scramble down the face of the steep canyon walls to reach the work. Construction required considerable precise drilling and blasting.

We hired Wesley, who resided at the village Forks of the Salmon. He had the California blasting permits the Forest Service required for this project. We had two Punjar gasoline-powered jack hammers for drilling the rock. I laid out the drill pattern and determined the depth of the holes. Wesley suddenly became the out-of-town "specialist," who thought we should drill more holes and use more explosives. I had used these "experts" before. I also had learned from experience how much explosives to use and NOT to use. We did it my way.

Don Winterholler, Fred Hyke, Ken Piper and Wesley.

We formed and poured the lower section of the fish ladder using a long-boom pump truck. We got the concrete from the local batch plant near Orleans.

We then formed the remainder of the fish ladder. The plans called for a concrete anchor a few feet above the upper end of the ladder, which would have required blasting in the stream bed. From the blasting we had already done, I knew that if I blasted it would destroy the falls. I also figured out that if I modified the top of the ladder, it would work just as well. I did not want to notify the FS because I knew they would shut us down for a long time while they scratched their heads. We completed the form work and went home for a short respite.

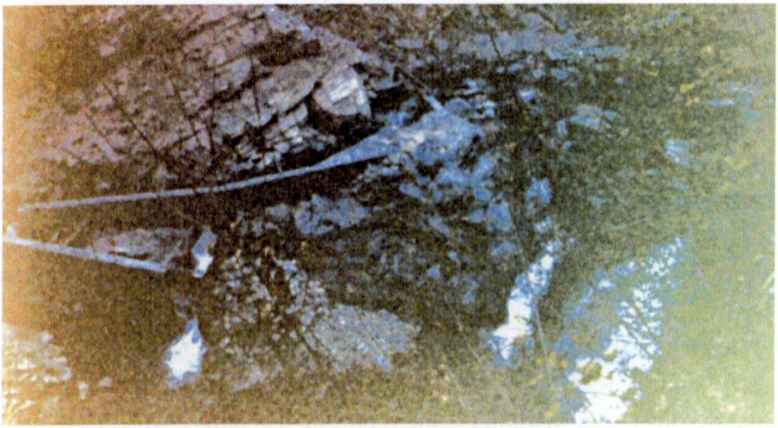

Fish ladder.

During the course of construction, we stayed at the Orleans hotel in Orleans. The proprietor, Barry, was a fishing guide. He kept the hotel open mainly to accommodate his fishing clientele. The hotel was old and dilapidated, and had been flooded a few times. The air conditioning consisted of swamp coolers in each room, which really didn't become effective until after dark. When we came in from work, we would sit in the shade on the hotel porch for happy hour. I always backed my pickup up to the porch.

One day a local Indian man joined us for a drink. He told us his name was Billy Two Shoes, and that he was a warrior. After a couple of drinks, he got ugly and we helped him leave. Later, we told Barry about it. He said, "Yeah, he's a warrior all right. He battles his wife every night."

A few days later, a very good looking Hoopa Indian girl showed up at happy hour. She had a drink and told us how proud she was to be a Hoopa. We were enjoying good-natured banter. My pickup was backed up to the porch as usual, the manual transmission in first gear position. As we were talking, the gal jumped into the driver's side of my pickup, which was aimed down the boat ramp.

A few minutes went by, and the local wood vendor and beer can recycler parked his Datsun pickup broadside in front of my pickup. It looked like someone had crapped all over it, and didn't have a single panel without a dent. These guys were the local "color," and would join us for a beer a couple times a week.

The gal was getting kind of high, and she repeated how important the Hoopa was. In my most diplomatic manner, I good-naturedly asked her, "Are you a mud-head or a blanket-ass?"

This upset her. She turned the pickup switch on; it started and rammed the Datsun. This put yet another dent in it. I told the guys to figure out how much it takes to fix the problem. The next day, they showed up and said, "We'll take a case of beer, and you guys can help us drink it."

I said, "I'll give you two cases of beer, and you can go somewhere else to drink it." However, since they did save my pickup from going into the river, and we didn't want to hurt their feelings, we helped them drink both cases of beer—and still made it to dinner on time!

One night at dinner, there were some special guests Barry invited. The dining room was full. Midway through dinner, in walked Billy Two Shoes. He was drunk and profane. Kenny told him to leave. He didn't listen, so Kenny picked him up and threw him out the door. Poor Two Shoes had lost another battle with the booze.

We finished forming the next day and went home.

While home, I called the batch plant at Orleans to arrange for concrete, only to find that they had gone out of business.

That meant that the nearest source of concrete was in Yreka. I decided to truck the sand, gravel and water to the job site, add the cement and place it with a helicopter.

I notified the USFS COR on Sunday that we were going to fly the concrete in Monday morning. Sunday afternoon, our crew headed for Grants Pass, where we planned on spending the night, driving on to the job site Monday morning.

Around 7 p.m. the COR called me and told me there was a forest fire on the ridge a couple miles north of our project. He said, "No helicopters, except for fighting fires, are allowed in the area, and we want the helicopter you were going to use."

I immediately notified the helicopter company, and waved them off.

We arrived on site early Monday morning and started cleaning up some loose ends. The COR showed up and told us there was an area-wide fire closure and we could not work. I argued that we were on the banks of a stream and in a rocky area. He wouldn't bend.

What really irritated me was that I knew there was a road contractor working just three or four miles away in an area that was closed due to high fire danger. I didn't rat on him, and we went home.

The specifications on this project required the contractor to submit a plan to use form-liners to give the concrete a natural look. They approved the same "crushed rock" form-liners that we had used on the Ozette River Trail Bridge. They also wanted us to color the concrete to match the slate blue color of the existing rock formation. We made samples and submitted them to the COR, and they were verbally approved. The proper color was obtained simply by adding lamp black, a powdered form of pigment, to the concrete mix.

After we were allowed to return to the project, there were no helicopters available. We changed our plans and brought in a concrete pump from Eureka. The sand and gravel also came from there. Ahead of time, we trucked in the required number of bags of cement.

The plan was to bring in three 8-yard loads of sand, gravel and water, and add the cement and lamp black on site. We had used this method many times before. We used the Swinger to lift the bags of cement up to the discharge end of the trucks, and dumped the cement into the bowl, and added the lamp black.

The three trucks arrived at 8 a.m., but the problem was that the first truck missed the running planks on the bridge. The driver panicked, slammed on his brakes, and broke through the bridge deck. We had a dilemma!

As luck would have it, one of the fire foremen showed up. He told me, "The Army has a large loader that was sent in to help our fire crews. I'll send the loader up to help you."

A few minutes later the loader arrived and pulled the concrete truck off the bridge. I told the driver, "Drive across the bridge, but stay on the running planks."

Running planks.

The driver had called his boss, who told him not to cross the bridge. My first thought was to tell him to get the hell outa there, but that wasn't going to solve the problem. So what I had to do was haul the cement across the bridge with the Swinger, and load it into the mixer truck. Once the concrete was mixed, we poured it into the Swinger bucket, and hauled it to the pump truck. I had planned on doing this concrete pour with five men: me on the Swinger, one man to break the cement bags into the truck, one man on the vibrator at the pour, and one man to help Kenny move the concrete hose around, but Wesley was a no-show. He went to work for someone else, which left Kenny to do a two-man job by himself. Only he had the power and will to get it done.

About an hour after we started the pour, the inspector showed up. He said, "You were supposed to do a sample patch of the concrete on the rock. Stop the pour."

We didn't hear him, and kept on pouring. He didn't know what to do. He had no way of contacting his office. We kept on pouring.

We were almost done when he discovered we'd made the modification on the upper end of the fish ladder. He told Kenny to stop pouring, but Kenny didn't hear him, so he ran up to where I was working and told me I had to stop pouring. I said "OK. We're done. Please notify the COR that we'd like to have the final inspection on Wednesday."

The COR showed up Wednesday morning and accepted the work. I handed him a bill for $14,000 for the delays the USFS had caused us.

It did NOT make him happy. I turned the bill over to Arnie Gray, my attorney, and spent $14,000 collecting the $14,000. (I should have done as I did in Delano: gritted my teeth and moved on. It would have saved me many hours of hated paperwork.)

1988
Ape Caves
US Forest Service
Gifford Pinchot National Forest
Original Contract Amount: $450,000

This job bid in 1987 and was completed in '88. The main feature of this project was the lantern rental building, but there was also a roadway, a parking lot and a trail and steps to the main entrance to the caves. We also built a trail to the upper end of the caves and two vault toilets.

Ape Cave parking lot.

Outhouse.

Doug and Grover, the Job Dawgs, in front of the lantern rental building. Getting ready for final inspection.

The job started in the fall and went well. We subcontracted the grading work to Dick Jones of Cougar, WA. He had a 200 Mitsubishi excavator that he used to do the grading. He was slow and had many excuses for not showing up for work, which put us behind schedule. This did not please Doug or me. Jones had failed to show up for several days. It was now Friday, and if we did not get the grading done this day, we were not going to have a place to work on Monday, and were going to have to reschedule our curb and mason subs.

To solve this problem, we worked Saturday and Sunday. Ken Piper got on the Mitsubishi and did the grading. Early Saturday morning, some hikers drove into the work area. Kenny asked them to park somewhere else. They said, as they were putting on their backpacks and hiking gear, that they would only be gone a short time, and left their car in the work area. Kenny did not believe them.

Kenny finished the grading early Sunday afternoon and the crew went home to Vancouver, returning to work Monday morning.

About 9:00, the hikers reappeared, but their car was nowhere to be seen…nor was it ever seen again…

At this time, some spotted owl protestors showed up and sabotaged some of our equipment. They then went to the Forest Service complex in Vancouver to protest. The Forest Service trapped them in between their two double sets of glass doors. I would have left them there without food or water until they begged for mercy. The Forest Service was more prudent.

The design of the interior of the lantern rental building was quite complicated, with copper countertops, fancy hardware and oversized beams in order to give it a rustic look. The overall design, along with expert craftsmanship and Doug's rapport with the USFS made for a very spectacular project.

CHAPTER 31

1988
MARBLE BLUFF FISH PASSAGE FACILITY AT PYRAMID LAKE
US Fish & Wildlife, Portland, Oregon
Contracting Officer, Lola Gannon

We contracted to modify a fish elevator for a lazy and endangered fish. This elevator was next to the Marble Bluff Dam, adjacent to Pyramid Lake, Nevada. We had previously modified this same lift in 1984. This contract required numerous modifications to the facility. It also required us to deepen the river channel below the dam and remove any obstructions.

Lloyd, Kenny and Dan.

The government had built a mile-long fish ladder from Pyramid Lake, which cost millions, but the Cui-ui were too lazy to swim up it. However, they did swim up the river to the base of the dam and into the elevator that we modified in 1984. The 1988 contract made modifications to the fish lift that allowed the fish to be directed into the fish-handling building where they were stripped of eggs, clipped and identified. From there they could be transported farther up the Truckee River by truck. We did many variations from the plans to make everything work.

Cui-ui fish: lazy, but endangered.

We enjoyed a very good working relationship with the Fish & Wildlife engineer, Ron Whaleen. He almost always agreed with our ideas, but liked to go into detail. If you asked him what time it was, he would explain to you how to put the watch together.

We decided to go home for a few days, as we'd been working every day for the past three weeks. I called my pilot, Marvin Alfred, and had him bring the Cessna 185 to the job site. We built a landing strip on the desert over 1,000 feet long and parked a pickup at each end. Marvin had been instructed to land between the two pickups. The 185 was STOL equipped (Short Field Takeoff and Landing) and should have landed in less than 100 feet.

I do not know what Marvin was thinking, but he did not land on the strip. Instead, he decided to land at a different spot on the desert. The left front wheel hit a clump of sage brush, causing the plane to balloon and nose into the ground, collapsing the landing gear and damaging the propeller, wing tip and other components.

Plenty of room to land.

This is called an "incident" and not a "crash."

Other than this "incident" with the 185, the job went very well. The $30,000 repair bill offset the profits. (It must be noted that this was the dumbest stunt any of my employees ever pulled).

Sage brush clump that caused the "incident"

Kenny Piper talking to the tow truck driver after the "incident."

Loading the 185 for transport to repair shop in Vancouver.

Chapter 32

1989
MY GOLD MINE
Idaho City, Idaho

In 1980, while we were working on the North Dryden Flume, Fred Meier continually bragged to me and Daryl Elliot about some rich gold claims next to Elk Creek, near Idaho City, Idaho. So in 1984, while in-between jobs, Fred and Daryl panned ten 5-gallon bucket of black sand that showed good color. Daryl called me and asked if he could bring them to my place and pan them out. I said yes. He panned out about an ounce of beautiful gold.

When I told Millie, she said, "I don't think he should stay here."

I said, "It will only be for a couple of days." It turned out to be six weeks. This was May of 1987.

At the end of the first week, as Millie was changing the sheets on the bed, Daryl asked, "How are you, Millie? Can I help you make the beds?" According to my last report from Millie, they made the bed about six more times.

While he stayed at our house, Millie did the cooking. Daryl was a vegetarian, and this complicated Millie's grocery shopping. She did not want me underfoot in the kitchen while she cooked. Daryl wanted to cook his own food but Millie didn't want him in the kitchen either. Period!

One morning Millie had gone shopping early and was putting the groceries away while I stood nearby. She was not in a good mood. Daryl moved into the kitchen and said, "How are you, Millie?" in a flirty voice that I had heard him say many times to other women. (His voice seemed to either flatter or shock them, but it got him plenty of loving anyway.

When Daryl saw me, he left the room. When he was gone, Millie yelled at me, "LLOYD, I want him the hell out of here!"

Later that morning, I told Daryl, almost apologetically, that he had to leave.

He moved out the next day, but a few days later he invited Millie and me to his apartment for dinner. Millie said to me, "You can go if you want, but I *sure* as hell am not going."

Daryl liked to brag—like when he told me about making out with his best friend's wife (he ran the Paradise store). Daryl had also dropped a couple of hints when he was having coffee with my friends at the Totem Pole Restaurant. I really did not *want* to believe they had been screwing around, so I did *not* believe it. Life went on as usual. Based on the fact that Daryl had just broken up with his long-time girlfriend, he was horny.... not that he wasn't *always* horny. She had wanted to get married and have a baby. Daryl did not want the responsibility of a family.

After he moved out, he and Doug met on the street one day. In jest, he told Doug, "I never worked so hard in my life as I did taking care of your dad's house and yard and being his houseboy."

When Daryl was working on different projects, I always paid him prevailing wage plus fringe benefits. Being my "houseboy", he naturally believed he was entitled to the "fringe benefits."

We started the process to lease the claims during this period. Daryl and my dog Grover made the first trip to the Idaho State Capital in Boise in my pickup, intending to lease the 400 claims that were available. Daryl parked the pickup in front and got out. Grover was loosely tied in the bed. Heading inside, he heard a scratching sound. Grover was hanging by her neck. Daryl rescued her. She celebrated by setting a bench mark on the Capital's lawn.

I also made several trips for the same purpose. The attractive woman in charge of claims was named Linda. She was quite cold at first, and considered us to be pains in the ass, but we finally sweet-talked her into finagling a way to lease the three of us the 400 claims. We had little knowledge of how to make a mining operation work, so we spent much time doing research.

All three of us had to come to the Idaho Statehouse building, as each lease had to be signed individually. The three of us each bought an equal amount of shares with the understanding that we would share the work and any profits equally. Daryl barely had enough money to pay for his share. Fred was *always* broke and didn't have any money, so I financed his shares.

After three years of waiting, we had the leases, and I called Fred Meier to tell him we were ready to mine. I also left messages for Daryl, but received no response. Fred showed up with his girlfriend and they camped in a small tent where he and Daryl had first prospected. Whenever Fred brought her to a job site, he immediately started an argument with her. This time was no exception, and when we got ready to start work, they were gone. I never saw or heard from Fred again.

In 1988, while Millie and I were attending the Annual Trailblazer's meeting in Reno, Jerry Clark invited us to his home in Fiddletown, California, to inspect his gold mine on the property he had inherited from this father. (Jerry was the president and founder of the Pacific Trail Builders Association, of which I am a charter member.) Jerry showed us what it took to make his mine work. He agreed to come to Idaho City to look at our claims, and advise us. We decided to mine in an area across Elk Creek that was completely out of sight.

We determined what equipment was needed and spent the next few months mobilizing.

The State's rules were that we were to provide a plan and get a permit before we started mining*...but we didn't have time for that!*

In the meantime, Daryl had returned to his and his sister's remote home near Ojai to attend his "secret garden" and other pursuits. He also did some prospecting near Lowman, Idaho, which netted him thirteen ounces of gold.

On January 12, 1988, Daryl and his sister Cheryl showed up at the motel where our crew was staying in Bend, Oregon. (We were finishing some work on the Crane Prairie job.) Daryl showed me the gold and I bought it for $6,000 cash. ($461 per ounce.) This was the last time I saw Daryl.

▪ ▪ ▪

Shortly thereafter, in the summer of 1982, I partnered with McCain to do a large US Forest Service project at the world's largest logging camp in Thorne Bay, Alaska. The job was accessible only by boat or float plane. Ron wanted to put amphibious floats on the 185, but I vetoed the idea. This turned out to be a wise decision. It was much more cost-effective to use the local air services, which were based in Ketchikan.

Not only did they deliver the daily mail, but they were in and out of Thorne Bay four times a day.

When the Thorne Bay job was complete in May of 1983. I used the 185 to fly around the northwest in search of new jobs.

In the late summer of 1983, we bid, and were awarded, a US Forest Service contract to build tree coolers at 15 sites in Idaho and Montana.

The 185 proved to be very useful in transporting personnel from our base in Vancouver. It was also very beneficial for transporting parts and equipment to the remote areas where we were working. The 185 gave our company an added dimension, which made us much more diverse, and as a consequence, increased our profits—up until the time Marvin Alfred wrecked it in 1987, when landing at the Marble Bluff fish facility at Pyramid Lake, Nevada.

On May 27, 1989, my colleague Jerry Clark, and I began a trip from my gold mine in Idaho City, Idaho, to Amador City, California. By the time we got to Boise, the weather turned bad, so we spent the night there. The next day we continued our flight. Jerry, supposedly a good map reader, directed us over restricted territory in his rush to get us to our destination. I suddenly realized that we had missed a check point and were far south of our route. I landed at Tonopah to rest and chart a flight plan to Amador.

When we approached the Amador City airport closest to Jerry's home in Fiddletown, it was obvious that there was a cross wind, but I could not find the wind indicator. I did see a glider parked on the taxi-way and mistook it for the wind indicator. Mistakenly, I proceeded to land in the direction it was pointing.

The south half of the runway was level. The north half was on an incline, uphill to the south. It was recommended that when a crosswind was blowing, one should land upgrade and to the south. I landed to the north with full flaps, which slows the plane down.

I soon realized that I was too high, and tried to "hang the plane on the propeller," a way to gently lower the plane's altitude. But I ballooned instead, going up instead of down, so I used full throttle to make a go-around. That meant that I had to hold both hands on the yolk in order to keep the nose down, and it left me with no way to reach the flap lever. At the same time, the throttle backed out while I was still holding hard right rudder. The plane turned 90 degrees right and hit the runway. At the edge of the runway, a 4-foot deep ditch with a fence behind it threatened to be my resting place, but I didn't want to put the nose into the ditch; somehow I nudged the nose high enough to clear both the fence and the ditch. As I was taught in basic flight training, I kept the plane from stalling out.

And then I flew it into the only tree in sight.

Oops.

Bottoms up.

I was momentarily stunned. As Jerry was yelling, "Lloyd, Lloyd," I heard a banging from the back. It was my dog Grover's tail wagging and thumping up against the back seat. I could see the fuel pouring out of the right wing tank, and could see the fuel vapor rising from the engine compartment. Fortunately, the right half of the windshield had popped out. Jerry scrambled out, and after passing Grover out to him, I climbed out, too.

We had lucked out. No fire and no injuries. This all happened because of poor pilot-training, compounded by mechanical problems, and extremely poor judgment on the part of the pilot. Me. The odds of being so lucky are indeed long. The throttle should have been fixed a long time before.

▪ ▪ ▪

In late summer, while mobilizing our equipment to the mine site, we encountered our first incident of "gold fever."

The site we picked to mine was adjacent to a claim owned by a resident of Idaho City. While I was looking at our claim, I parked my car on his claim and left the door unlocked. I had been taking some medication and had left my prescription on the seat. When I returned to the car, the doors were locked. *Now what do I do?* I sat down and gazed at the sun, which was getting low. All of a sudden, a brand new Chevrolet four wheel drive pickup roared out of the brush and drove up to me. A big burly guy started hollering at me, wanting to know what the hell I was doing on his claim. We talked for a while and he calmed down. He finally said, "Okay, and by the way, here's your medicine."

Once things were smoothed over, he went to get into his truck, which was parked on a side hill. He could not get the door open as the truck was wracked. I helped him bounce on the bumpers until we finally got the door open. We were good friends after that.

Our second incident of "gold fever" occurred when the truck hauling the Hitachi EX200 LC rolled into Idaho City. A local yahoo followed it all the way out to Elk Creek. While unloading, the guy kept telling me about a hard rock mine he owned three miles farther up the road, which was rough and overgrown with brush. He told me it was rich and could be easily mined with the EX200. I agreed to take a quick look, as long as we used his Jeep to get there. We headed out.

Shortly after we left, Jerry Clark showed up at the excavator and asked the crew where I was. They replied, "He's gone up the road to look at a mine." Jerry jumped into my shiny orange and white pickup and headed up the road.

The Local and I were just leaving his mine when Jerry showed up. My pickup was all scratched up, but I saved my breath for breathing. It was done and we had more important things to do. This Local bugged us all the while we stayed in Idaho City, trying to get us interested in partnering with him. He had bought the mine with the proceeds of a security agency that he owned in Hawaii, which gave us reason to believe he was truthful! Later on after we had found gold, we paid him to help separate it. I left Jerry to watch but he didn't like the idea, so we both watched. I'll never know how much he stole. "Gold fever" again.

Jerry furnished his trommel, two pumps and his front-end loader. The trommel was okay, but the pumps and front-end loader, as I was to learn the hard way, were worn out. It took two semi flatbed loads to haul the trommel, front loader, pumps, etc., to the site, and one low-boy to haul my EX200. I bought a new sluice box, a new shaker table and a few other items—about $12,000 worth.

We started leveling off the area upon which to set the trommel. Jerry, who claimed he was a good backhoe operator, simply was unable to operate the EX200.

I had left Kenny behind in Vancouver to finish up another job, which I had hoped would only take a day or two. We screwed around all week trying to set up the equipment. Kenny finally arrived on Saturday with his pickup jammed full of parts and other items we needed. It only took him about 20 minutes to level off the spot for the trommel and another 20 minutes to finish unloading the trucks and set the trommel in place.

We then started building the retention pond, using the excavated material to construct the dike on the downslope side. Our goal was to make sure that the pond would pass all tests if we ever formally applied for a mining permit. We wanted to make absolutely sure no muddy water got into the creek. We set the two pumps next to the creek and installed about 600 feet of water line to them. We tested, and the system worked perfectly. The muddy water percolated out through the bottom of the pond, filtered through the gravel, and was clear long before it returned to the creek.

Once the trommel, sluice box and shaker table were set up, we started the pumps. All worked well for about ten minutes and it looked like we were on a roll. Suddenly the water stopped. We scampered down to the creek to find out why. The pumps were running but not pumping. They were simply worn out. I headed for Boise and rented two pumps. While I was gone, the rest of the crew, Ken, Don, Steve Stamper, and Jerry, did maintenance on the loader and other equipment. By late afternoon the new pumps were installed and we had water.

Loader on access road; hopper and trommel in background.

The plan was to use the loader to haul gravel to the trommel and load it with the EX200.

It was time to mine. We loaded the trommel and worked all day fine-tuning the operation, but found no trace of gold. Jerry ran the loader and was having trouble picking up the gravel. That's when we discovered the loader had barely enough power to get out of its *own* way. I could have rented a new loader for less than it cost me to haul Jerry's from Fiddletown to Idaho City. In order to make things work, we loosened the gravel deposits with the EX200. By loosening the gravel, Jerry was able to scoop it up with his loader, and stockpile it at the trommel.

We operated this way for several days, with no sign of gold.

Suddenly one day about noon, a fine line of gold began walking across the shaker table. The line got heavier and heavier and lasted about four hours and abruptly ended. We had accumulated five ounces of gold. This was the first and last time we saw color. It took us a few more days to realize that the old timers did not leave much behind. We packed up and went home.

If I had spent $5,000 in the beginning to retain a consultant, I might have saved a lot of time and money—but we never would have had the pleasure of watching the gold marching across the shaker table.

We were now experts. The $2,500's worth of gold only cost $100,000…forty thousand for the fun of learning and $60,000 for wrecking the Cessna 185.

To save argument and end the story, I gave all the gold to Jerry. It was time to travel on.

CHAPTER 33

1989
MORE WATER WORKS

Coleman National Fish Hatchery
Anderson, California
U.S. Fish and Wildlife
Contract amount: $70,000

This project consisted of a small pre-fabricated building that housed equipment for disbursing polymer into the settlement ponds, the ones we built in 1986. The polymer was stored in two 200-gallon plastic tanks, and was metered and disbursed as needed into the ponds. The purpose of the polymer was to attach itself to any dirt that was in the water, and sink it to the bottom of the pond.

It was the contractor's responsibility to supply the first 100 gallons of polymer, so we put 50 gallons in each tank.

The equipment supplier had not yet provided the polymer meters. These meters had to be installed before we could call for final inspection. Not knowing for sure when the meters would arrive, I went to help Doug on his historical building restoration (Heather Meadows) job near Mt. Baker, Washington, a distance of 800 miles from Anderson. The day after I arrived, I received a telephone call from the gung-ho assistant manager at Coleman, informing me that one of the polymer tanks was leaking.

I headed for Coleman. When I got there, I found that the hatchery had added 100 gallons of polymer to the tank that was leaking. I called Nalco to find out if the product was toxic, and how I should handle it. They suggested that I pump the polymer into a Baker Tank.

It took three days for the tank to be delivered, and by the time it arrived, I was becoming suspicious of one of the fittings we had installed. I had also determined that it was safe for a man to get into the tank. Instead of pumping the polymer into the Baker Tank, I pumped it into the other polymer tank. I crawled into the empty tank and turned the fitting around. We had simply installed it backwards. Same for the one in the other tank. I pumped the polymer from this tank into the one I had just fixed and corrected that fitting.

Just as I was finishing, Nalco's crew showed up and installed the meters, and started their four-day testing ritual. When they were done, I called for the final inspection, which usually takes about two weeks. At this time, the assistant manager informed me that he had more polymer on the way. I told him, "Whatever you do, do not put it into the tanks until after the final inspection." This made him very unhappy. He said, "We have the right to use the facility any time we want." I disagreed, and said, "Let's call Lola Gannon, the Contracting Officer in Portland, and verify what you just told me."

We called, and Lola said, "Lloyd's right. You don't have the right to use the facility until after inspection."

I had done several jobs for Lola, and she liked our work, but she also got great pleasure from conducting final inspections. After some more conversation, I explained to her that there really wasn't anything to see, and that is was really a small job. She agreed to let the assistant manager do the final that very same day. This was good for all parties. However, it would not be the last time I had to deal with this #$%^&* to get something done!

1991
Black Canyon Reservoir Park Facilities
Bureau of Reclamation
Emmett, Idaho
Original bid: $827,611
Final total: $1,010,000

The main features of this project were a concrete block maintenance building, three picnic shelters, keystone block retaining walls and a boat launch. The design team was two ladies from Iowa. They thought the whole world was flat and it was even flatter when they drew it out on a piece of paper. This was particularly noticeable when you looked at a picture of the keystone retaining wall. The plans showed the wall no more than three blocks high. Some of the walls turned out to be seven blocks tall. As the picture of the finished product shows, if the roads had been properly engineered, there would have been no need at all for a retaining wall.

Finished park.

Block retaining wall.

The maintenance building started out well, but we were plagued constantly by the inspector, Reid, who had no written authority. He was a thorn in our side until the Bureau ran him off for interfering with the contractor who was doing maintenance on the dam.

We soon discovered there were no qualified masonry contractors available in the Emmett—Boise area, so we imported the masonry contractor who had done the masonry work for us at Truckee, California. These guys were fast and did excellent work.

Maintenance building.

It was necessary to build the boat ramp and floating boat ramp docks in the winter when the reservoir was drained. The Bureau had set a benchmark for the reservoir's high water level. We used this benchmark and built the docks accordingly. When we connected the floats to the anchor block, most of the first section was above the water line. When the Bureau saw this, they tried to put the blame on the contractor. Good ole Fred Hyke, our longtime savior, had no problem in convincing them that they had made a one-foot elevation error.

Boat ramp and floating docks.

It was found that some of the material at the upper end of the boat ramp was unsuitable. When I explained this to the Bureau, they didn't want to pay for extra ballast. I argued with them, and they wrote me a work order to use the reject material that the maintenance crew had picked up along the highway. I argued some more. They insisted—and also insisted that I use this material to fix soft spots in other road areas! I knew better, and even had the material tested at my own expense. It was definitely unsuitable and also had lots of six-to-eight-inch round rock in it. As per the contract, I had no choice but to proceed.

Boy, I wished I hadn't. The final outcome is that I wound up digging out all of the bad material, and importing suitable ballast from the local quarry.

The plans called for 180 yards of excavation in the roadways and parking areas. They also called for 1,200 yards of embankment. (It might be noted that this was about the time of the advent of the Computer Assisted Design—CAD machines.) When we calculated the quantities, there were 1,200 yards of excavation and only 40 yards of embankment. The Bureau said we could put the excess excavation material into an embankment at a future construction site next to Black Canyon Dam, and that we had to compact it as per specs. They didn't want to pay for the loading or the trucking. We went ahead and finished the job, and Doug spent the next year trying to get us paid for the extra work. Finally, I called the contracting officer directly and explained the situation to him. He said he would "put a man on it immediately, and he and Doug can work this out." It took a month to negotiate the $182,389 we received for the extra work.

The contracting officer called me afterward, and told me that he gave the two COTR's on this project two choices: early retirement—or termination.

Once again, the government benefitted from our engineering and construction expertise. The job was challenging and fun, and we made a very good profit.

1991
Irrigon Fish Hatchery
Army Corp of Engineers, Walla Walla District
Irrigon Fish Hatchery, Morrow County, Oregon
Contract No: DACW68-91-C-0036
Contract Amount: $386,635

We bid this job in May of 1991. As we were second low bidder, we moved on to other work. This would be the first of six jobs that we did for the Corp of Engineers.

A couple of months later, as we were leaving the office for the Black Canyon Park project, we received a call from a vendor congratulating us on being awarded the Irrigon project. We chuckled a bit and told the guy we had not heard anything about it, but on August 8th, we received a certified letter giving us notice to proceed, and that we had been awarded the job on July 31st, .

We began the submittal process as per the Corp's rules, which we really didn't understand too well at the time. They required considerably more detail than the other government agencies we worked with. Getting proper details from our vendors was not easy. We got enough submittals completed that we were able to proceed. This work had to be done during a fish window, and at least three months had already been wasted.

This job was unexpected and I had to be in other places, so I designated Ken Piper as our Job Superintendent. Kenny struck up a good rapport with the onsite inspector, and he helped Kenny smooth out the submittal process. The onsite work went well.

The largest bid item on this project was for the installation of 1,540 lineal feet of 24-inch High Density Polyethylene pipe (HDPE). The installation went well. The only problem being there wasn't enough pipe to reach from one pump house to the other, which meant we had to order more pipe. Of course we wanted to be paid for it, but the Corp took the position that the plan clearly showed the pipe running between the two pump houses and that we should have checked that dimension.

Here's what happened:

On Friday, the crew finished welding the 1,540 feet of pipe. However, they did not bolt the loose end to the pump house. Don Winterholler wanted to put a couple of bolts in it. (It would only have taken five minutes.) Kenny yelled, "Come on, Old Don! Let's go home." Don had no choice; Kenny was driving the "hard-on express". When they came back Monday morning, the pipe had shrunk four feet. They spent the next three days straightening out the ditch so they could gain back the four feet of pipe.

Once the pipeline was completed, it was necessary to divert the water from the existing pipeline, carrying many thousands of fingerling fish valued at about $3 each. We built a slide gate with a long operating bolt in the pipeline for this purpose. The Federal Fishery Representative was there to make sure the operation was done properly. He told Kenny not to start the operation until he called the engineer to make sure we had submitted a diversion plan and a backup plan. Our plan was to remove the operating bolt and slide the gate shut.

Kenny called me before making the change-over to tell me his plan. I asked him if he was sure it would work, and he said yes. Was the core driller sure it would work? He said that Vern Balkowitsch, who was working for Concrete Coring at the time, said he was sure it would work. I told Kenny, "This business isn't for the faint-hearted. Go for it."

The FF Rep had to go to the fishery office to call the engineer in order to confirm that we had submitted the proper plan and back-up plan, saying he would be gone for five minutes. What he didn't know is that Kenny had disconnected the operating bolt from the gate. As soon as the Rep was out of sight, Vern finished coring the pipe, and Kenny pushed the gate closed with the excavator bucket. It didn't take more than a second. The Rep came back and said we could NOT start. Kenny told him it was already done and no fish were lost. The Rep never did figure out what happened.

While the main contract was going on, the Corp gave us a separate contract for $25,000 to finish the plumbing in a building the previous contractor had not completed. I really didn't want to do this contract but Kenny talked me into it because the nature of the main contract was such that there was a lot of stand-around time.

When it came time for the pre-final inspection of this extra contract, it turned out that my crew had violated our company policy of always double priming when installing plastic pipe (PVC). Our employee Bob Henry, had been a maintenance man at Memorial Coliseum in Portland, and thought he knew everything, did not double-prime the pipe before gluing it. When he turned the water on, every joint leaked. Bob told me he could fix it. I said, "Sure you can. Cut out every piece of pipe and start over." This exercise did not enhance our credibility with the Corp.

All in all, the main contract went very well and the field inspector was very happy with our work. But the bean-counters in Walla Walla weren't. A meeting was set up between the contractor and the Corp in Walla Walla to resolve our differences. When Kenny and I got to the meeting, the Corp's accounting crew said, "We are going to do this, in this order. We'll do the talking, you do the listening." They had big egos and were trying to prove to the contracting officer how important they were. I objected. They told us that this was just the way it was going to be.

I thought to myself, "Here we go again. Do I have to get our lawyer involved?" I whispered to Kenny, "Let's go." We got up and walked out the door. They came running after us yelling, "Wait! Let's talk about it." We went back in and got most of what we thought we were entitled to.

The important thing is that we learned their system and earned commendations on future jobs. We also made a good profit.

CHAPTER 34

1992-'93
HISTORIC SKI LODGE RESTORATION
Snoqualmie National Forest at Heather Meadows, near Mt. Baker
US Department of Agriculture—Forest Service
Mountlake Terrace, Washington
Original bid: $252,644
Final bid: $326,000

Entry sign reads "Welcome to Heather Meadow."

This was a negotiated contract based on price and contractor experience. The final determining factor in the selection of the contractor was the sample graphic design presented by my daughter, Karen Kessler.

Due to a late snow melt, we did not have access to the site until mid-July, 1992.

Doug and crew, Owen Kessler, Mike Waterfield, Don Winterholler, and Annabeth, started demolition work in the basement.

In renovation work, one problem often uncovers another problem. Over the course of the two-season job, there were eleven separate change orders. However, most of those change orders included numerous different items.

During the summer of 1992, the crew made all the interior repairs to the basement and the rest of the structure. They also replaced the roof and painted the outside of the building, formed the footings for the serpentine wall and other outside stone work, and did the rock excavation for the vault toilet.

Interior basement demolition.

As this was an historic building, all building materials had to be the same as the original, including the stone fireplace. Specifications required that all stones be numbered before they were taken down so they could be put back in the exact same places. It was also necessary to remove the fire brick in order to replace the metal fire box liner. Greg Paul, of Louis Guinett Masonry, followed the specifications to the "T."

During the course of the repairs, the government decided they wanted a smaller fire box, which meant it took more stone to fill the void. We informed the Forest Service that the smaller liner was causing the masonry work to be much more expensive. They understood and issued a change order for the extra cost. The mason re-installed the stones any way they would fit. This did not change the overall appearance of the fireplace, and no one ever noticed the difference.

Finished fireplace; finished floor and timbers restored to natural color.

Owen removing 1935-era brown paint from timbers.

The contract required some existing outside stonework to be replaced. And there were extensive retaining walls and pedestrian walls to be constructed. The quarry for this stone was a short distance away. When the mason went there, he discovered a natural serpentine formation of stones all about the same size. Greg suggested installing the stone into a serpentine design. The government concurred. The results were striking.

Existing handicap walkway and walls.
New serpentine wall in center of photo is now part of the historical restoration.

Ole Don and Grinnin' Ken backfilling the inside of the serpentine wall.

One bid item required removing and replacing the shakes on the roof. Once the shakes were torn off the roof, considerable water damage was discovered and substantial repairs were required. Doug had to negotiate a change order as the work proceeded, and hired extra help to get the roof on before the end of the first season.

Tearing off shakes.

Owen finishing tear-off.

Ryan (the mountain climber), installing new shakes on steep 1.5:1 roof—no need to bend over.

The crew worked very well together. Annabeth lived in Glacier, and turned out to be our most productive worker. Mike Waterfield was fascinated by her, but Annabeth told him she wasn't a charity. And besides that, her logger husband was just as big as Kenny (6'6″ and 200+ lbs.)—and almost as mean!

Annabeth—And if you called her "Annabelle," she'd break your nose.

Mike, Don and Owen framing vault toilet.

The crew excavated and installed the rebar for the various retaining walls. This left the rebar sticking up through the snow during the ski season. We did put red safety caps on the rebar, but many got lost or stolen.

Red safety caps on rebar for stone retaining walls.

We lost a little sleep about this during the ski season, but as far as we know, no skier was injured, nor did they lose any family jewels.

One of the contract requirements was for building a vault toilet. This required excavation in solid rock. No blasting was allowed. We drilled holes and used a concrete splitter, but were not able to break out the last two feet. Doug hired a local "old wino" to do the drilling and splitting. He was happy to work in the hole breaking rock all day. We fired him after his first paycheck because he was drunk every morning when he came to work.

As luck would have it, Kenny was on his way back from an errand in Glacier when he saw a truck-mounted rock breaker working on a guard rail installation. Kenny contracted with the owner to break out the remaining two feet of rock. It took him about an hour, and he was happy to make a quick $500. It's always good to have a little cash on hand for greasing the gears.

What are the odds of that breaker being there the day we needed it?

Brutus, our main operator, patiently waiting for the crew to get out of the way so he can finish excavating the retaining wall trench.

Kenny and Owen forming vault toilet.

Owen and "Ole Don" Winterholler forming the vault toilet.

The second season, we needed a crane with a long reach to place the flag pole. The nearest crane was in Seattle. Kenny and his girlfriend Lois rode his Harley to Seattle to pick it up. They loaded the Harley on the deck of the crane and drove the rig to Heather Meadows and set the flagpole.

Truck crane setting the flag pole.

We also used the crane for a couple of other lifts. When the crane work was finished, Kenny drove the crane to the motel parking lot in Glacier.

That night, after a few beers, Junior decided to practice repelling.

Kenny put the boom straight up (about 100 feet). He lifted Junior clear up until the headache ball touched the sheave. Junior repelled down on the rope that he had bought from someone in the bar. This was repeated for the entertainment of the motel guests long enough for Junior and Kenny to consume a case of beer. The next morning Ryan, who had planned on teaching Junior how to repel, got mad at him when he found out he had been using a cheap rope. Doug didn't learn about this event until years later. Good thing. I don't know where he would have gotten help to finish the job if we had canned them.

This was a fun job. The craftsmanship was exceptional, as was the rapport between Doug and the Forest Service.

Attending the dedication of the new facility:

Top to bottom: Nick, Doug and Owen Kessler.

Owen and Doug.

Beverly and Doug Kessler at dedication.

Letter of commendation:

September 23, 1993

To: Lloyd H. Kessler, Inc.

We are quire enthused about the works your firm has done on this project. The result is both striking and beautiful, making for us a visitor center with few equals.

William. C. Whitson
Contracting Officer

View of the valley from the Center.

Chapter 35

1991-1993
A ROUGH COUPLE OF YEARS

Outlet Malls
Woodland, Washington and Boulder City, Nevada

The Outlet Mall Fiasco began in 1991, my friend Harold Coffman was working in Woodland, Washington, when he met Bob Bjerke there. Coffman had been talking with Mrs. Boys, owner of Boys Woodland Freightline. (I had known her late husband Lenny since he moved my household goods from Vancouver to Chelan, Washington, in 1963. He also had done many trucking jobs for me.) Bjerke had been a long-time employee of Woolworth's department stores, and had recently sold an outlet mall that he had built in Hilo, Hawaii.

He was proposing to build an outlet mall on the east side of Interstate 5 on property owned by Boys. In order to finance the operation, Bjerke was seeking investors, so he set up a corporation called REB Real Estate. The buy-in was $150,000 per investor. Coffman and I each invested $75,000 with the understanding that we would have first opportunity at any earth work or site development. REB needed our expertise in acquiring ingress, egress and easements from the existing infrastructure. Coffman was also elected a member of the board. The plan was to build three outlet malls: Columbia Crossing in Woodland, Washington; Blaine Crossing, in Blaine, Washington and Boulder Station in Boulder City, Nevada.

One of Bjerke's tenants and good friend in Hilo was Garry Fredericksen, who was the owner of the Levi outlet at that mall. His wife Louise was owner of a Merle Norman cosmetics salon in the same mall. When the mall sold, Fredericksens invested in REB. They moved to La Jolla, California, and spent $1 million building a beautiful 7,000 square foot home on an $800,000 lot. Louise acted as her own contractor. They planned on living in the house, and Louise exclaimed that they expected to "make a whole bunch of money from the profits of REB's outlet malls." Bjerke bought a home in Carlsbad, about thirty miles north of La Jolla. Bjerke lived in high style, as did Fredericksen, who joined the expensive La Jolla Country Club.

REB was able to raise over three million dollars from twenty-one investors. Bjerke was President of REB, and Fredericksen was Vice-President. Bjerke's main duties were obtaining financing and purchasing property. Fredericksen's main responsibility was recruiting potential tenants such as Levi and other name brands. He signed up tenants for almost every space.

Bjerke (REB) leased office space in Carlsbad, California, and staffed it like he was still working for Woolworth. He paid himself and Fredericksen large monthly salaries. He had an office manager, a couple of secretaries, and Bob Baxter, an engineer from Boston, also drawing salaries. There were considerable start-up expenses, including wining and dining potential investors. There were also extensive travel expenses, especially for the Blaine project, due to REB's repeated efforts to obtain the City's approval. The amount spent on salaries of unnecessary personnel was more than any start-up could afford. As a result, they burned through most of the money in the first year.

Though Coffman and I were equal financial partners, I let him take the lead (he had talked me into this to begin with). He was good at land development, knew how to deal with local authorities, and was a first-class promoter. We were both determined to make the project work.

One of the investors was Alan Stromberg Engineering, a firm from Boulder City. He had drawn the building plans for the malls in both Blaine and Boulder City, had done a very good job, and hoped to be rewarded for his efforts.

LHK and crew, along with Coffman, spent many unpaid days working with Bob Baxter developing plans for both on- and off-site work. This work was done in my Vancouver office. Baxter was more hindrance than help, and was a real pain in the ass!

Purchasing the Blaine property became complicated as the owner was long in years, and was represented by a crooked lawyer. However, Bjerke did obtain a tentative sales agreement. The summer working weather was disappearing fast. REB's board decided to pay Kessler and

Coffman $50,000 to prepare the site in advance of the winter's rains so that the mall could be built the following spring. We completed the work, along with environmental protections to prevent winter rains from causing damage. This made Bjerke and the shareholders very happy. All were convinced the building work would start after the spring rains.

The Woodland mall (Columbia Crossing) project got bogged down due to politics and zoning issues and was abandoned early on.

Meanwhile during the winter, Fredericksen managed to obtain tentative agreements from Levi and other name brand tenants for most of the outlets at Blaine. Bjerke continued arguing with the Blaine city council to get building permits. The council acted like they were in favor of the project but one of the owners of the nearby airport did not want it, and claimed it would interfere with their operation. This killed the mall project. Bjerke then advocated building housing on the site. This idea failed for basically the same reason and it was questionable if there would have been enough buyers. The project died.

Near the end of the first year, Bjerke called a meeting of the investors at the Carlsbad office and asked for more funds. Most refused, but enough was raised to keep things going for a short time. Bjerke whined and cried, but he and Fredericksen agreed not to draw any more salary. The only employee they kept was a part-time secretary. Boulder Station was the only option left. Work could be done there anytime. The zoning was in place, the property was available and could be leased from Boulder City.

The major problem was construction financing. Bjerke had previously met with Washington Mutual. They had indicated they would provide financing once the properties were secured. However, the savings and loan debacle was in full force, so no loans were available.

Desperate, Bjerke paid $100,000 to a mortgage broker, who guaranteed to provide financing. Bjerke immediately scheduled a groundbreaking ceremony. A couple dozen people showed up for the groundbreaking, including a local reporter and the broker. The broker was dressed in a black hat and long black overcoat, gangster-style. I asked the broker a question. He looked at me like "How stupid can you be?" I then realized that Bjerke had been scammed, but he still believed he would have financing in 30 days. We never saw or heard from the broker again.

Coffman and I had spent weeks planning ingress and egress to this site which was adjacent to State Highway 93. Alan Stromberg Engineering worked with the city and state so that everything was tentatively approved. We were ready to build, but there was no money. Coffman and Kessler decided to sue REB for the losses that we had incurred. In June 1998, we won a judgment for $502,002.94 in the U.S. District Court in San Diego.

Prior to the trial date, the court attempted to talk both parties into mediation. The court explained to Coffman and Kessler that if we won a judgment, Bjerke and Fredericksen would file bankruptcy. Bjerke refused to compromise and Coffman was adamant in pursuing the claim. He believed Bjerke and Fredericksen still had the money from the sale of the mall in Hilo.

After we won the judgment, I wanted to hire a top-notch bankruptcy attorney to pursue Bjerke and Fredericksen. I have always believed in hiring "the best", but Coffman did not want to spend the money to bring another attorney up to speed. This is what I call, "cheap Charley-ing." In the long-term, we spent a ton of money on a lost cause.

It took Stacy Brandt, our attorney, two years to schedule the bankruptcy hearing for Fredericksen in Indianapolis. It took another year to schedule Bjerke's hearing in Las Vegas. This gave both parties far too much time to hide their assets. If we'd retained a good bankruptcy attorney, this whole process would have taken about six months.

During Fredericksen's testimony, Stacy asked him, "How much cash do you have with you right now?" Fredericksen answered that he had $58. Stacy said, "Okay, you can leave that on the table." She asked, "Are you wearing a watch?" He said yes. She said, "Okay, you can leave that on the table too." We didn't take the watch or money but Stacy managed to extract a total of $6,000 from the Fredericksens.

A year later, on December 20, 2001, I hired a cab to take me to the Federal building in Las Vegas for Bjerke's hearing. After getting dropped off at the wrong building, I managed to arrive at the courthouse twenty minutes late, carrying my duffle bag. Stacy's plane was late and she arrived after I did. The old judge, who looked like an undertaker and was listening to all the tales of woe, looked my way and asked me why I was there. I told him I was there for the Bjerke hearing, which was already over with, and that my attorney would be here soon. He said, in a hollow tone with a faint twinkle in his eye, "You are not going to need that bag."

Installation of underground PVC sewer lines and pump stations—Neskowin Oregon Regional Sanitation Authority

This job was a disaster even before it was awarded. It was delayed four months from bid to start date, plus it was held up another two weeks because of lack of permit. It suffered from several things:

- Confusing leadership
- Changes not communicated in timely manner
- Defective design
- Mis-identified existing conditions
- Denial of timely review and response

Bids for this project were opened September 7, 1993, the intent being that the work begin in September, the driest part of the year when the water table was the lowest. Due to a myriad of facts, including not having the proper permit from Tillamook County, funding problems, and many other administrative snafus, the Notice to Proceed was not issued until January 17, 1994, well into the wet season when the water table was ten feet higher.

The bid documents indicated that BST's Dave Thomas and Paul Trahan, in partnership with Kevin Long, were the project managers. Thomas signed documents as Project Engineer and Trahan signed as Project Manager. You could not believe much they said. Thomas and Trahan were nicknamed "the BS (bullshit) twins." Kevin Long was silent.

Of the three, Dave Thomas was a graduate engineer with somewhat limited abilities. Trahan had no engineering experience, but he did know that "crap flows downhill." Being a lobbyist for the Oregon Midwives Association was Kevin Long's claim to fame. How was this team conceived?

HGE of Coos Bay designed the project from aerial photography and made little or no attempt to determine the location of existing facilities. For example, we discovered when excavating for a pump station, existing and conflicting utilities. This required BST and NRSA to have

HGE do a re-design, and forced LHK and Skyline, the Prime Contractor, into numerous start-stop situations.

Another example was the Salem Avenue bridge crossing. Tillamook County mandated that NRSA comply with Tillamook County's utility permit, which was not a part of the contract. Once the design was done and the pipeline across the bridge was installed, it could not continue as planned because NRSA did not have the proper easement. This meant a new line had to be designed on the opposite side of the road. Even though we had bought and paid for all of the bridge material, BST refused to pay us because we had not done other work that could not be tested until after the re-design work was completed.

Due to the lack of funds, the engineer refused to acknowledge required redesigns as cost change orders. Dave Thomas told Pat Balbi of Skyline Construction, that "he would do anything to break Lloyd Kessler," and "did not care if Lloyd Kessler went broke." Dave didn't like the fact that Pat and I, along with everyone else, knew more about construction than he did and we were not bashful about telling him so – particularly Pat.

A person can get a sense of his classic administration attitude by reading this letter he wrote:

Dear Pat:

Thanks for the copy of Nick Castorina's letter. It's amusing to hear him accuse BST of not requesting the referenced information at an earlier date, when in fact Nick represents himself as Lloyd Kessler's claims "expert". When Nick first put forth his diatribe about "measured mile" several months ago I told him that we needed factual information, not inductive and subjective nonsense. I'm surprised that he didn't think of it first, particularly when it would be obvious to Helen Keller that the only claims we gave credence were those for which factual (as opposed to imaginary and inductive) backup information was provided.

Sincerely,
David M. Thomas, PE

In the long run, LHK Inc. was still in business after the claims on this job were paid. BST went the way of the Gooney Bird, and was never heard from again.

CHAPTER 36

1993
JEWETT LAKE
Port of Portland, Oregon
Original Contract Amount: $164,015
Final Contract Amount: $201,263

Template and sheet pile.

Jewett Lake is a seasonal wetland on Government Island in the Columbia River. The project was installation of a sheet pile dam near the end of the outlet channel from Jewett Lake at the high point of the Columbia River's south bank. The dam incorporated one-way flood gates to retain water in the lake after the spring runoff or other high-waters. The only access to Government Island is by water.

The only structure on the island was a house leased by Pete Girodano, the same Girodano that did the excavation for us at the Coleman National Fish Hatchery. His caretaker/foreman lived in the house and took care of Pete's herd of beef cattle. Pete had two elevating scrapers on the island. He wanted to rent these scrapers to us to haul sand. He and his foreman would operate them. As it turned out, as almost everyone knows in earthmoving, you cannot move sand with elevating scrapers.

For this project, we rented a three-yard front end loader equipped with oversized tires to haul the sand.

Fred Hyke and I laid out the dam, the excavation and the templates for driving the piling. Once the templates were set, we started driving the piling.

Junior (Waterfield) placing the piling.

Our consultant was "Pile Buck Pete" Kelly, who had worked for Riedel, Hoffman and Peter Kiewit construction companies. Pete had the reputation of being the best pile driving boss ever. I hired him to make sure everything went right. It did and we completed the pile driving in less than half the time I had estimated.

Collin guiding the vibratory hammer.

Once the sheets were driven, some of them had to be cut off to grade. This is always a slow and painful process as the piling are loaded with oil and grease. I asked Pete how long he thought it would take to cut them off. He said, "Two and a half days." I told him I had a special tool for that, "It's called a Petrogen touch." He laughed. I said, "I'll show you." Collin lit the torch and cut the piling off in less than four hours. Pete shook his head. "I learned something today," he said. I laughed, "It's the first time in a long while you learned something new." The torch paid for itself in one day.

The dam and pilings.

Mostly at my suggestion, four change orders were initiated. Change order number one was for additional earthwork. Change orders two, three and four were minor modifications to the original design, necessary to make everything work properly.

The only time the inspector was on site was the day we finished,

The job turned out especially well. We did have to come back a year later and adjust one of the gates in the dam that was not closing properly. It took more time to get to the jobsite than it did to make the correction.

This job was fun and profitable.

CHAPTER 37

1995
ABOVE AND BELOW

Parkdale Coe-Eliot Bridge Replacement
US Forest Service
Hood River Ranger District
Near Randle, Washington
Contract Amount: $241,591

Original Eliot log stringer bridge.

The purpose of this project was to replace two aging log-stringer bridges. This job was scheduled to be done during the 60 days between Labor Day and October 31st. It required pre-fabricated temporary bridges to be installed at each bridge site. The temporary bridge for the Eliot site was 80 feet long and was presently installed on an abandoned Forest Service road near Randle, Washington.

The road to the bridge in Randle was closed and required some construction to access the site for bridge removal. The specifications indicated that this bridge had been hauled in by one truck when it was first installed. Once we did the clearing and construction, it was obvious this was not possible. After some research, we learned the bridge had been dragged the last mile with a D-8 Cat. The bridge was composed of two eighty-foot sections, dragged in one at a time. I decided to drag it out the same way, and hired a contractor from Randle to do the task.

The first section was no problem. While going back for the second section, the D-8 hit a bump and the fan tore a hole in the radiator. It took the contractor over a week to make repairs. When completed, he dragged both sections out the three miles to a place where we could load them on to trucks for transport to the Coe-Eliot site.

While this operation was going on, we were busy preparing the sites for the temporary bridge. The whole operation took about two weeks.

We moved the prefabricated bridges to the site and set them in place with a Campbell Crane. Once set, we built the temporary roads to them and started excavating the downgrade footing for the Eliot Bridge. This took a couple of days of hard digging. Once the footing excavation was complete, we formed the footings.

The plans called for the rebar to protrude from the footings clear to the top of the pier, but we cut the rebar off five feet above the top of the footing. The Forest Service didn't like this and made us dowel in some extra rebar. I didn't mind, as it was much easier than putting it in as spec'd—and allowed us to pour the entire column in one pour rather than two.

We made the pour on Friday and went home for the weekend. When we returned on Monday, the entire excavation was flooded.

The Flood.

We moved to the other side of the creek and started building the access road to the other footing. The water subsided and we were able to excavate for it. We used the same procedure on the rebar as we did before. We finished pouring the pier and started placing riprap to the top of the footing excavation. During the night, the water rose again, clear to the top of the riprap we had just placed. If the riprap had not been in, the entire bank would have washed away.

De-watering.

We got lucky. What are the odds? The operator at the dam told us these were the two highest stream levels they had ever recorded.

Still de-watering.

While the concrete was curing, we started working on the Coe site, removing the wood portion and prepping the existing concrete piers for the new stringers. This required some drilling and doweling.

Removing 80 foot prefabricated section at Eliot site

Junior was doing this work. For some reason, he short-holed for the dowels on one of the footings. We set the planks on them anyway.

The Forest Service had directed us to place the logs we removed from each of the bridge sites into Coe Creek, several hundred feet upstream from the bridge. (A few years later, heavy runoff from a snow-slide caused a wall of water to come down the creek, which washed the logs out and caused a logjam. When the logjam broke, a huge wall of water washed down the creek and swept the bridge into the river—never to be seen again. We blamed Junior because he short-holed the dowels.)

After the concrete cured, we installed the stringers.

Installing the stringers and removing the temporary bridge at the Eliot site.

It was now time to pour the curbs, but winter had set in, making the roads icy. There was a steep area near the east end of Clear Creek Road that the concrete truck could not climb. I had Junior walk the EX200 the three miles out to Clear Creek Road to help the trucks up the steep section.

A few days later, Junior was walking the EX200 back to the bridge site when he slid off the road and went over the bank. The road was paved with asphalt concrete and had a steep out-slope. He swung the boom to the left in an attempt to stop. He slid over the bank with the boom pointing towards the road. Luckily two large trees stopped him from going to the bottom of a canyon.

As luck would have it, a machine operator working for a local logger happened by. He was an excellent operator and was used to getting out of tough situations. He called back to Parkdale and had them send a loader, which he used for an anchor. He hooked the chain to the loader and hooked the other end to the bucket of the excavator, and had it out in less than a minute. Junior walked the machine the rest of the way. However there were obvious tracks where the machine went over the bank. We disguised them somewhat. The next day, the COR noticed the tracks and wanted to know what happened. None of us knew.

The plans called for grouting between the stringers prior to paving. I knew we wouldn't be able to pave until the next season, but I didn't want to leave the joints open between the stringers and have to clean the dirt and rock out of them the next spring, so I bought some five-minute grout and we started grouting the seams. It was a bright, calm, sunny day and the grout set up very fast. The COR came along and said, "Hey it's 20 degrees. You can't place that stuff when it's below freezing."

We were over half done, but he made us stop; we went home for the winter.

When we came back in the spring to pave, the grout was set up perfectly. Few contractors will believe what happened. The grout froze instantly when we placed it and set up when the weather warmed up in the spring. What are the odds?

Before and after—the original and newly constructed bridge.

1995
Trout Creek Fish Ladder—Wind River Ranger District
US Forest Service
Gifford Pinchot National Forest, Washington
Contract Amount: $63,300

This job was for construction of the fish ladder at Hemlock Dam. On Saturday, August 5, 1995, our three-ton truck arrived on site with form lumber, rebar and pipe. We had to hand-tote the material across the creek from the pump station on the north side.

On Monday, Aug. 7, we began the form work and the rock excavation. My original job plan called for using a large electric pump to de-water the work area. After studying the contour map of the creek bottom, I realized there was a deep hole well outside the work area. *It flashed into my mind that siphons were used on the Grand Coulee Project to move water into Banks Lake*, so I decided to use two ten-inch PVC pipe siphons to de-water the work area, thereby eliminating the need for an electric pump. I named the siphons "Grand Coulee 1" and "Grand Coulee 2". This system saved a lot of time and money.

I decided to build a flume to divert the water from the top end of the existing fish ladder and dump the water into a rocky formation where it disappeared. The siphons completely de-watered the work area.

Bypass flume.

Siphoning water from pond.

Once the water was diverted, we began forming the first section of wall at the lower end of the fish ladder. We also started the rock excavation.

We went home Saturday afternoon. Monday morning we were just completing the first section of forms when the designer, Helen, showed up. She had the Forest Service fish expert, Ken, with her. He said, "The fish windows will not work in the location shown. We need to re-design."

My thoughts were, "We cannot afford to be delayed." I asked him where the windows needed to be. He explained where the openings needed to be and why. He did make sense.

Helen said, "I'll start the re-design."

I suggested that we rotate the structure about two feet into the rock to make everything work. It will require some additional rock excavation, for which we get paid by unit price. We also need to be paid for the entire 16 yards of concrete, as shown on the schedule of items. Everyone agreed, and we continued with the work.

Forming concrete.

Blasting was not allowed on this project. As on many previous jobs, we were drilling holes and using a concrete splitter to break the rock. As we got closer to grade, this method was not working.

3-man work team drilling rock: Mike (Junior) Waterfield, Collin Surbert and Owen Kessler.

18-man inspection team watching 3-man construction crew.

I decided to use a water ram to break the rock. A water ram works by drilling a hole in the rock, filling it with water, and inserting a 12-gauge shotgun shell. A long cord is attached to the water ram. When jerked, it triggers the shell, which explodes, exerting a great force, which shatters the rock, sometimes throwing chunks of rock a hundred feet or more.

By law, this method is not called "blasting". However, we did not use this system if any Forest Service personnel were present. It worked very well, even though we blew a couple of rocks across the river, which struck the hand rails at the pump station. We quickly disguised the marks.

I had rented the water ram from Cessco in Portland. A few years later, I tried to rent another one, and the proprietor said, "We sold our rams. We did not want the liability."

We poured the 16 yards of concrete on August 25th, stripped the forms, and installed the 24-inch HDPE water line. This line was designed to bring water from behind the dam and into the lower end of the fish ladder to attract fish.

We completed the project on August 31st, and a month later received a hand-written letter from the COR Neil Oliver, who wrote, "Thank you for your good work on this project."

Neil was a good COR, unusual in that he was wise enough to stand back and let the contractor get the work done using his *own* methods.

Finished project.

Tough job. Good profit.

CHAPTER 38

1997
THREE BUREAU OF LAND MANAGEMENT PROJECTS:

- **Cascade Streamwatch**
  Clackamas County Oregon 1997
  Contract Amount: $710,882

- **Vincent Creek, Smith River Falls & Park Creek**
  Recreational Areas,
  Coos Bay District, Oregon 1999
  Contract Amount: $203,443

- **Lone Pine Recreation Area, Roseburg District, Oregon 2003**
  Contract Amount: $254,420

In the late 1990's, we were doing the majority of our work for different government agencies. Each agency had its own 'personality' and the level of supervision from each one varied greatly. The most feared by contractors was the US Army Corp of Engineers. They were the toughest to work for, but the upside was that they had a good understanding of what they were building. Once a contractor and the Corp were on the same page, the job went well and got done right the first time. If there were conflicts, they were resolved expeditiously.

Cascade Streamwatch

We were contracted by the Bureau of Land Management to build an underwater fish-viewing structure—and an informational kiosk with related trail information—in Wemme, Oregon, near Mt. Hood. This was the first of three jobs we did for the BLM. Their supervision and engineering only got worse on the next two jobs.

Fish viewing facility under construction.

Informational kiosk.

Pedestrian walkway to the Streamwatch window.

For Streamwatch, excerpts from our letters written to the BLM describe vividly the wild swing in everything from our working time frame, to inconsistent surveys for trails and design modifications for buildings:

- We were not allowed to regulate Cork Creek, which caused us to lose one supervisory day chasing keys to unlock the head gate.
- We waited six weeks for clarification on strange and unworkable trail and walkway alignments on the upper trail. We lost many supervisory days in making design changes and corrections of deficiencies.
- Width of entry structure, alignment "D," did not match profile chamber entry, so we widened it, losing another day to design considerations.
- Some villain of unknown identity locked the headworks open on Cork Creek, causing us to lose half days in both working and supervisory days.
- As originally submitted, the diversion would have used a 12″ culvert, a size that would easily have maintained the 3-5 cubic feet required by the contract, and which was verbally approved by the COR. Then someone remembered something: there were fish in the stream. And last year someone put a 12″ corrugated pipe in a diversion somewhere,

and the fish wouldn't swim through it. So the contract requirements were changed because simply conforming to the contract requirements just wouldn't do. We were instructed to take out the 12″ diversion and put in a bigger one that could double as a fish bypass.

- And then someone remembered something else: Even if the fish swim through our pipe, they can't get through the head gate if the contractor is regulating Cork Creek as per the contract. The solution this time is to take away the contractor's right to regulate cork creek at the head gate as provided in Section 02140.02.
- In fact, one fine dry day someone from the BLM office got it into his head to open the head gate and lock it into a compromising position. Too bad. This time, instead of remembering something someone forgot—It rains here. The river goes up and down, and the channel with it. When it did rain, this BLM employee had carelessly endangered the safety of my crew, the property, and me. And it came within a hair's' breadth of violating those very aspects of the permit which are to my mind the most important—by filling the channel with silt, construction debris, and toxic substances. We are only on site 8 hours per day. It's at best only one in three chances that this calamity was diverted.
- You and others have made a great big deal out of the fact that one of your staff feels intimidated in some vague and indescribable way to Lloyd's personal manner. "Threatened" is the way you've put it. This is nothing compared to this: Your employee, a person with a demonstrated bent for criminal negligence, has no place on my project. I want him gone.

The survey on this project was crude at best. There were many areas where it was necessary to make adjustments. Once we had convinced our COR, Bruce Runge, that the changes were needed, he'd wave his arms like a magic wand and get them approved.

During the course of construction a few things went our way. When we formed the pathway walls to the viewing chamber, we used Waferboard. We'd used this material on many other jobs because it gives a pleasing, distressed-finish to the walls. It costs less, doesn't blow like plywood and it's easy to dispose of.

My company policy is to pour concrete and to strip the forms the next day. In this case, the crew did not follow the rules and left the forms on for many days. When the forms were stripped, portions of the Waferboard were embedded in the face of the walls. I wasn't happy, thinking, "How in the hell are we going to fix this?" I lost a couple of nights sleep over it. The architect showed up and I didn't have any solutions. Before any conversation started, he looked at the walls and said, "They are beautiful. The embedded wood looks just like stream debris. I love it." What are the odds?

The specifications called for us to remove large boulders of a certain girth from the river. The only problem was that there were no boulders of that size. They were all at least four times larger. Luckily, our EX200 Hitachi was still on site and was able to move the boulders to the kiosk area, where they were intended to define a stream effect at the walking path trailhead. Some of these over-size boulders weighed 10,000 pounds, but they greatly enhanced the kiosk area visually.

The walking trails were designated to be surfaced with a product called Road Oyl®, manufactured from pine sap. The idea was to get rid of the black surfacing typical of asphalt. This material was designed to be placed on natural ground or dirt. The natural ground was interlocked with tree roots, which if cut would damage the trees. It was specified that four inches of crushed rock be placed over the roots. I sensed this product was not going to work well on certain sections. I tried to talk the BLM into using asphalt to no avail. We went ahead and imported the resin from the Midwest and transferred the material into the water trucks and surfaced the trails.

Completed fish viewer.

All looked well for a few weeks until certain sections of the trail started to deteriorate. After about three months, the BLM paved all of the trails with asphalt.

Vincent Creek

We were awarded the Reconstruction of Vincent Creek, Smith River Falls and Park Creek Recreation Sites near Coos Bay, Coquille and Fairview, Oregon in August of 1999. This was the second in a series of three jobs we did for the BLM. The plans on this project were well drawn. The only problem was that each campground had a different set of details. The crew would get used to doing the work one way, only to have to do it a different way on the next campground. We had to be very careful not to make any mistakes.

We got a late start on this one. Our operator, Junior (Mike Waterfield), left for greener pastures after two weeks. We suddenly realized that Collin Surbert, who happens to be my grandson, was a natural operator. We started work, only to be shut down for two weeks due to fire closure. This forced us into a winter shutdown. During the winter and late end of the summer we worked on other projects. Communications on this project between the contractor and the contracting officer were very poor, and delayed final inspection and payment. Overall, however, the project turned out very well.

▪ ▪ ▪

Lone Pine

The third BLM job was in the Lone Pine Recreation area just outside, Idleyld, Oregon, an RV campground.

The start-work date on this project was delayed by an overdue survey. The government's excuse was that it was too wet and rainy. However, once the survey was completed we were given notice to proceed the following Monday.

It was Thursday by then. Doug told me he had not ordered the 24-inch pipe for the drinking fountain sumps. I looked at the plans and decided it was concrete pipe, similar to what we'd used in other campgrounds.

I ordered the pipe and had it delivered to our shop the next day, which was Friday. I then had Accurate Concrete drill two inch holes in the six pieces of two foot-long pipe. As it was the weekend, they gratefully did the work for $2400. Sunday night we loaded all our building materials onto a flatbed, and Monday morning at 6:00 a.m. we left Vancouver for the jobsite. We arrived just after lunch, and pulled the truck up next to the pump house site, which was just a few feet off the paved road.

The first thing that happened was that Tom, the inspector who was undocumented to us, started telling us what to do. "You can't unload there. That's not the designated staging area." We went ahead and unloaded. It was the only place we could. "That concrete pipe doesn't meet spec. Don't unload it." We unloaded it... and finished the layout from the centerline road survey, to the pre-fabricated restroom and pumphouse sites. The restroom itself was manufactured in Spokane.

The next morning, the COR, Randy, showed up. He said, "Oh, we want to move the pump house twenty feet farther south; that way it will be closer to the road and easier to maintain."

I should have known better than to agree. Experience should have taught me that every time you change something on the plan, it affects everything else on the plan and always costs the contractor more money.

But, we went ahead and graded for the footings and installed the pipelines; we poured the footings and built the pump house. This took two or three days. Everything seemed to be going well.

Tom, the inspector, told the crew that we had to chlorinate the water lines and test them. A pressure test had to be on for 48 hours with no drop. We installed the pressure test late Friday and went home for the weekend. When we returned, there was a leak in the test line, so we fixed the leak and re-started the test. We also closed the valve between the pipeline and the test pump. After a couple of hours, another leak showed up in the test pump.

Collin and I were standing in the ditch next to the pump. Mike was up on top of the bank standing next to Tom, who said, "You guys will have to start that test over again."

Collin replied, "The pump's not affecting the test."

Tommy replied that we were stupid, and with that, Collin started to lunge up out of the ditch towards Tom. I grabbed Collin, and Tom ran to his truck. As I was to learn later, he called the BLM police.

That evening Doug and I each got a call from the contracting officer, Shapiro, to stop work until we had a meeting the following Wednesday. He also said that Collin need not attend. He indicated that the BLM was going to file assault charges against Collin. I called my attorney, Jan Sokol, who agreed to attend the meeting.

When we arrived for the meeting, Shapiro, several assistants and three BLM law enforcement officers were there. Shapiro gave a speech on how the government had the right in instances of criminal activity to remove the contractor or any of their personnel from the project.

The law enforcement people started asking us questions about what happened. Jan Sokol immediately intervened and said, "No, no."

Collin was our key man and campground expert. He and Mike were also a team. They worked together all day long, seldom talking, each one knowing what the other was thinking. Not having Collin was a great hardship on us. There were no other machine operators available. Mike hated Tom, considering him a coward and a liar. Tom was Tom, and that's all there is to it, but Mike would not work if Tom were present. The result was a long, miserable summer.

The surveys on this project were entirely screwed up. The invert for the culvert pipe at the entrance was two feet higher than the existing pavement. That's when we should have packed up and left.

When the final inspection was complete, the forest engineer said to me, "The workmanship is excellent, but why are these roads so high above the natural ground level?"

I said, "That's what your engineers insisted on."

He said, "That's not the way we like to build a campground."

I said, "I know that." I told him that this was the only job we'd ever done that didn't come out better than was expected. I've always regretted not having challenged Shapiro's removal of Collin from the project. This is still the USA, and a man's still innocent until he's proven guilty.

To this day, Doug insists that Shapiro was just trying to "get revenge" for the letter that Doug had sent to him on the Streamwatch project. Shapiro said that Collin was to be removed from the job permanently – perhaps because of 9-11, as the government was being very particular about personnel security.

The only satisfaction we enjoyed from this job is that I got enough concrete pipe for Millie's raised tomato garden.

Millie's raised tomato garden, made of concrete pipe; still raising tomatoes every year.

CHAPTER 39

1997
THOSE DAM DIKES

Kirkendoll-Holder Project
Revetment Repair on Cowlitz River
Corps of Engineers
Cowlitz County, Washington
Contract amount: $658,000

These revetments were severely damaged by the flood of 1996. This contract was for placing rip rap to provide protection to sloping banks in such a manner as to allow the water to pass through without damaging the area on the dry side.

The specifications required the contractor to establish a baseline and take cross sections every 25 feet where the bank protection material (riprap) was to be placed.

Excavating for a toe trench and placing the riprap therein was a simultaneous operation: dig out the toe, and place the riprap. And then continue placing the riprap to the top of the revetment slope.

Due to our crew's surveying experience, we were able to do most of this work with our own forces. We used a crane and a weight to sound the river in the area the riprap was to be placed, and cross-section the dry areas. Once the cross sections were done, we turned them over to John Barbieri Engineering to do the quantity calculations.

We started work on the downstream end of the Kirkendoll section. When working with any water that flows, it's always best to start on the downstream end.

Colin and Junior survey sounding for x-sections.

The flood of 1996 tore thousands of yards of gravel from the existing stream bank but left some of the riprap in place. A savvy contractor always takes advantage of anything that is given. We harvested the riprap.

At the time of the flood, the county hired a local quarry to haul in riprap in an attempt to stop any more damage on the dry side. This riprap was so big that you could only get one or two pieces on a low-boy trailer. We had planned on buying our riprap from the same quarry, but it did not meet government specs for hardness. This meant I would have to haul rock in from Oakville, the nearest Corp of Engineers-approved quarry.

I called the quarry salesperson and he drove down to look at the site. He suggested that I put all of the material in a stockpile and move it along the top of the dike with a front end loader and cast it over the bank with an excavator. I listened to him but I didn't say anything. In my mind, stockpiling did not make sense. That would require an extra move.

He quoted me a price and left. I was just getting ready to leave when in drove Sam Tooms (Sam-Sam the Rip Rap Man). He said that he had a quarry at mile post 57 and would like to sell me some riprap. I explained to him that it had to meet Corp of Engineers specs. He said he was sure it would. We sent six samples to the lab and they passed with flying colors.

Hitachi is excavating material at the down-stream end of project. Truck is dumping material on the dry side of the dike.

Overall view of bank being repaired.

Digging out for the revetment toe, placing riprap and hauling gravel to dry side of dike that was washed away by 1996 flood.

Kenny Piper and Mike Waterfield did the grading work on the lower end, Kenny being the superintendent for this job. Sam showed up and told Kenny that if he didn't have to break the boulders down, he would sell it for less. As it turned out, we used Sam's rock on this job, and the future Ridgefield and Troutdale jobs. Oakville wanted to sell it to us by the ton. It takes about two tons to make a yard. Sam would sell us one yard for Oakville's one-ton price. The Corp was paying us by the yard. The quantity was determined by the survey. The Corp did not require a re-survey. The quantity was controlled simply by building to the specified percentage of slope.

What this really meant is that Sam was only charging us half price for the rock. Besides that, we were able to back the dump trucks right to the spot where we needed the material. One excavator on top of the bank swung the material to the excavator working at the toe.

Placing toe material—in concert.

For the most part we were able to do this job with two excavators and two men. A Cat D-6 was also used to shape the slopes in some areas. The job went very well, and we were able to place the riprap as fast as the trucks could haul it in.

The COR, Joe Ekahl, although he only came on-site a couple of days per week, was very pleased with our progress. We showed him a few areas that we thought needed more protection. He agreed and paid us by the truckload. He was delighted to have the oversize riprap, particularly at the Holder location. This section was in front of a private residence and had tended to wash away for a long time.

Joe was also very particular about how the finish slope looked. He wanted us to chink in between the large boulders so that the slope had a smooth look. For this purpose we fabricated a chinking tool at considerable cost, shown in the picture below. This is the first and only time that anyone used a tool of this design.

Smoothing the slopes with our custom chinking machine.

Junior and one of the large boulders.

Joe was very pleased with the finished product, as was the contracting officer. They said this was the best looking riprap job they had ever seen. We received a letter of commendation from the Corps.

As this job went smoothly with very few problems, our costs ended up being just less than half of the contract price of $658,000, coming in at $325,000. Our profit was just over 50% and as it turned out, was a cushion for our next riprap job.

1998
Dike Repair
US Department of Fish & Wildlife
Ridgefield National Wildlife Refuge
Ridgefield, Washington
Lola Gannon, Contracting Officer
Contract amount: $1,020,300

The name of this job was very misleading. Its purpose was to armor the stream banks that were allegedly damaged by the flood of 1996. This job was primarily funded by federal disaster relief money. FEMA money could be used for dike repair, but not dike protection. Though the name of the job was Dike Repair, there was only one very short section of dike (less than 100 feet out of 3400 feet of work). The specifications required that all work on this project be done from a barge. This made sense as there were no roads. The specifications also stated that the only dredging allowed was what was required for the toe trench.

As the areas that needed bank protection were not continuous, it was the contractor's responsibility to survey the entire area so that F&W engineers could determine the exact locations they wanted riprapped. These areas were then cross-sectioned every 25 feet in order to determine the top elevation of the riprap.

Finished bank in foreground and dike above in the background.

The engineer was very slow in getting this information back to us, making it very difficult to schedule the work. It was very important that this work be completed simultaneously with the fish window. This was strongly emphasized at the pre-work conference.

During the conference, we had presented pictures of the Kirkendoll-Holder Bank Protection project that we had just completed for the Corp of Engineers, and for which we had received a letter of commendation. This didn't help our cause. Lola Gannon, the contracting officer for Fish and Wildlife didn't like the Corp of Engineers, as we suddenly learned.

Fish and Wildlife issued us the revised drawings and specifications for the job, which had eliminated any reference to lines and grades. We later found out that F&W had initially issued the *un-revised* drawings, which did show lines and grades to the job COR—and the inspector. This meant that from the very beginning of the job, our relationship with the COR and inspector was contentious. Added to this, the COR was from Denver, and the inspector originated in Yakima. Getting this water job done with two dry-landers was bound to be difficult.

On most of the jobs we had done for Lola, her CORs and engineers were in-house and were very helpful in working with the contractor to smooth out the bumps that exist in all jobs. Lola was very protective towards those contractors she had taken under her wing and done multiple projects with. During this time, there were few contractors who would even do this kind of work.

Hagedorn Inc. survey crew.

It is important to realize that the reason lines and grades were eliminated is because all riprap material was to be paid for by the ton. This makes sense because the inspector, at the COR's discretion, had the right to add more spalls (small rip rap) to any areas that he wanted to modify. This also eliminated the need to re-survey. Unfortunately, we were ordered to re-survey anyhow.

The first line item on all construction jobs is the clearing. Below is a picture of the contractor's personnel clearing work area RS-3. Across the water are three piles of clearing debris that has to be stacked beyond the dike on Bachelor Island.

Clearing the work area.

To make matters worse, the COR, Ken White (in Denver), wanted us to measure the toe trench, which was underwater, before we placed any spalls in it. I went into Lola's office and we got on a conference call with Ken. He thought we were digging the toe trench like a pipeline trench. He did not understand that we were side-digging the trench and immediately filling it with spalls before it caved in. He reluctantly agreed which gave us a little breathing room.

It was very important to determine where the banks were to be protected because, as on any job, the clearing must be done first. Even more so on this job, because much of the debris to be cleared was under water. Also, the specifications required all in-water work areas to be surrounded by filter fabric, which was to keep any silts from settling in the *spawning areas* in the middle of winter when there are no fish spawning.

The designated disposal area for clearing debris was on Bachelor Island, behind the dike and twenty feet from the access road. Remember the specs required all work to be done from a barge—an impossible spec! Nevertheless, the excavator had no problem climbing over the dike and stacking the burn pile according to the Washington State Department of Forestry rules.

Once the original survey and the toe trench excavation problems were temporarily resolved, we started moving riprap. The water was lower than normal for this time of the year, lower than the averages shown on the plan. This required us to put lighter loads on the barges, and required an extra one for the overload. We made good progress, and completed all the work except the very last upstream section on Bachelor Island.

Our entire fleet of equipment for this job: 5 barges, 1 long-boom Kobelco 912A excavator, 1 EX-200 Hitachi excavator and one 950 front-end Caterpillar loader.

Placing spalls from sunken barge onto bank.

Tugs Light Duty and The Chief pumping out a sunken barge. The only reason it isn't any further underwater is because it's on the bottom of the river. When working on the water, something bad will happen sooner or later; you just never know when.

We had sailed in at high tide and unloaded the riprap onto the beach. Kenny and I were at the staging area when the inspector, Chuck Palmer (who incidentally was also the inspector on the Yakima-Tieton job in 1981) was watching the unloading happen at the upstream dike. He told the operator to stop. The operator called us and told us that Chuck had told him to stop. I handed the phone to Kenny, who could yell louder than I could. He told the operator, "Keep unloading!"

The operator said to Kenny that Chuck was telling him to stop.

Kenny said, "Keep unloading! We need to get the barge unloaded before the tide goes out."

He finished unloading the barge and managed to get the whole rig back to the dock. As was his forte, Palmer made a big deal out of it. This made the CO Lola very unhappy and she issued a stop-work order for the rip rap. This left us with a large quantity of it at the staging area —material which we never did get paid for.

The rip rap work was stopped, but we were still doing cleanup work and tree pruning. (The government had ordered us to hire an arborist to prune the cottonwood trees.)

It was the government's responsibility to mark the trees they wanted to save. The problem was that they should have marked the trees before we did any clearing, as the specifications called for the removal of a precise number of trees. The inspector, Palmer, never did mark the trees, probably because there was brush and blackberries growing around them, or maybe because he was just too damn lazy. As contractors, we couldn't wait, so we took down the trees that looked like they should be removed—until we reached the contract quantity.

I asked Palmer to please mark the trees he wanted pruned. He marked about twelve trees, and we had the arborist prune them. We thought we were done and started to demobilize when Palmer came up and told us that there were a bunch of damaged trees we hadn't pruned.

I said, "I know. We pruned all of the ones you marked. If I recall right, the government negotiated a separate contract with the arborist to repair the damaged trees."

A damaged tree that Palmer didn't mark for pruning.

In the meantime, we were paying rent on the staging area where we had stockpiled the riprap for the last section of bank repair prior to the stop-work order. As mentioned above, the government never did pay us for that material and we wound up hauling it to a bank repair project in Troutdale, Oregon.

The material we never got paid for.

The government wanted this tree removed but they had not marked it. It was not damaged by the construction activities.

The Beaver Tree

About once a week, the local schools brought a group out to view the "Beaver Tree", as we called it. I refused to remove it. Nor was I obligated to.

Once the clearing was completed and the riprap installed, the specs called for "fish trees" to be anchored at twelve different places on the east side of Bachelor Slough. The specs showed these trees bolted down to concrete anchors. When reviewing the specs, I suddenly thought, "What would happen after the trees disintegrated and the bolts were still sticking up?" I visualized a boat traveling through and what would happen to the engine if it hit the bolts. Then I thought, "What would happen if the top of the bolts were slightly underwater and a swimmer or water skier ran into them? Or how about a sled?" I called the design engineer and suggested that we use chain instead of bolts. It was a hard sell but the USFS finally agreed to a change order to use chain.

Scuba diver installing fish tree anchor chain.

Sometime during the last few weeks of construction, Palmer was replaced by another inspector. We basically told him what was required and he eventually approved all our work, which was started in October 1997, and was substantially completed five months later. The claims on this job, however, started the first week of construction and were finally resolved in May of 1999. These all resulted from the fact that the government was working from the wrong set of plans and specifications.

Unfortunately I did not figure this out until long after the final settlement. The bad rapport on this job continued to influence future decisions on requests for proposal at the Wildlife Refuge. All of these issues could have been easily resolved if there had been a meeting between the design engineer firm, the US Fish and Wildlife Service and the contractor.

Finished product.

We had many comments from other contractors about what a good looking job we did. The work was good, but the profits were thin.

1998
Beaver Creek Bank Stabilization
City of Troutdale, Oregon
Contract Amount: $172,336
Final Amount: $228,751
Awarded in June

The baseline for this work was in the roadway next to the top of the bank that was to be stabilized.

Access to the work required us to erect a temporary bridge over the top of an existing bridge owned by the local homeowners association. The temporary bridge was necessary in order to get trucks and heavy equipment to the project. It worked so well that the homeowner's association wanted to keep it; however, they did not want to pay for it. Our contract could not be finalized until it was removed. Much to their anguish, we loaded it up and hauled it away; sometime later we sold it to a logging company.

Collin and Mike placed the temporary bridge.

Upon receiving notice to proceed, we ordered the temporary bridge components, sheet piling and template material for the sheet piling.

Once the temporary bridge was installed, we moved our excavator and loader to the work site and started clearing.

Temporary bridge in place.

When we bid the job, the area was completely obscured by blackberry vines. We cleared the vines and started laying out for the sheet piling and toe trench. We soon realized that the dimensions shown on the contract drawings indicated only half of the units of the material required. We were not sure what the engineer did wrong. *We believed he reduced the drawings to half-size and then used the wrong scale to measure distances.* The results were that the job was twice as big as shown on the schedule of items. Also, the sheet piling was twice as far from the baseline as the drawings indicated. This created a myriad of problems. It's always six times harder to fix a mistake than to do it right the first time.

One problem was that we had sub-contracted the pile driving to Jerry Miller. Jerry owned his own crane and pile hammer. As he had to reach twice as far as the plans indicated, this meant that his hammer was too heavy for his crane to handle, forcing us to rent a lighter hammer, which cost an extra $6,000.

During the clearing operation, we became aware that the reason the bank had failed was because the engineer had used filter fabric on the steep slope after the bank had slid in due to the 1996 flood. We soon realized that the engineer had also worked for the same firm that designed the '96 repairs. Now the engineer had to explain to the owner (City of Troutdale) that the project was going to cost more than double. The City was not pleased, and called the contractor and engineer to a council meeting. The engineer tried to justify his actions. The mayor was not impressed, and turned to me, saying, "Why didn't you notify us during the bid procedure?"

I didn't know what to say, so I didn't say anything.

After a few days of negotiating, the City agreed to pay the extra costs, and we proceeded with the work.

Kenny Piper was superintendent on this job, and did most of the negotiating. He and Mike Waterfield took turns operating the EX-200 excavator and front end loader.

Once the toe trench was in, we began installing the gabion baskets, using the rock to fill them that was left over from the Ridgefield job.

Even though it wasn't called for, at our own expense we added rock to the slope above the gabions before installing the blankets containing top soil.

To understand the complexities of administering this project, one needs to look at the chain of command, starting with the owner. First, there was the Mayor; then the City's Engineer Inspector, Travis Hultin, who answered directly to the Mayor. Travis' responsibilities were to ensure that OTAK, the engineering firm hired by the City to design the project, was doing a proper job. OTAK's engineer, Steve Blanton, had to answer directly to Travis. OTAK hired a survey firm to stake the project. OTAK also hired an inspection firm whose field engineer, Azad Mohammadi, inspected and made sure the contractor was doing the work according to specifications. This meant three inspection teams were doing what one man could do all by himself. All of these people attempted to direct the contractor at various times, and attempted to hold him to the exact line and grades shown on the drawings.

The main problem was that the engineer designed everything "straight-line". This project was built on curved ground. Azad constantly complained in his daily reports that the contractor was deviating from the straight lines. We didn't like this much because it stirred everyone up in the chain of command. Azad was educated in Iran, and graduated from engineering school there. He indicated to us that engineers in his country ran the show, and he expected to be treated with respect, even though he treated contractors like dogs.

Crane rigging the pile hammer.

One day, Azad tried to boss Kenny. Out of my hearing range, Kenny lectured him in "contractor's language." and told him that if he said another word he would bury him so deep that he'd never be found.

Azad came to me and said, "Kenny's not treating me with respect."

I replied, "He's treating you with all the respect you deserve. If you don't like it, tell your boss."

Steve Blanton, Azad's boss, *did* say something to me, and I said, "Steve, let Kenny and me do what it takes to make the job fit the ground."

Steve replied, "It's obvious that you guys know how to make everything work. Do it your way. I will see that you will get paid for any extra work. Regarding Azad, I will keep him out of your way."

We all had a good laugh.

Lacing piling.

Rigging piling.

Excavating toe trench and filling with rip rap.

Collin & crew installing soil blankets.

Finished project.

The neighbor across the river facing the project was very concerned about their view, and it was my job to try and keep them happy. As you can see from the photos, there are many shrubs planted on the face of the work, which made the neighbor happy. I checked the site a couple of years later, and the entire work site was again covered with blackberry vines.

This job was very labor-intensive. Because of the design problems, it was a real challenge, over which we prevailed due to our rapport with Steve.

We finished the work on Sept. 24th, 1998. After lengthy negotiations with the City, we wound up getting paid for all our work on Feb. 4, 1999. The price of the work increased by $56,415. We had a lot of fun doing this job, and our anticipated profit more than doubled.

1998
Steinborn Track Flood Repair
US Fish & Wildlife
Bureau of Reclamation
Pacific Northwest Office, Portland, Oregon
Original Contract Amount: $90,220
Contract Amount with Modifications: $165,187.00

This contract was awarded September 25th, which was late in the season for doing this type of work. We had only 45 days from notice to proceed to complete the work.

The main purpose of this project was to allow fish to get into the spawning bed. All the structures were small and it was up to the contractor to make them fit the existing conditions, which included the rearing pond. The pond was partially on private land, which was still owned by Steinborn. Some of the work required making minor changes to Steinborn's driveway. This sounds simple enough, but Steinborn still believed he had the right to fish in the rearing pond.

This put the contractor in a very delicate position. Steinborn wasn't happy with the Bureau of Reclamation—and vice versa.

Sheet pile holding pond.

We had the first phase of the project almost done when we had a severe rain and flood. The flood brought out the deficiencies in the overall plan, and the engineer and contractor worked together to correct the problems. The total cost of the corrections was $74,967.

The main problem with correcting the problems was that the contractor could figure out what to do in 15 minutes, but it took 15 days to get the government to agree. This delayed the job. During the delay, another contract was taking place at the project entrance. This completely cut off our access, which meant we had to travel over private property. The Bureau insisted it was our responsibility to obtain ingress and egress. We did—simply by *sneaking* in and out.

We left on good terms with the private property owner, and the Bureau of Reclamation was pleased with the work. This project later became known as the Tualatin River National Wildlife Refuge and is a popular wildlife observation spot.

Sign at entrance to Tualatin River Natural Wildlife Refuge.

CHAPTER 40

2001
IT WAS A VERY BUSY YEAR

1. **Vista House, Crown Point State Park**
   Historic Columbia River Highway; Corbett, Oregon
   Oregon Department of Transportation (ODOT)
   Contract #1—Contract Amount: $1,057,710
   Final Contract Amount: $1,292,960
   Contracts #2, 3 & 4—Contract Amount: $1,382,780
   Final Contract Amount: $1,497,479

Award of this contract required that the contractor had experience in doing masonry work on historical buildings. This job was bid at 9 a.m., July 12, 2001. There were 3 bidders:

Low:	**Lloyd H. Kessler, Inc.**	**$1,057,710**
2nd:	**Skyward**	**$1,069,500**
3rd:	**Western Waterproofing**	**$1,115,352**

Engineer's estimate: $1,000,000 to $1,250,000

Two weeks passed, and Doug Kessler called the contracting officer for a status report. The CO informed Doug that the second bidder had filed a bid protest, claiming that our company did not meet the historical criteria.

Doug immediately began researching the second bidder's experience. He discovered that the two buildings Skyward worked on were concrete. He also discovered that Skyward had not done any *stone masonry* work. Doug passed this information on to the CO, who called back and said the other bidder argued that the two buildings he worked on were concrete, and that concrete is considered masonry.

A month later, Millie and I were driving home from a family reunion in Minnesota when Doug called and said, "Hey, I've got some good news. We've been awarded the Vista House."

ODOT wanted us to start as soon as possible in order to get the work done by the end of the work season. Nearly two months of the work season had already been lost, and the roof tile was a long lead-time item.

Doug continued, "I've already called our bonding agent, Doug Hunter, who said the bond would be ready tomorrow and that he's working on the insurance."

The next day, Doug Hunter called back and said, "None of the insurers want to write earthquake or flood insurance, but I'm still searching for one that will."

The problem was that there had been an earthquake a few months before the bid opening. There had also been recent floods on the Columbia River (the flood of 1996). We did considerable arguing with the insurers. We explained to them that the Vista House was 400 feet above the river, and the last flood that reached that high was the Missoula Flood that occurred ten thousand years ago. They issued the flood insurance. As for the earthquake insurance, the same company said they were mandated by the government to write it.

We were awarded the work and a pre-work conference was scheduled.

Attending the meeting were Saul Zaik of Zaik Miller Architects, Herb Shaw of David Evans Engineering, Henry Kunowski, an Architectural Historian working for the State of Oregon, and Doug Kessler, Project Manager, and I. During the early stages of the work, it became evident that Henry Kunowski was going to make most of the decisions regarding restoration. He didn't like having to pay David Evans for doing inspections that Henry could do himself.

Henry and Saul Zaik had collaborated to do the restoration design and outline the work to be done, based upon historical information and recent investigations. This work was put into contract form, upon which the contractors could bid. As always happens in remodel work, there were many surprises, which dramatically increased costs. (The job was awarded based upon funds available.)

When conditions are not as shown on the plans, the job has to be re-engineered. Engineering costs money. The State's way of dealing with this was to contract with professionals of their choosing as long as the amount was under $20,000. These funds were separate, coming from the State's General Fund. This was a time-consuming and unwieldy process, which directly affected LHK Inc.'s progress. Some of these experts were aloof and were reluctant to consult with the contractor, even though our crews solved most of the problems encountered.

This was the first of two separate several-part contracts we did in the next three years on Vista House.

Verdigris green copper roof—The Vista House as it looked before we started renovating.

■ ■ ■

The first part of this contract was to repair decks, clean and replace outside stonework and windows, and re-tile the dome. We immediately started demolition work on the deck, as it was very important to get the outside work done before the high winds started in late fall. We also ordered the replacement stone and other long-lead time items.

We decided to erect a covered geodesic dome over the entire structure to protect it during severe weather. The manufacturer had convinced us that it could withstand winds of 90 mph.

One Friday night in early October, we completed erecting the dome a little after dark. We returned the next morning before daylight to find the dome had been vandalized. Several 80-lb. bags of sand holding down the cover had been thrown over the eight-foot-tall fence. We never did find out who the culprits were, but we always suspected it may have been a local football team.

Geodesic dome after vandalism.

It was necessary to remove the concrete deck and the lower course of stonework from around the entire building in order to install liquid-applied waterproofing. The same water-proofing was applied to the top of the dome.

Erecting the dome: Removing pedestal deck and lower stonework.

The plans indicated that the existing deck was four to five inches thick. It turned out to be closer to nine inches. We planned to break the four-five inch slab with a concrete breaker mounted on a Bobcat.

Deck thickness.

This wasn't working, so we hired a concrete cutting company to saw the nine inch slab into chunks that we could lift out with a small excavator. This was difficult and time consuming, but it worked. The reason the deck was nine inches thick was because the state had poured a four inch slab over the top of the original deck in an attempt to waterproof it. This created a four-inch high-hazard step.

Eliminating the hazardous steps required removing the top three stairway steps and re-pouring them.

To meet our minority goals, we hired a woman-owned subcontractor to remove the five inch deck slab. Her crew attempted, but simply did not have the equipment or the expertise to remove the slab the way I wanted it done. I gave them a lot of flack. Once they had done the required minority contract dollar amount, I made it so rough on them that they told me to go to hell and left. I'm sure they had easier work somewhere else.

The balcony and the dome required removal of the existing tile and concrete. We erected a stair tower with runways connected to a long orange chute, and dumped the debris down the chute into a dumpster.

Debris chute (orange).

The original dome roof was concrete tile. Over the years, the State thought the tile was leaking, so they covered the dome with copper, which had turned a verdigris color from copper sulfate. The standing seams had discolored and the stonework had turned nearly black from 85 years of exhaust smoke from passing trucks—not a pretty sight.

As soon as the balcony deck and dome demolition was completed, we began prepping the dome for the new tile. When the State installed the copper dome, they used ram sets to anchor the roofing. These ram sets fractured the original tile. During the roof removal, it was evident that the dome had never leaked. If not for the ram sets, the tile would have been good as new. However, the concrete substrate had deteriorated in a few places.

I negotiated a change order with Henry to fix the damaged area by placing a layer of high strength grout over the dome surface. It did not stick, and cracked everywhere. We immediately removed the grout before Henry saw it.

I then went to Saul Zaik, and we designed a system of wire mesh and concrete anchors. We then poured high strength concrete. Henry never knew the difference.

(In historical restoration, the idea is to replicate the original installation as closely as possible.)

Dome prep for high-strength concrete

Sometime during the design, someone decided the new roof tile should be shingled. I knew this would not work and told Saul. He was reluctant to change plans and told me I needed to prove it. I discussed this with my foreman, Collin Surbert, who told me he'd make a mock-up of the shingled tiles.

Shingled tile model

He made the mock-up, placed it on the roof, and showed it to Saul, who then conferred with Henry, who had been adamant about staying with the shingle method. Collin was able to show him how the wind would lift them right off.

Henry finally decided to have us install the tile exactly the same way as the original. He had us get some sample tiles from Pratt & Larson, the manufacturer, so he could check the color. They sent the samples to us. Henry wanted more samples. *This was all a very time consuming process.* The factory said, "Use the samples we sent. You must order now as this is the only window we have in our production schedule."

I sent a deposit that same day.

Original roof tiles— shades of light green. Maintenance workers shot ramsets into tile when they installed copper roof. Deteriorated concrete shows on darker area at right.

New tile roof

The Vista House was built in two phases. The first phase was the basement, main floor and two stair towers. We discovered that the first phase workmanship was very good. The poured-in-place concrete shell and dome in the second phase, however, was poor. It may have been because the second phase was built during World War I with unskilled help.

What is known is that the two decks leaked from the very beginning. Lazarus, the original architect, also placed vents above each skylight. When the wind blew, these vents leaked. The Vista House sits above the Columbia River Gorge, where the wind blows up to 100 miles per hour, and blows hard many days out of the year. The vents were a disaster—and we eventually sealed them up.

While waiting for the tile for the dome and balcony, we prepared the substrate by grinding, sandblasting, scraping, etc. Meanwhile, the architect was deciding what systems to use for waterproofing. Some of their ideas we knew from experience simply would not work. We had water-proofed many decks and were very aware of the best products available. It turned out that they used our recommendations throughout the project.

The main problem with Saul and Henry was that they had no conception of time. They could spend days and weeks dallying around with manufacturing reps and other out-of-town experts. Yet they were like lightning compared to the wizards who ran the second contract we did on Vista House. Even though Henry and Saul were very slow in making decisions, they were nevertheless easy to work with. Henry was always worried about where he was going to get the money for the change order work, and Saul was always complaining about how slow the State was in paying him.

One day, Henry said to Doug, "How much contingency money did you have in this project?" Doug told Henry, "If we put contingency money in a bid, we don't get the job." This is hard for a public servant to understand. This contract was finally completed in the fall of 2002. As it turned out, we would have only needed to add $235,250 to our original bid for contingencies.

This job turned out really well due to the help of Henry and Saul, and we felt privileged and proud of our work on this historical landmark.

Multnomah Falls Access
Columbia River Gorge Scenic Area; Troutdale, Oregon
US Forest Service
Original Contract Amount: $612,025
Final Contract Amount: $699,032

The main purpose of this job was to make the Multnomah Falls Lodge and the trail to the bridge viewpoint handicapped-accessible. This was mandated under the Americans with Disabilities Act, (ADA) and the government threatened to close down the Lodge if this work wasn't done, and wanted the work done prior to the busy tourist season. For this reason, this work was awarded late in the fall.

That September, Doug and I were sitting in the Vista House office trailer when I suddenly remembered, "Hey Doug, isn't there a bid coming up on Multnomah Falls?" He said, "Yeah, the closing is at 3:00 today. I have a set of plans." I said, "Let's figure it." He looked at me like I was nuts, as always. We started figuring, based mostly upon memories of costs of different items on earlier jobs. The main item here was the masonry. We called Guinett Masonry; Greg Paul had already prepared a bid. We put the prices together and I made it to the bid opening in Sandy with five minutes to spare. The CO Carl Culham, said, "Being as this is a request for proposal, you had up until 5:00 to turn in the bid." If I had known that was the case, I'd have probably gotten there at five minutes to 5:00.

A few days later, Carl called and said, "This bid looks like it was hastily thrown together. Can you review it and revise your prices? They are over our bidding range."

I asked, "How much was the second bid?"

He replied, "I'm not allowed to release that information."

Doug and I were sure we were the only bidder. This was a Hubzone project and we were the only Hubzone contractor on the plan-holder's list. Hubzone is a government program (SBA) for small companies that operate and employ people in Historically Underutilized Business Zones.

Doug and I reviewed our numbers, and were able to take a considerable amount out. Two or three weeks passed. We called Carl, who said we were still high but within their range: "The problem is that we don't have enough money."

A few hours later, the engineer called back and said, "We have awarded you the work, and you have the usual 14 days to provide bonds and insurance, but we want to get started as soon as possible."

We had the bonds and insurance up to them the next day, and then faxed Carl to say we wanted to schedule a pre-work conference as soon as possible.

Not receiving any reply, I called a couple days later and talked to him. He said, "The COR, Greg Neely, is on vacation and won't be back for a couple of weeks." This did not make me happy. Since it was the intent of the contract to get the work done before the main tourist season started, I decided I wasn't going to wait on Neely, so we went ahead and installed a protective fence and gate, and started the demolition.

Security fence and Theresa Logan, our traffic control person along with Kuila, our Traffic Control Dog.

The first day on the job, we backed our tool trailer next to the lodge. When we came to work the next morning, we found that someone had broken into the trailer and stolen our $3,000 generator and another $4,000 worth of tools. Fortunately, we had enough tools for the work we had to accomplish that day, but from then on, we made sure the doors to the trailer were up against a rock or secured by a piece of equipment.

The contract required a temporary trail so that people could access the trail to the bridge. This required a six-foot-tall set of steps to get foot traffic over an existing rock wall.

We were just completing the trail when Greg Neely called and said he wanted to have a pre-work conference in the lodge the following morning, January 23rd. I told him we'd see him there.

The next morning, Greg showed up early and wasn't very happy about what he saw. He said, "You're supposed to have turned in submittals for all of this work."

I said, "Doug will bring them to the pre-work conference later this morning." Greg grumbled but didn't appear too unhappy. He said, "I'll have to explain this to the Contracting Officer at today's meeting."

At the beginning of the meeting, Doug turned in the submittals for the work that we had already done. The Forest Service personnel had their game faces on, and scolded us for breaking the rules. The specs implied that we had to allow foot traffic through the work area. Doug had warned me about this possibility. However, at the meeting, the Forest Service was adamant that we were *not* to allow any pedestrians into the work area. They did not want the liability. We lucked out.

We started demolition of the existing trail. As soon as we were finished, Barbieri, our surveying company, laid out the lines and grades for the new work. It soon became evident that many of the lines and grades needed to be adjusted. This meant that some of the existing masonry walls would have to be removed or altered. We had to work through the COR to convince the Historical Review Committee that the changes were necessary. Once the Committee conceded the changes, it was then necessary for us to convince the USFS to pay for them.

We were now working concurrently on the Vista House, Multnomah Falls, the Oneonta Trailhead, the John Yeon Trailhead and Elowah Falls projects, which were just down the highway from the Vista House. This allowed our crews to move from one project to another while problems were being solved on one job or another.

We were required to submit a traffic plan showing how we were going to safely move foot traffic across the Historic Columbia River Highway from the parking lots to the lodge and trail. The plan worked fine. During the six months of construction nearly one million people were safely guided across the highway. There was not one incident or complaint—and *that* made the Forest Service personnel at the lodge very happy.

Original trail with (non-ADA) steps everywhere.

Reconstructing trail to meet ADA standards.

Lloyd ram-rodding the construction.

One of the other purposes was to enlarge the area and make it comfortable for more visitors, preserving the stonework's original motif.

Guinett Masonry crew—Steve Crom, foreman in yellow pants.

Monica enjoying the new seating wall area.

Seating wall area.

Although the contracting officer for this project was fully aware of LHK Inc.'s ability to do difficult jobs, the COR, Greg Neely, was not. Greg had just finished dealing with a contractor at the Angel's Rest Trailhead and was not pleased with the contractor's delays and inability to stay within the specs. It took him a while to realize that our methods resulted in a quality product the first time out. Having gained his confidence, we formed a good team and were able to speedily resolve the many unforeseen problems encounted.

Aerial view from bridge.

There were numerous changes that we did with our own forces, for which we were paid profit and overhead. We did not mark up the $45,000 worth of extra stonework that Louis Guinett Masonry did. This pleased the Forest Service, as they had run out of money.

Collin on the excavator, Owen standing next to the box shoring for the hole that Collin is digging to access the basement, and Greg Neely, our COR. No cover charge for the guests in the dining room watching the show.

On the performance rating, the Contracting Officer gave us "excellent" in all categories. This job was fun and profitable and another example of how problems can be solved when the contractor and engineer work together.

Oneota & John Yeon Trailheads
Columbia Gorge Scenic Area
US Forest Service
Contract Amount: $165,996
Final Contract Amount: $198,353

This project consisted of parking lots, stone masonry curbs, kiosk and signage at the Elowah Falls Trailhead, the John Yeon Trailhead and the Oneonta Trailhead. We started this work in March of 2002.

Here again is the same old story of trying to make the straight lines on the drawings fit the curves on the ground, complicated by the fact that we had to deal with ODOT (Oregon Department of Transportation). Their ideas and US Forest Service ideas were different. Fortunately, our USFS COR on this project, Fred Netzel, had many years of surveying experience. He was kind of grouchy, like old surveyors get. As a result, he and I got along very well. He knew what had to be done to make everything fit, but that didn't stop ODOT from giving us fits. For this reason, the job took a little longer than it should have, but we had fun —and made money.

Owen, Collin and Mike at John B. Yeon State Park.

Owen, Collin and Mike installing the Elowah Falls Trail sign.

■ ■ ■

Bonneville Lock & Dam, Low Water Fishing Access at Hamilton Island
Contract Amount: $47,100

We received notice to proceed on August 7th, 2002, to build a parking lot, handicapped-accessible fishing trail and bank protection (riprap) between North Bonneville and Bonneville Dam on Hamilton Island. We were doing this work at the same time, with the same crew of beauties pictured above.

The only problem on this job was that the local supplier of riprap and gravel trucks seldom showed up on time. If five trucks were due, three would show up; the other two would be broken down along the way. When the first three went for the second round, sometimes only one would come back.

What should have been done in four or five days, got spread out over a month, which forced us to reschedule the paving. Fortunately, we were also working on the John Yeon project, and were able to jump back and forth. Overall, this was a fun job and turned out very well. No fuss, no changes, good profit.

▪ ▪ ▪

Second Contract at Vista House—September, 2003

The requests for proposals were issued on June 9, 2003, for rehabilitation of the Vista House interior, as listed below.

These proposals were issued by the State of Oregon Purchasing Division. Agency: Parks and Recreation.

Phase I

1. Mobilization, including setting up LHK office trailer and concession trailer for Friends of Vista House—including electrical connections to the Vista House panels and security fencing
2. Marble restoration
3. Terrazzo restoration
4. Plastering and stucco

Phase II

5. Install new mechanical system, which included two 500-foot, vertical bores for the closed-loop Geothermal heating system
6. Install new electrical system
7. Install new plumbing system

Phase III

8. Build interpretive exhibits and signage

Phase I of the Second Contract

We were the only bidder on this project, submitting our proposal in June. However, Parks & Rec didn't award the contract until mid-September.

The majority of the work on this contract was stone and marble repair, which we sub-contracted to Pioneer Masonry, the only company in the area that met the historical qualifications for this project. Due to our rapport with Pioneer on the exterior restoration of the Vista House, we bid this job as the prime contractor. Our crews were experienced in preparation, and most all other items of work that were required.

We were the tail wagging the dog, putting us in the position of having to argue with the project manager and architect when processing change orders for Pioneer's extra work.

When bidding a project like this, the contractor must rely upon the plans and specifications in order to determine the scope of the work. Vista House specifications were drafted based on assumptions and historical data, which included the original plans and specs. The spec writers for this project did not allow for the changed conditions that are found in every historical restoration. The specs were very rigid and they gave no direction about how to deal with changes.

The contractor must prove to the owner that he has the ability to do the work according to the specs, and the contractor must assume that the owner's representative has the knowledge and experience to administer the work.

When the work began, Jean Castillo signed her letters "Engineer-in-Training" and "Project Manager". Once the work started, it soon became clear to us that she was not qualified. Jean had set the job up whereby we had a contactor-engineer meeting every Wednesday at 1 p.m. The purpose was to schedule the following week's work and resolve the usual construction problems. As project manager, Jean's duties included interpreting the plans and specifications for the job as they related both to the owner and the contractor on an impartial basis. As a trainee, she had not yet learned how to do this. She chose to read the specifications to the letter, but often failed to understand their intent.

She was slow in making any interpretations, one very important one took thirteen months. She acted like she was the engineer, architect and designer, and at times she even attempted to direct both the contractor's and subcontractors' workers. One has to wonder who made the decision to make an engineer-in-training a project manager for a complex, million-dollar restoration project. Her decisions and indecisions created much chaos.

It must be remembered that the intent of Parks & Rec was to get this contract awarded in the early summer so that the work could be completed in the dry season.

The bids were open June 9, 2003, and finally awarded on August 22. The delay was partly caused by Parks & Rec's lack of understanding about insurance company's rules, so the order to proceed was not issued until Sept. 19th. It took another eleven days for Jean to schedule a pre-construction conference for Tuesday, Sept. 30. This did not make me happy.

As a result, we jumped the gun: a day before the conference we removed all the obsolete pipe and other items in the building that were scheduled to be scrapped.

About the conference, Jean wrote to Doug, "I was frustrated that you began work without notifying me, and did not provide the required submittals for my approval prior to the construction meeting. While we are on a tight schedule, it is still required that all procedures outlined in the specifications be followed."

The letter from Doug below described the unforeseen problems encountered in this project:

October 8, 2004

Jean Castillo, Contracting Officer
Oregon Parks and Recreation
725 Summer St NE, Ste. C
Salem, Oregon 97301

Subject: Reply to your letter from October 6, 2004
RE: Limestone Vista House (2 options)

Dear Ms. Castillo,

Throughout this project there have been numerous discoveries creating changed conditions and expensive delays.

1. *Insulation not included in Phase I*
2. *Insulation not included in Phase II*
3. *Water infiltration*
4. *Defective concrete columns*
5. *Rock pockets concrete columns*
6. *Rotten East stairway*
7. *Leaky balcony windows*
8. *ADA and safety requirements before building permit*
9. *Others*

At the pre-work conference, Jean and Saul advised us that they wanted insulation in certain sections of the building. *It must be noted that there was no insulation included in Phase I or Phase II and it was only* ***after*** *the work started that insulation was mentioned.* They also indicated that there were problems with the balcony windows leaking, and asked for our advice on how to stop the leaks.

They also asked if we knew of an insulation system that would work. LHK Inc. suggested using spray-on foam insulation, as it would bond to the concrete substrate and also provide a suitable substrate for plaster. We made it very clear to them that any insulation work must be done *prior* to plastering; that this was critical to our construction schedule, and would require an extension of contract time.

It was now October 16, and all the surfaces had been prepped and primed for either insulation or plaster. Jean asked us to plaster the walls first, in order to give her engineer more time to approve (design) the insulation. (It's normal to plaster the ceilings first. Doing the walls first takes more time and costs more money.)

The spray-on foam was approved by Saul, the architect, on November 13th, but rejected by Jean on November 19th. The reason given was that SHPO (State Historic Preservation Office) didn't want the spray-on foam. We didn't know why. Parks & Rec then hired Dick (Mac) McBride's architectural firm to engineer the insulation system. This should only have taken a few days.

We also discussed the old world system of plastering that Euro Plastering wanted to use. Jean said, "I like it. It will take me a few days to get it approved by Parks & Rec and Saul Zaik."

I told Jean, "Euro Plastering will start in the morning." She balked. I told her that no matter which system we use, the primer is the same. She said okay.

We then proceeded with the plastering, which went well for the most part. But the insulation design delay had made it necessary for James, the owner, to work on another job and leave his foreman in charge. (James was working on a time-and-materials basis.) As the work proceeded I noticed that the foreman was skipping certain small areas near the doors that should have been done at the same time as the main areas. This was increasing costs, so I notified James.

His foreman had gotten into the habit of driving to the Corbett store for lunch, about 3 miles away. Sometimes he would be gone an hour or more, leaving the crew unsupervised. The crew was fully aware that the foreman was screwing up. I informed him that our contract with Euro Plastering & Stucco only allowed a half hour for lunch, and the crews were not allowed to leave the project during the shift. The next day at the end of the lunch break, there was again no sign of the foreman. When he returned a half hour late, I told him to get off the job!

He replied, "I don't have a ride. I came in the crew truck." He used my phone to call his wife, who agreed to come and get him.

I said, "Good. Wait for her OUTSIDE the gate."

Later that day I talked to James, who said, "I apologize. We also had trouble with him on the last job."

Immediately production doubled. As there was still no decision on insulation, we finished plastering the ceilings. Jean, Friends of The Vista House, Parks & Recreation, Saul Zaik and Henry Kunowski all raved about what a beautiful job Euro Plastering had done.

Later, we submitted the cost for installing spray-on foam insulation system. This was the same system that was accepted by Saul (Nov. 13, 2003) and then rejected by SHPO (Nov. 19). It was still contingent upon MacBride finalizing the design. By late April of 2004, we finally had the building dry enough to install the insulation. This was a window of opportunity, and we had to take advantage of before it rained again, so we installed the insulation.

That very same day we were having a meeting with Jean and Teresa Moritz, the Department of Administrative Services' contracting officer. They asked me, "When do you plan on installing the insulation?"

I replied, "We're insulating the ceiling right now." You should have seen the look on their faces.

They weren't happy. They said, "You don't even have a signed change order."

I said, "I'll have to take the risk. The weather doesn't wait for formal signatures."

Waterproofing around the windows was still under discussion. I knew what would work, but Jean and her engineers did not.

I convinced James Hambrick, head of OPRD's parks department, to visit the site and look at the windows. I explained the spray-on foam system to him, and he said, "That sounds okay to me."

I, of course, took this to mean that he was giving OPRD approval. A few days later, we installed the foam, much to Jean's dismay. She wanted to know what guarantees there were if the window leaked. I explained to her that we were installing the foam system per the manufacturer's recommendations. Again I explained to Jean that I'd spent much time drying the area around the windows, and the installation had to be done before it rained. I told her we'd worry about leaks if and when they occurred. The windows did not leak, and have not leaked to this day, even though Jean claimed they did.

When we finally got started on the Phase I work, about October 1st, everything went well for the first seven weeks. We set up the concession trailer for the Friends of the Gorge and our office trailer, and installed electrical service to them from the panel inside the Vista House. The scaffolding was installed and the masons started removing the paint from the Kasota Stone. Our crews began preparing the substrate in the basement for plaster and paint.

On November 24th, when I returned from running an errand, our foreman Collin Surbert said, "An inspector was here from the City of Gresham and said we had to shut down. He said he'd be back in a couple of hours to talk to you."

When the inspector returned, he said, "You do not have a building permit."

I said, "OPRD says I don't need one."

He said, "Doesn't matter. Multnomah County says you do. You need to call Al Lajimodiere, head of the Building Dept. He will be in his office at 9 a.m. tomorrow."

I immediately called Saul Zaik, OPRD's architect of record for this project. Saul called Henry Kunowski. Henry said, "We don't need a permit." Henry was no longer with Parks & Rec, but he had played an important part in the design of the previous project and acted as a consultant on this one. He was also the spokesman for Friends of the Vista House.

This would become the beginning of a losing argument for OPRD, Henry and Saul. The next morning, I met with Al Lajimodiere. He said, "We need to do a plan review prior to issuing a building permit. This requires an up-front fee and a set of stamped plans from the architect of record."

I asked, "How long will the review take?"

He said, "I don't know, but due to the urgency of the situation, we'll start the review right away." Ten days later, Jean finally managed to provide Al with the plans.

I explained to him that if we had to shut down, there were a few things we needed to do in order to make the building safe. He said okay. I went back to the Vista House and Pioneer and did what we needed to do to make the scaffolding and stonework safe. (I cheated a little and finished the demolition in the basement.) Pioneer's crew spent the next couple of weeks finishing up jobs at other locations, and I moved our crew to Multnomah Falls.

I presented Al with the check for the fees for the plan review. He had a big ego and a loud, authoritative voice, and left no doubt about who was running the show in this part of the county.

A few days passed and Lajimodiere sent me the list of work that would have to be done before the permit could be issued. This list included design and approval to make the building ADA accessible, and design and approval of an alarm system that allowed for emergency exiting while keeping the door-swings moving inward. OPRD and the SHPO claimed that they did not have to alter the building to comply with ADA regulations—for historical preservation reasons. However, Oregon's Governor finally convinced OPRD that ADA was required.

Lajimodiere was very reasonable and allowed us to continue Phase I masonry work while the ADA access and alarm system were being designed. In the meantime, we did Phase II mechanical work without a permit simply because some of this work had to be done before Phase I masonry could be completed. The design process for the ADA and alarm system went very slowly, as the architects and engineers wanted to be assured how they were going to be paid. By the time the alarm system was approved, the Kasota Stone panels next to the doorways had been repaired or replaced.

The ADA design took much, much longer.

In the meantime, Jean ratted on us. She informed Lajimodiere that we were doing the Phase II work without a permit. Al made a special trip to the job and gave me a severe lecture. I did not interrupt him. He was not happy, and said, “You have to tear out the duct work you’ve been working on.”

I said to him, “I will,” and explained that it was a risk I was forced to take. “If you have the time, let me explain it to you why it is critical for the work to proceed in a particular order.” For an example, I showed him why the marble and terrazzo floors couldn’t be finished until the new ductwork was installed, as well as many other details that needed to be done in sequence. Al indicated that he then understood how OPRD’s inability to complete the alarm system design was impacting the entire project. The actual permit was finally issued on June 15, 2004, a full six months later.

Alarm system installed on cracked Kasota Stone.

Monica and Kuila inspecting light spots caused by water infiltration in the rotunda.

This panel disappeared many years ago and probably broke apart due to water running down the stairway. It took 13 months to replace it.

As is normal procedure, the designers had been paid before the contract was out for bids. Once the work started, we encountered many changed conditions.

Most of the people involved in the design had been paid for their services prior to the construction contract. It is normal for this type of work to encounter changed conditions. Due to these conditions, other experts had to be retained to solve the problems. On the previous contract, Henry Kunowski acted as the Job Captain, and was able to find the funding to pay the experts.

But there was no job captain to coordinate the myriad of designers. The State had negotiated separate fixed-price contracts with the mechanical designers, HVAC designers, insulation designers, architects, and historical architects, to name a few.

It is important for all parties involved that progress, *time, cost, and profit* decisions be made expeditiously. If the project manager had been an experienced engineer, most of the problems could have been resolved in minutes or hours. Major problems requiring an expert should never take more than a week or ten days to solve.

Jean's major problem was that she had to rely upon the architect to find the expert. The next problem was that Jean did not know how to find the funding. In most cases, the architect, Saul Zaik, consulted with us to determine how the problem should be fixed. The architect would then hire an expert to design the procedure. *(It should be noted that the very best contractors were selected to do this project.)*

An example: When we discovered that portions of the columns in the rotunda were defective, LHK Inc. agreed to pay WDY (the engineering firm) up front out of the negotiated cost of doing the repairs. This way we could keep the job going without delaying the masons (Pioneer). We proceeded with the repairs, but there were some minor issues with WDY's design, which caused some delay. Jean refused to pay for this work until it was 100% complete. While this work was going on, we discovered other areas in the building that required WDY services. WDY agreed to do the design work for these areas, but since we had not been paid for the column work, we could not pay WDY, and they refused to release the design until paid. Jean's refusal to pay us was unjust punishment, in particular due to the fact that all the other work in the building was on or ahead of schedule.

All the above was particularly difficult because of the way the contract was set up, and Jean's to-the-letter interpretations of the specs. I had to deal through Jean and Saul to communicate with WDY, preventing me from having one-on-one relationship with Wade Younie, owner of WDY. In order to make the job go smoothly, I paid WDY out of proceeds from other projects. From then on, we had a good relationship.

This also meant that OPRD had to work through Saul Zaik and Associates to do the design work, which meant that the architect was responsible for hiring a qualified engineer, which meant that OPRD had to find money to pay both Saul and the engineer. This took time, and caused LHK's office rental, fence rental and many other expenses to accrue each day. Plus, the project was pushed into the winter season and while the work was indoors, there were many days in the winter when a person couldn't even get to the door.

The first phase of the interior rehabilitation work was to clean and remove paint from the Kasota Stone, replace any broken Kasota Stone (marble), plaster the basement, and install new utilities (which should have been in contract #1). The paint had to be removed from all surfaces before it could be determined which stone panels needed to be replaced, and what methods would be required to repair or clean it. Once it was determined which stone had to be replaced, the contract was modified to pay for the cost of the replacement stone. The same held true for repairs to the substrate in the areas to be plastered.

For instance, we gave Jean the required submittal on how to remove the Kasota Stone. We gave her drawings of each piece of stone, showing match marks and dimensions. Everyone knew that the stone was very fragile. Our submittal simply stated that we would remove the stone in the reverse order that it was installed. (Remember, the very best masons were being used on this project, and had many years of experience installing and uninstalling this type of work.) She had all kinds of concerns: How were we going to protect the work? How were we going to protect the stone? How were we going to transport it?

Regarding transport, there was a clause in the specifications stating that some of the stone would be removed and transported and repaired at the OPRD warehouse, which was located three miles down the road.

The idea was to get it out of the way so that the other repairs could be made in the rotunda. These are some of the dumb things that get written into the specs by design personnel who have absolutely no idea of what it takes to get the job done. LHK, Inc. was the Prime Contractor and Pioneer was the Sub. When we bid the job, it was with the idea to take what's given and help each other make it go. It took considerable time for Pioneer and LHK to convince Jean that the stone should be taken down a few pieces at a time, repaired and replaced using the fewest moves possible to minimize the chances of damage to the stone. After much arguing, Pioneer finally got Jean to agree.

In the meantime, Al Lajimodiere informed us that the building, including the stone, had to be updated to 1997 Uniform Building Code, which included seismic upgrading. This meant that OPRD had to hire an engineer to design the upgrades for the stone. This took a couple of months.

When Jean learned about the upgrade, she wanted us to stop work until the design was complete. Tom Crawford, the owner of Pioneer, said to Doug and me, "Pioneer has work in other places. If we leave here, we may not be able to get back for two or three months."

I didn't want this to happen. It would have put us way behind schedule and increased costs by many thousands of dollars. At our own risk, we decided to hang the vertical stone. Tom's friend was the designer for OPRD, at KPFF Engineering, and told Tom which fastening system would be specified.

Shortly after we began taking the stone down, it became obvious that the only stones that were damaged or missing were on the faces of the stairways and next to the doorways. We asked Jean to determine which of the panels she wanted repaired or replaced. Jean, the engineer-in-training, on her own, determined which panels she wanted replaced. The specs called for any replacement stones to be 'in kind'. Jean never could get it through her head that there was no 'in kind' stone available.

Our supplier informed Pioneer, as he had informed the designers before the contract was bid, that the stone *available* was from a different part of the quarry and of a much lower grade than the 1916 stone. The resulting situation caused an argument that would last for thirteen months.

Pioneer ordered the replacement stone per Jean's list. The supplier advised Pioneer to order ten times the amount needed and expect a 100% breakage. It turned out that he was 100% correct.

Once the paint was removed from the stone, we were able to see that 300 pieces of stone had no cracks, and that 16 pieces near the doors and stairways were cracked, broken or missing. The question was: what caused this stone to fail? I decided to go by the old rule "if something doesn't work, something must be wrong."

I started researching, and discovered by reading the Vista House Historic Structure Report that the original cladding specified for the building was Vermont Marble, a much stronger material than Kasota Stone. *(It should be noted here that during the original construction, in order to save money, Kasota Stone was substituted for the Vermont Marble.)* If the Vermont Marble had been used as originally specified, the work we were doing would probably not have been necessary. The trade practice up until 1916 and continued to this day, requires that any panel be a minimum of 7/8″ thick. That meant that the recessed panels (Vermont Marble) specified for this project would have had to be 1-1/8″ thick. Eureka! The reason the Kasota Stones with recessed panels next to the doors failed was because they were only 5/8″ thick, and therefore structurally unsound when installed. This was the same for the panels on the stairway.

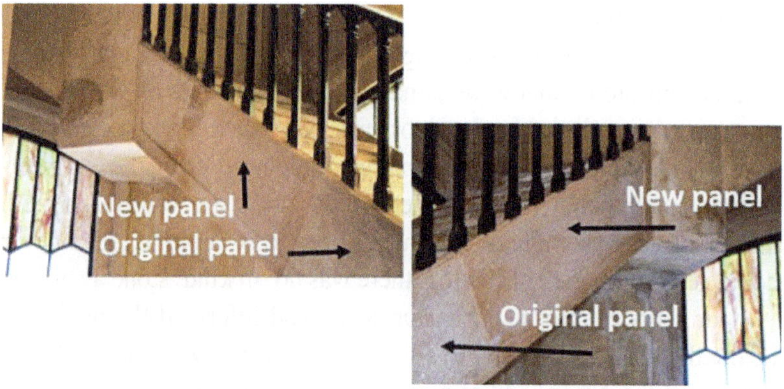

Both East and West stairways show the light patina of 84-year-old Kasota Stone panels in comparison to the new, raw stone.

2010 demolition at the top of the stairway caused more cracks, further indicating that this panel was defective when originally installed.

Doug suggested to Jean that there was Vermont Marble available that could be used to replace the damaged recessed panels on the stairway face. As we expected, there was no response.

Vermont Marble, green in color, would contrast nicely with the Kasota Stone and compliment the greenish colors of the art glass windows and the roof tile on the dome, while keeping it historically accurate.

Doug, our project manager, Pioneer Waterproofing, Mankato Stone, Geo Loop Tec, The Heating Specialists, Devco Mechanical, Heil Electric and others wrote many letters explaining how the work had to be done. Most of these problems, in one way or the other, related to the replacement of the broken Kasota Stone.

The following is an example of the kind of responses we received while arguing about rejected stone pieces:

October 6, 2004

...At this time you have two options:
1) You may install the unbroken rejected piece
2) You can replace the unbroken rejected piece

If you choose to install the rejected piece and it is determined by OPRD, Zaik/Miller & Associates or the representative from SHPO to be unacceptable, you will be responsible for removing the unaccepted piece and replacing it at your expense.

Sincerely,

Jean M. Castillo, EIT (Engineer-In-Training)
Project Manager

The argument about the Kasota Stone went on for thirteen months delaying monthly payments and contract completion, costing the contractor a lot of time and money—for no good reason.

Upgrading to 1997 Uniform Building Code meant the stone had to be inspected twice, first to ensure the stone was hung right and again when the extra fasteners were added. This doubled the inspection costs. It did not make sense for KPFF's inspector to stand by all day waiting for Pioneer to fasten a panel. Some days no panels were placed, and other days a dozen could be placed. All the KPFF inspector was qualified to do was make sure the correct number of fasteners were installed. Jean wanted to make sure that the authorized inspector actually counted the fasteners, so she decided to have an OPRD inspector watch the KPFF inspector! This myriad of inspectors made the project onerous and the relationship between Jean and LHK more adversarial. We, the prime contractor, technically were the only ones who had contact with Jean and OPRD, even though Pioneer was doing the stonework. The whole process was convoluted.

Jean was there one day when Collin and one of the stone masons were modifying a door in the concession area. She was telling Collin how wide to cut the door opening so that a wider door could be installed. I could see that her measurements were all wrong.

At the same time one of the workers had just installed an Exit sign over the door opening, and a few feet away one of the masons was removing some tile. Jean exclaimed, "I want that sign taken down and replaced with a different type!" She then exclaimed to the mason, "I want that tile replaced with one that matches better."

Everyone was able to hear what she was saying, including me. I said (in a loud voice that everyone could hear), "You guys keep doing as you were directed. If Jean wants anything done differently, she can write a change order." This did not improve our relationship.

The following is the continuation of the letter dated October 8, 2004, from LHK to Jean Castillo, summarizing the Kasota Stone repair and replacement problems:

LHK, Inc. has discovered that the original flat-panel limestone of sixteen wall locations and six stairway actions is/was defective. The specified thickness was 7/8". The panels installed were only 5/8" thick.

The result is fourteen of the twenty-two panels cracked or broke. There were approximately 350 flat-panel limestone pieces 7/8" thick. Of those, two pieces have one crack each. All of the rest of these panels are sound and have stood the test of time.

Approximately 64% of the original 5/8" thick panels have failed. The specs state to replace in-kind. It has been discovered that the limestone available today is of a much lower grade. Simply put, there is no in-kind material available. Even if there were, panels only 5/8" thick would still be defective.

On September 14, 2004, I called the CO in an effort to resolve the situation. On September 16, 2004, the CO replied, stating the material is rejected and there will be no discussion. On September 28, 2004, LHK, Inc. sent a letter putting OPRD on notice (that there is no limestone durable enough to meet construction requirements).

The project manager and architect have refused to discuss the situation; therefore, I am requesting OPRD to pay for the limestone replacement change order in full. The contractor has done all work required by the defective specifications. The defective specifications were conceived when the original 1917 panels were cut too thin, 5/8", as opposed to the specified 7/8" thick panels, and have matured into an impossible specification in 2004.

As discussion are closed, please reply via e-mail by Monday, October 11, 2004, so that the mason contractor can de-mobilize in preparation of final cleanup of project.

Respectfully yours,

Lloyd H. Kessler
President

A SURPRISE!

Towards the very end of the Phase I of the project, we received an email from Jean dated July 13, 2004, at 4:40 p.m. "We are getting ready for company." The Friends of Vista House planned to host a party for donors the following week. Jean's email included a list of tasks that needed to be completed before the party. Both Pioneer and LHK Inc. protested vehemently. We were only *ten days away* from having all the stonework done in the rotunda. Unfortunately, now we had to burn six of our ten days removing the scaffolding and doing other work. At first, Pioneer's Tom Crawford and I told Jean we would not comply, but we relented—for the cause, since The Friends had worked long and hard to raise the funds to help pay for the project. Since scaffolding took up the whole inside of the rotunda, it took a full day to remove tools, supplies and equipment from it, and another full day to take it down. Pioneer had to lay off six of their masons, and much of the work had to be done out of sequence. By doing some work on Saturday and Sunday, we were able to get everything on Jean's list done by the 21st. The next two days were spent cleaning and stocking for the "Big Shebang," as Doug put it.

Scaffolding built to access entire surface area of rotunda; tools and supplies placed at levels where they were to be used.

The party was a great success. Everyone was very impressed and pleased with quality and beauty of the restoration.

We were still optimistic that we could get the work completed by the end of July. However, an unscheduled demobilization at a time when the work is nearly complete would severely disrupt and delay any project. Re-mobilization was challenging enough as it was, as we now had to install scaffolding in such a way as not to damage the newly-polished floors. This forced us to do the work in bits and pieces and we could only work one or two men at a time. As referenced by the dates in the letter above, this added two and a half months and much cost to the project.

And then, there was this issue with the clock:

The story of the clock: The clock had been installed in later years. The specs required us to remove it from the building. Jean spotted it and decided to have it repaired and reinstalled. Toward the end of our contract we took it down for safety reasons and stored it in our shop. A few days later Jean noticed it was missing. She asked Doug where it was and Doug told her, "It's ours and we're not giving it back." (Doug had become fully frustrated with Jean's management skills.) Jean called the CO, who ordered us to return the clock the next day or she would call law enforcement. I told her we'd have to clean it up again, but that it would take a few days. As you can see, we put it back.

Phase II of the Second Contract on Vista House

Before Phase I was complete we were awarded Phase II, a mechanical contract. *That should have been done first, before the marble restoration, as parts of the marble restoration could not be done until after the mechanical was complete.*

As in Phase I, we were having the same types of arguments with Jean about the intent of the plans and specifications. The insulation problem was still up in the air, as was the ongoing argument about the low-grade Kasota Stone.

We sub-contracted the geothermal heating and air conditioning system to the Seattle firm Geo Loop Tec. The plans showed one of the 500-foot bores on the east side of the Vista House access tunnel, and the other one on the west side. It was very important that these wells be separated by a minimum distance. The problem was that it was impossible to get the required piping from the east side of the tunnel to the mechanical room. This should have been obvious to the designer. After much negotiating, Steve Snorsky of Geo Loop Tec was finally able to convince the engineer that we could get the proper separation by drilling both wells on the west side of the tunnel. This took two weeks of arguing, but just two days to do the work drilling the wells and installing the piping.

Several months later, after the other items listed above were completed, our HVAC subcontractor, The Heating Specialist, completed the heating system. Everything went as planned—except The Heating Specialist was unable to balance the system. The design engineer, who was based in Eugene, Oregon, had not allowed for the two open stairways that led from the basement to the main floor. Apparently, OPRD and the architect had not provided the designer all the necessary information. The designer had never been on site. If he had been, the open stairways would have been obvious.

Again, after much arguing, we sealed the open stairways and the engineer responsible for checking the balance signed off. Once the stairways were re-opened, the warm air escaped and rose to the top of the rotunda, as we expected. This caused the heating equipment to work much harder and shortened its life span from twenty to ten years.

Installation of geothermal wells.

■ ■ ■

Phase III consisted of additional interior work consisting of fabrication and installation of interpretive exhibits and signage for the upper and lower levels.

We had the usual arguments with Jean. And as usual, Jean wanted to make changes. Most were minor, and agreed to soon enough that they fit the interpretive vendor's (PPI, Inc.) schedule and did not affect the cost. Fortunately, PPI was easy to work with.

■ ■ ■

Conclusion of Vista House and other OPRD contract work

At this same time, many OPRD workers were taking advantage of Public Employees Retirement System's (PERS) generous early retirement benefits. Henry Kunowski, who had been job captain on the first Vista House contract, was one of them. The more experienced they were, the more likely they were to leave. Inexperienced people like Jean replaced them. However, even if Jean had been qualified, there was no one to support her.

Having worked with numerous government agencies over 33 years, the final stages of Vista House mark the most exasperating experiences LHK, Inc. encountered. Most of the problems stemmed from the fact that OPRD failed to follow their own guidelines, lacked leadership *(had no Job Captain!)*, and had little knowledge of building construction and engineering. Oregon Department of Administrative Services, who directs all state contracts and makes payments (except for ODOT contracts), is separate from OPRD, and adds yet another layer of difficulty to the bureaucratic process.

It's interesting that despite all the fuss about preserving the historical fabric, that the "historical architects" changed things as they saw fit. Example: all of the metal windows and door frames were originally painted a grass green color. The stairway guard rails and balusters' original color was verde, but for some reason, the architect could not resist painting all the metal black. It's not hard to visualize how much more beautiful the building would look if it were trimmed in the original green.

They also covered the "No Dogs Allowed" sign at the base of the north door with black metal.

Some of the art glass in the upper windows are original. The original architect was probably trying to show the early sunrise and sunset colors, and probably the blue color of the Columbia River. The replacement art glass for the other windows is not nearly the quality or beauty of the original glass.

Finally, we were paid for all of the deficiencies claimed by Jean in our bid when she denied our bid for Phase 4 of Vista House. We were paid $157,442 in August 25th, 2005. This seemed a small amount for our pain and aggravation.

The Vista House refurbishment was unique, requiring special skills. The structure itself, the location, the history and the refurbishing of Vista House made this a one-of-a-kind project. Everyone was proud of the end results. On Jan. 22, 2004, LHK, Inc. received the Hammurabi

Award for Meritorious Achievement in Craftsmanship from the Masonry and Ceramic Tile Institute of Oregon for our work.

Vista House today.

CHAPTER 41

2003
CAPE MEARES LIGHTHOUSE REPAIR AND REHABILITATION PROJECT
(near Tillamook, Oregon)

Oregon Parks and Recreation Department
Bid date: Dec.12, 2002
Base Bid: $289,400 plus alternates of $38,700
Engineer's estimate: $250,000 for all items
Change Order for Painting: $67,000
Change Order for Window Repairs: $19,229
Final Contract Amount: $361,936.90

Refurbished Cape Meares Lighthouse.

The engineer's estimate was low, as usual, and the State did not have enough money to do the job. Jean Castillo, OPRD's Project Manager, requested that we revise our bid.

Doug Kessler, LHK Inc.'s Project Manager, re-figured the bid. He notified Jean in a letter, pointing out the "savings of $34,000, about 57% of which resulted from costs cuts, and 43% from contract deletions."

The contract was finally awarded in March, 2003. A notice to proceed was given in April.

Prior to the bid opening, a mandatory pre-bid conference was held. A large portion of this job was sand blasting and painting the surfaces of the lighthouse. There were several painting contractors at the meeting, and their first question was, "Is there any lead paint on the project?"

OPRD's reply was, "No. There is no lead paint on the lighthouse. It has been recently sandblasted and re-painted, and the long-standing prohibition against the use of lead-based paint would have precluded its use in the painting."

One of the painting contractors pointed out a small metal cupboard that appeared to have a (red) lead oxide finish in its interior. As a result, OPRD issued an addendum to the contract, requiring a per-square-foot unit price for lead removal from the cabinet.

Deck lights.

These deck lights were originally specified to be clear because they were directly above the stairway. We made them opaque to give those climbing the stairs a little "privacy."

Lantern clockworks gears before and after polishing.

After the work started in early April, our painting subcontractor removed the deck lights and took them to his shop in Portland to prepare them for installation of new glass and new paint. They discovered the paint contained lead. We immediately notified Jean Castillo. She hired an independent engineering firm to test the paint at the lighthouse. They found that all the painted surfaces contained lead. Unfortunately, the presence of lead-based paint on the exterior of the structure reflected a condition not included in the original scope of the contract.

Our attorney, Jan Sokol, wrote to Jean, "Obviously, Kessler needs guidance from you *immediately*, to avoid further cost and schedule impacts. The painting and coating are now the next phases of work on the critical path. Many work items that could have been done prior to or concurrently with the coatings have necessarily been deferred. Kessler very much wants and needs to resume work on all phases, but feels it cannot do so without agreements on contract price and contract time extension. Accordingly, Kessler looks forward to your immediate response."

And furthermore, we informed Jean that we needed a precisely engineered specification for doing the lead removal. National code demanded the entire lighthouse be encapsulated with plastic sheeting.

Security motor home for site.

Scaffolding around lighthouse—If damaged or broken, replacing the lens inside the would now cost $2 to $3 million. Six years later on January 10, 2010, two drunk punks shot holes through the glass and lens.

This forced us to shut down until the lead paint removal plan was engineered. During the shutdown, we hired Gary Hermiston and his motor home to watch the job until we could resume work.

Finally, after much hassle, we came to terms regarding the cost of removing the lead paint. The actual cost was $67,000 or roughly 24% of the original contract price.

We soon discovered a second, serious engineering problem. One of the contract items was to remove, clean and reinstall the exterior glazing (windows). Our subcontractor for this item was Morehouse Glass of Portland, a long-established, reputable firm. Shortly after we signed a subcontract agreement with them, they sold their firm. This concerned me, but I was assured that they would have the same mechanics do the glazing work. The specifications explicitly stated that once the windows were reinstalled, they were to be water-tested. As the prime contractor, we made all of the testing equipment available to Morehouse, including the water. I went over the testing specifications with Morehouse's foreman and he assured me that he would do the testing. Our crew left and went back to our ongoing work at the Vista House.

At the end of the month, Morehouse notified us that the windows were installed and presented us with a $16,000 invoice. We paid $11,000 and notified Morehouse that the balance would be forthcoming upon final acceptance. This made Morehouse very unhappy as they thought they were 100% complete. In the meantime, the lead paint change order work was being done. Once done, for safety reasons, we removed the plastic sheeting. We then notified Jean that the windows were ready for inspection. She showed up at noon on a Wednesday, about the same time as a sou'wester. Some of the windows leaked.

Had Morehouse tested the windows at the time of installation, repairs could have been made prior to the start of the rainy season.

Newly polished astragals on the lighthouse.

We contacted Morehouse and told them to fix the leaks. They were not very cooperative, but they sent two men down the next day. I sent them home after about four hours as it was obvious that they didn't know what they were doing. That left Collin and Doug to determine what was causing the leaks. They soon discovered a design flaw. The engineer had failed to provide for sealing the gaps where the astragals (bronze frames) butted together. We notified WJE (the engineer hired for the project), who sent their designer to the job site. He agreed with them and rewrote the specs accordingly. Doug and Collin painstakingly sealed the gaps. Doug even used a hypodermic needle to seal the tiniest gaps. We, along with OPRD, monitored the lighthouse throughout the winter. After a hard storm, water would be found in the lantern room and in the basement. We finally discovered two bolts had been left out in the area above the windows. Once we replaced the bolts, there were no more leaks. The cost of correcting the original design error and sealing the windows properly more than doubled the cost of the window repair.

The Friends of Cape Meares Lighthouse, who do a great job running tours, concessions and a gift shop, lost the entire tourist season because of the lead paint and leaky windows due to the poor performance of OPRD's engineers and architects.

Lloyd standing next to the lantern room astragals, smiling because the windows are no longer leaking.

As was the case in the Vista House project, the owner again benefitted from the contractor's ingenuity, only to be punished by the owner stating that we weren't qualified when we bid the next job for Jean and the OPRD. My son Doug summed this up in a letter about the lead abatement argument with OPRD to our attorney below on July 2, 2003 (about the same time this job was scheduled to have been completed and ready for the tourist season):

Contracting climate: The increasing change from 'low-bid' to negotiated contracts has forced us to consider each agency as a long-term partner. We have found good relationships with these agencies to be of considerable value, and bad relationships a tremendous liability. We have lost years' worth of contracts from casual remarks from agency representatives who regard changed conditions as a personal affront on the part of the contractor...Being diplomatic enough to convince an agency we're acting in [their] best interest is something [we] have to work at constantly.

CHAPTER 42

2005
LONGMIRE BRIDGE, and other Minor Bridge Repairs
US Department of the Interior
National Park Service
Mt. Rainier National Park
Contract Amount: $296,847

This job bid on March 18, 2005, and was awarded on April 14, 2005.

The *major* item of work on this contract was replacing the deteriorated towers on the Longmire suspension bridge. It is next to the National Park Inn in Longmire, Washington, the main gateway to the Mt. Rainier National Park. The original bridge was built in 1923, and the support towers were replaced in the 1950's.

The challenge was designing a support system to hold up the suspension cables while the wooden towers were being removed and replaced. We hired John W. Parkin, Consulting Engineer, to design the system. He calculated that we would need to lift the suspension cable a minimum of four inches in order to install the top timbers. Doug built an exact scale model to prove Parkin's calculations, and we were convinced that his design would work.

Scale model of new tower.

The red dots on the scale model indicate the steel "false work." The green dots show the suspension cable.

Temporary steel support structure.

Jack in place, holding up suspension saddle and cable.

Orange-colored jacks support the suspension bridge cables, which were jacked up four inches above the top timber. This allowed enough room to slide the old timber out and guaranteed enough room to slide a new timber in.

My grandson Collin—installing top timber for new tower
Monica is supervising.

We took the old towers down and were ready to install the new ones that were scheduled to be delivered at the end of the week. Unfortunately, the treating plant broke down and the timbers did not arrive until a month later.

The contract required that the bridge be kept open so that Longmire employees could access the old bunkhouse lodge on the far side of the river. The problem was that the false work had cross-braces that prevented vehicles from crossing the bridge. Another problem was that I needed to be able to access the far side of the river, as it was much closer to the town of Packwood, where we were staying.

I explained the situation to the Longmire resident engineer, and told him that if we modified the cross braces, there would be room for a vehicle to pass. We agreed to keep the gates locked on both sides of the bridge except when we needed to cross. He said, "I only have one man who needs to get across the bridge on a daily basis. The rest of those girls can get along just fine without daily meetings."

Once the timber arrived, it took us two days to complete the north tower. We moved to the south side of the bridge and were able to complete the job in seven days.

While waiting for the timbers, we moved to the Kautz Creek Bridge site, about ten miles west of Longmire. The main work there was filling the area behind the west concrete retaining wall with concrete. This required boring two 6-inch holes into the bridge deck to pour through.

The only source of concrete for this project was Andy Noel Construction in Morton, Washington. Andy ran a good operation. The day we poured concrete, we needed four truckloads. Andy only had two trucks, which meant that each truck would have to make two rounds. The trucks were scheduled to arrive 30 minutes apart, but they both showed up at the same time, a half hour early. I was sitting in my pickup finalizing the paperwork so it would be ready before the inspector arrived.

There was a steep grade a short distance before the bridge. The concrete truck stopped there, as traffic was backed up. For some unknown reason, the driver began adding water to the concrete. Concrete started spilling out of the back of the truck onto the pavement. Traffic cleared and the truck pulled up to the bridge; Collin started pouring. I had not wanted to start the pour until the inspector arrived. I told Collin to stop pouring, I saw that the concrete was nothing but soup and was running through the riprap and into the creek. I had the driver pull the truck to one side so that the concrete in the bowl would set up. An hour later the driver said to me, "The truck's almost empty." This was news to me.

Exasperated, I muttered, "Get going." We had wasted considerable time and money.

The concrete retaining wall was supposed to stop the concrete, but it was undermined, letting the concrete run under it, through the riprap and into the creek. By the time the inspector arrived, I had already decided not to say anything. I did show him that the retaining wall was undermined and that it was going to take several extra loads of concrete. I wasn't very happy with Andy Noel at the time, but we got enough money for the additional concrete to make both of us happy.

Upon completing Kautz Creek Bridge we moved to Laughing Water Creek Bridge, a few miles north of Highway 12 on Highway 123, and about thirty miles from the town of Packwood.

The work at Laughing Water Creek Bridge required jacking up the uphill end of the bridge a couple of inches and installing elastomeric pads under the ends of the steel bridge stringers. Our plan for doing this was to lay heavy timbers on the ground and place hydraulic jacks on top of them in order to raise the bridge. We unloaded the timbers at the end of the shift and drug four of them under the bridge before it got dark. Just after daylight the next morning when we arrived at the bridge site, we found the rest of the timbers had been stolen. I left Collin and Mike at the site and set off to see if I could find some more timber. At noon when I returned, Collin said, "We don't need any more timber. Everything's done." I didn't believe him. He explained that he set the jacks under one of the stringers and decided to test it. The whole bridge came up. He and Mike quickly installed the pads under the stringers and let the bridge back down. Due to Collin's decision-making ability, he did in a few hours work that we estimated would have taken at least three days. However, I did chew him out for bending up the $100 steel plate he set the jacks on!

The only problem with this was that we had not put the road closure date on the traffic control signs that the bridge was going to be raised. In order to get paid for the signs, we had to pretend that the work hadn't been done. We rushed around to date the signs: I went one direction and Collin went the other to the many different locations scattered around Mt. Rainier, about 200 miles of roadway.

A day later we called for inspection on the bearing pads. The inspector was late in arriving, and of course, by the time he got there the work was done. We got paid on time for all items!

Next we loaded up our tools and headed for the Backbone Ridge Viaduct, which is about five miles west of Highway 123, near the east entrance to Mt. Rainier National Park. The purpose of the work was to seal the expansion joints on Piers 2, 5 and 8, so water would drain off the bridge instead of running through the joints and onto the steel below, causing rust and also eroding the soil beneath the viaduct.

This required sawing through the pavement, which the plans showed as being two inches thick. As it turned out, the pavement was a foot thick. We attempted to do the sawing with our hand tools—but were forced to bring in a concrete cutting company. We planned on doing the work in two days, with one mobilization. It took three separate “mobes” (mobilizations) to get the work done. The total time was six days, but due to the changed condition the Federal Highway paid us for the four extra days. We continued on to Longmire and set the new suspension bridge towers, which completed the project.

We had learned early on that inspectors are seldom on time. Our schedule usually showed us starting work at 8 a.m. If we had daylight, we started at 6; otherwise, at 7. This gave us three or four hours to work without being pestered by inspectors. We normally accomplished 75% of the day’s work in the first four hours. Whatever minor adjustments were needed, we made. By the time the inspector arrived, the work was done, and we didn’t have to do a lot of explaining.

Despite delays that were beyond our control, we were able to take advantage of unexpected opportunities (as at Laughing Water Creek Bridge), had a great rapport with the DOT, made a nifty profit, and had a lot of fun.

The moral of this story is: *the further you stay ahead of the inspector, the better the work goes, and the more fun you have doing it.*

CHAPTER 43

2006
PARKWAY TERRACE SUBDIVISION
Battle Ground, Washington

This story actually began in 1978. My son-in-law owned a carpet business in Battle Ground, called Rick Adam's Floors and More. He lived in Vancouver, but was looking for a home closer to the store. A twenty-acre dairy property was being sold off. The north ten acres of the property had recently been sold and divided into eight 1¼ -acre lots upon which eight single-story houses were being built. The other ten acres were divided into two 5-acre tracts, each with a single family residence. I bought the north five for $65,000, contingent upon survey, which revealed that there were actually 5-1/2 acres, caused by a 100-foot error made when the section was originally established. I sold the house and one half-acre to my daughter and son-in-law for $25,000, which left me with five acres. I borrowed the remaining $40,000 from Northwest Bank, repaying it with five annual payments of $10,000. At the time, I considered this an opportunity to help Maxine and Rick, and considered the investment a hedge against inflation.

Ken and Judy Cobb bought the other five acres. The house on this property was the original home place.

I paid little attention to the property over the next 28 years or so, but I did remove the main barn and did weed control. I also let the Cobbs and others graze their cows and horses on the property, which also helped to control the weeds.

One Saturday in early January, 2006, Ken Cobb called me and asked, "Can you come to a meeting at my house at 10 a.m. tomorrow morning, Sunday?" He explained that two guys from a land developing company were interested in buying our properties.

The next morning Cobb introduced me to them. They were happy I was there, and said they would also need my property to make their project work. They thought each five-acre tract was worth a million dollars plus. They offered each of us a non-refundable $50,000 retainer so they could do due diligence, and making sure they could get proper approvals from the City of Battle Ground and other government entities. They said, "Think it over, and we will call you back next Friday."

They called back on Friday and I told them I needed another week.

In the meantime, I had conversations with Eric Holmes and Robert Maule who were with the Battle Ground Building Department. They assured me and my engineer, Norm Harker, that if we met all the requirements for our proposed 52 lot plat. We could start construction by June 1, 2006.

I decided to go ahead. I didn't realize at first, that the City of Battle Ground was being completely reorganized. The city engineer left, and so did his assistant. Remaining were Mark Herceg and Robert Maule, who were really not qualified, to check and approve our proposal. To make matters worse, the information the city gave us regarding the location of existing water and sewer were erroneous. One example is that they informed us that the water line was privately owned and ran up North Parkway Avenue past the west end of our project. It took us a while to learn that there had never been a water line in this area.

As the west end of the subdivision was the highest point, and the east end the lowest, we designed the sewer line to fit the natural lay of the land. We presented this plan to the city engineer, who only then informed us that the sewer line had already designed and approved to run east along the proposed extension of Onsdorff Avenue, and that we could connect to it. He said, "As soon as you pay for the permits, you can start work."

Digging to connect into existing sewer manhole on North Parkway.

We started work at Manhole #2 as we wanted to get across the lowlands while the ground was still dry. (Manhole #1 was in the center of North Parkway and was a major operation that was going to require removal of rock and water. This work could be done in any weather.)

We hired Lawson Engineering to do the construction staking. The grade on the sewer was at the absolute minimum: .15 % (1-3/4" per hundred feet). It was very critical that Manhole #2 be set to the exact grade so that we had the proper fall in Manhole #1 when it came time to construct it. I explained to the survey crew how critical this was. They replied, "We know what we're doing. We've staked a lot of other sewer lines." They proceeded to set the grades electronically. This method was simply not precise enough to meet the tolerances required to control this work.

I asked them if they had checked the grades using a differential level. They said, "No. It wasn't necessary." I called their boss and told him to bill me for the services to date, as I no longer needed their services.

I then hired Kyle Feeder, owner of KPF Surveying to check Lawson's layout. This was a wise decision, as Lawson had an adverse grade between Manhole #2 and Manhole #1.

Kyle did all the staking for the sewer, streets, roads and utilities and plat-work for the entire project.

We completed the sewer work from Manhole #2 up to the point on the plat where we were stopped by rock.

It was now time to install Manhole #1 and connect into the existing manhole, which was 20 feet deep. Ken Piper and I gave Doug and Mike Waterfield Jr. explicit instructions on how to make the connection, as Kenny and I were scheduled to go pheasant hunting in South Dakota.

Junior (Mike Waterfield) signaling crew at beginning of excavation into existing manhole at North Parkway.

As the crew attempted to excavate the existing manhole, they encountered solid rock less than four feet from the manhole face. They'd expected to find rock, but not so close to the manhole. The crew had to attach the breaker to the EX200 and break on down to subgrade. When they got within five feet, a surge of water poured into the excavation from the gravel backfill of the existing sewer line. The crew immediately dropped the suction hoses from our pumps into the water.

The problem was that there was too much head for this type of pump. The worst part of this was that, unbeknownst to Doug, we had three submersible pumps stored in our shop!

Breaking rock for sewer line, heading east on proposed Onsdorff Blvd. toward Manhole #2.

Doug immediately called PACO for a pump, and it took about two hours for it to get there. In the meantime, Junior had put the pumps in the bucket of the excavator and lowered them down into the hole, and was able to pump the water out. They then excavated enough rock to install a section of shoring. This allowed them to core into the existing manhole and connect the eight inch sewer line. In all, it took over a week to install Manhole #1 and make the connections to Manhole #2.

The rent for the PACO pumps we did not use was only $4,000.

By October, we had the off-site sewer completed, and the on-site sewer installed to the point where we hit rock. I then contracted with McCallum Rock Drilling to drill and blast the rock for both the sanitary sewer and the storm sewer. All other work was shut down for the winter.

Setting trench box heading east on proposed Onsdorff Blvd.

We continued the sewer line about 300 feet into the plat, at which point we encountered solid rock.

Monica monitors drill holes.

Tarpaper cones mark each drill hole. Operator is drilling for side sewer.

Breaking rock at west end of subdivision; installing storm drain.

We had not planned to do the off-site work until after the plat was developed. However, because the Battle Ground engineers did not approve our plans by June of 2006, as promised, we had to pay we had to pay interest on money for work that normally would not be done until after plat acceptance.

When we started the project, the economy was booming and all the best workers were busy. Ken Piper was superintendent for Ostrander Construction at the time, and the company was in a temporary lull. Ostrander loaned me their crew to do the off-site sewer. The off-site work went well and we continued digging on-site until stopped by the rock.

As previously stated, I called Don Bradshaw at McCallum Rock Drilling, and we made a plan for drilling and blasting. Don's idea was to drill through the over-burden to the top of the rock, and on down to three feet below subgrade. The depth of rock for each hole was recorded, and the information used to determine the amount of explosives needed. I had used this method myself on other jobs, so I knew it would work.

Before any blasting was allowed, we were required to retain a licensed firm to do a pre-blast survey of all buildings within 300 feet of any blast.

The western 200 feet of the project was less than 300 feet from the houses on the west side of North Parkway. We used a breaker mounted on a 60,000 lb. excavator to remove the rock in this area. This is time-consuming and very costly.

We dug the retention pond. The outlet for it had not yet been designed, so when it filled with water, we snuck in and pumped it onto the church's grassy field. The grass didn't mind and no one else noticed.

Sacred Heart Church's south property line was the center line of the proposed extension of Onsdorff Blvd. The designers had intended for the sewer to be built on the church's half. This required us to get an easement from them, a long and drawn-out process. At this time, Osprey Homes had a three-phase development on the south side. They were eager to have the sewer line in. When they learned that we would pay for it, they were happy to give us the easement that allowed us to get started immediately, even though it did require us to dig an extra fifteen feet of rock trench on North Parkway. A couple of weeks later the church gave us an easement to cross the east end of their property.

McCallum started the drilling operation. When the drilling and blasting was completed, we excavated and installed the sewer line and other utilities. When we blasted, the rock near the bottom of the trench broke into small enough pieces to run through the rock crusher. The rock above did not fracture, and remained in its native state, separated by tiny fissures caused by the cooling of the lava that came from Battleground Lake caldera. These rocks were so large that we had to use a Hitachi EX400LC, a 100,000 lb. excavator, to move them. The largest of these rocks we used to build a rock wall along the west and south sides of the subdivision; some were used for retaining walls, and many were sold to landscapers. The remainder were crushed and used as base rock for the subdivision roads. What wasn't used was sold and hauled away.

This boulder was dropped in by the Missoula Flood 10,000 years ago. It was too big to move, so we buried it on the corner of Lot 13 and used the top portion as a landscape feature.

These two boulders were also used as landscape features.

Crushing rock.

Monica directing rock-crushing; yellow crusher in background breaks boulders into 4-inch minus; the blue crusher then breaks 4-inch minus into 1-1/4-inch minus.

Stockpiling crushed rock.

Rock wall at Parkway Terrace entrance.

Parkway Terrace's only entrance and exit—North Parkway and NE 17th Street

Rock retaining wall at Lot #33.

Looking east along NE 17th Street.

Entry.

Lot #1—South property line wall in background.

Once the subdivision was complete, it was time to record the plat. What should normally take a few days took seven months. Prior to the time this property was annexed, the Clark County engineers' Master Plan designed the street system so that NE 3rd would extend onto the Catholic Church's property. There were also two trails, between lots 5 and 6, and lots 15 and 16, that exited onto the church's property. The church did not want public access onto their property. But, they did want a water line and fire hydrant for their future temporary classroom.

We installed the fire hydrant and water line as the church requested, but the church would not sign off on the required easement, even though the City no longer required us to build that section of NE 3rd Avenue. They called it 'Tract B', maintaining it for utility easements only, and left the trails as designed. I finally threatened to sue to prod the Church into signing off.

About the water lines: The nearest source of water for the project was an existing pipeline at the intersection of NW 2nd Avenue and Onsdorff, a distance of 462 feet west of Parkway. The complication here was that the route of the pipeline conflicted with off-site sewer line Manhole #1, which had been moved 15 feet farther south than originally planned, in order to stay on Osprey Homes' side of the Onsdorff extension. This required zig-zagging around sewer manhole #1. As this work had to be done in a trench from which the rock had already been excavated, I had our superintendent Jack Trimbo pre-assemble the zig-zag above ground so that it could be installed in one piece. The installation went well until we pressure-tested, which indicated there was a minor leak.

We called in an expert who attempted to sonically locate the leak. The problem was there was so much noise that we could not find the leak. I directed Jack to go back to the beginning and check each section of pipe all the way up to the manhole. Jack protested, saying, "You know we've already paved over the pipe." He thought we should spot check.

I learned long ago that leaks are seldom found where you think they should be, so I told him to start at the beginning and check each joint and to make sure all the bolts had the proper tension. Everything was good up to the zig-zag. When testing it, we found the two bottom bolts had not been installed. Once the bolts were installed, the line tested perfectly.

As explained above, we installed the line for the temporary classroom. To do this, we had to tunnel under the rock wall and do a 90 degree turn to the east and then continue several lengths of pipe. And then we did a 90 degree turn to the south in order to connect to the fire hydrant. We did our preliminary test and there was a leak. Jack convinced me it was underneath NE 17th Street, which had already been paved. I didn't think so. I had him go back and check all the joints that we had just installed. It still leaked.

We cut across the new pavement and tested all those joints, all of which tested good. I told Jack to dig up the whole line, joint by joint and put it back together again. When digging up the first 90 degree bend, by the rock wall, we discovered that the two bottom bolts were loose. Who can you trust?! *You would think we would have learned our lesson.*

A note of interest: When constructing the trail next to Lot #33, we encountered rock. We drilled holes and filled them with Dexpan, an expansion agent used for breaking concrete or rock. It takes several hours for this material to expand enough to crack the rock. In this case, it was overnight. About noon, I was looking at the layout, and there were no cracks. Suddenly, there was a loud "pop" and at the same time, a twenty-pound rock went sailing about forty feet in the opposite direction from where I was standing.

I called Dexpan, but they didn't believe me!

Recently completed homes.

Looking west on NE 17th Street from intersection of NE 3rd Avenue.

Two-story, 3,000 sq. ft. custom home.

Handicapped-accessible home; A covered deck was built in lieu of the third bedroom.

I'm 87 and still totally involved in this project, the culmination of many years in the construction business, and a legacy for my family.

Chapter 44

2013
AFTER MILLIE'S MOVE TO HIGHGATE

One day, while looking through a dresser drawer in the spare bedroom, I found a shoebox full of letters that Millie and I wrote back and forth to each other when I was working for BPA in Pasco, Arlington and Enumclaw. We had not looked at those letter for 62 years. I also discovered a diary that Millie started when she was a junior in high school, and kept up until a month before we were married.

Armed with those documents, I received the command from Great Spirit to write this book. I could not have written it without them.

I would read from these letters and diary to Millie every chance I got, in hope that her memory may return. She enjoyed these very much.

On October 9, 2012, as we were sitting in the Hub about 10:30 a.m., I was reading the letters to her when suddenly she said, "That boy (pointing to one of the care givers with long, dark hair) looks like a boy I made love to."

I asked, "After we were married?"

"Yes."

Neither Millie nor I could remember his name at the time. We remembered that he worked for a fish-packing company operating a tender, and had a reputation for being an outstanding navigator. I remembered that I rode with him a time or two, and that he also taught navigation to company employees. I also remembered the address of the trailer court where we lived and the name of the housing project he lived in.

As a result of this recollection, I put an ad in the local newspaper in Mt. Vernon asking for information about anyone who might have remembered him. A few days later, Monte Riley called me to inform me that he had worked with him—and his name was Kenny Childs. I mentioned his name to Millie and she brightened. "Yes, that was his name. His wife's name was Donna. We had a lot of fun when we lived in Anacortes."

During Millie's admission to Highgate, Jeremy Glover, the Communications and Relations Coordinator, explained to me that many people with Alzheimer's could remember things that happened from their early twenties back to their earliest memories. Over the next two years, I was surprised by how few doctors, and even the caregivers in supervisory positions, were aware of this. I certainly found this to be true from my own experience with my beloved Millie. Most of the residents at Highgate were widowed and had no record of their younger years. I was fortunate to spend many pleasant hours with Millie talking about the good times we had in our early years together.

CHAPTER 45

2013
RESCUED!

On Saturday, November 30, I put on my White® Boots and decided to hike up Angel's Rest trail, on Old Columbia River Highway, three miles west of Multnomah Falls. It was the first time I'd been on a hike in over two years. I wasn't sure how far I was going to get. I started hiking at 9 o'clock, and my boots felt really good, like a foot massage. I decided to make it to the Missoula Rock, which is half way. My legs were a little tired, but I decided to keep going. I was doing fairly well but by the time I got to the rock pile, my legs were very tired. As the rock pile is only five minutes from the top, I staggered on up and sat down to rest. It was 11:30. It had taken me 2½ hours to reach the top. It used to take me and hour and twenty minutes up, and an hour down.

I looked at my cell phone and there was a call from Kenny that had come in at 9:30. I noticed that the battery was low on the phone, so I decided not to call him back. I also realized that I was going to have trouble getting back to the trailhead. I did take a couple of pictures just to prove I was there. I had difficulty standing up and knew I was in trouble. I started down. When I got to the rock pile, I engaged in conversation with a hiker who was sitting there. I sat and rested for a few minutes and headed on down to the Missoula Rock.

Once there, I decided to sit on a log and rest. The log up-ended and I landed on my butt. I sat for a few minutes, struggled to my feet, and headed on down to the bridge. I leaned on the bridge railing for a while, giving my legs a chance to rest, then headed on down to the flat above Angel Falls. I sat down on the bank, rested a bit and knew I was going to have trouble going down the rocky area, which is about half a mile from the road. I leaned against the bank several times to rest. The last time, I slid down. My legs had turned to rubber.

At that very moment, three gals stopped to adjust their gear, not knowing I was in distress. I asked them to help me up. They helped me get on my feet. I told them I needed help to make it to the road.

These three good looking women had just met each other last summer on a back-packing tour around Mt. Hood. Nancy, a physical therapist from New York, had come over Thanksgiving to visit the other two, who both lived in Portland. The second gal told me her name several times but I didn't have my hearing aids in so it sounded like "God-ella." She was a hiking tour guide. The third woman also indicated that she had some physical exercise training. They tried to support me by holding onto my arms, but we only made it a few feet. Nancy said, "Put your hands on my shoulders and I'll walk ahead of you."

This worked much better, and we made it quite a ways, but my legs got weak again. I sat and rested for a few minutes, and they helped me back up. They suggested that I use their walking sticks, which worked well as I was able to take weight off my legs. We moved smartly along to the very bottom of the trail. The problem here was that there were four rock steps leading to the road. There was also a dirt detour where people went around the steps. I had my hands on Nancy's shoulders and started down the detour, but slipped and fell on my butt and slid to the bottom.

They got me up and I was able to walk the last hundred feet to the car. The trip down had taken three hours, with the ladies' help. I handed them my business card and asked them to send me an email. Among many hugs and thanks, we said goodbye.

I sat in the car and rested for a few minutes before I started for home. My legs ached, but they worked! When I got home, I was afraid to get into the shower, for fear that my legs would collapse, and I didn't want to get into the tub because I didn't know if I'd be able to get back out, so I flopped on the couch and watched the Oregon/Oregon State football game. After the game, I ate my dinner and went to bed. When I got up Sunday morning, my legs ached but they were strong. I walked around the house for a few minutes and then went for breakfast at the Peach Tree. I felt surprisingly good. I went to church. My legs ached just enough so that I didn't fall asleep during the sermon like I usually do.

After church, Dolores invited me to go with her to the Sons of Norway lodge for 'pancakes.' We drove to her house and parked the car in front, only a block away from the lodge. Breakfast consisted of pancakes, sausage, and scrambled eggs. Very enjoyable, with excellent company.

I said thank you and goodbye to Delores, and headed to Costco for gasoline and groceries. I was surprised at how strong my legs were, and my stride was longer and faster than it had been for many years.

What are the odds of those three ladies finding me at the exact moment I needed them?

CHAPTER 46

EPILOG

After we moved into our lake house in 1956, Millie was completely dedicated to raising the kids. She was PTA President three times, and an honorary life-time member; she sold Avon products, worked at Bemis Bag, and was a teacher's aide who was devoted to helping handicapped children. (She got so involved emotionally that I persuaded her to quit.) She did not believe that married women should fool around. She was as possessive of me as she was before our marriage. She continued to knit my socks and sew my shirts; she cooked excellent meals and kept them warm into the wee hours, and kept the house in order. She was a marvelous wife long after the kids were on their own. She loved to go to the Shakespeare Festival in Ashland, Oregon.

She was always as excited and happy to see me as the dog was when I arrived home from working out of town.

She loved to have her sorority meetings at the house, and was a wonderful hostess for many such gatherings. If any of her sorority sisters asked how Lloyd was doing, Millie wouldn't tell them because she was so protective of us as a unit – since some sisters weren't bashful about asking how things were going with us. (In her mind, there was no reason to broadcast anything that might have been temporarily amiss. She didn't want her sorority sisters to hit on me.)

Neither Millie nor I discussed these events with anyone else. When Millie did mention one of my "sins", the conversation was only one or two short sentences. I said nothing.

Millie liked to brag to her sorority sisters and friends that Lloyd always brought her coffee in bed on Saturday and Sunday mornings before I went hiking. This made them jealous. They would reply, "Our husbands would never bring us coffee in bed!"

She continued to help with our business, making sure the bills were paid. She loved to read and accumulated a large classic library. Since sewing was her #1 hobby and greatest joy, she also spent a lot of time making quilts and clothes for our children and grandchildren. Her sewing room was located so that she could see the shop operations and grounds from her vantage point at the house, as well as keep an eye on the employees.

As a testament to the strength of our marriage, with its ups and downs, in Millie's 2009 Sixtieth Reunion Yearbook (The Alki—from Fort Vancouver High), she wrote this:

Lloyd and I are still married, still healthy, and happy.
He has survived my cooking for sixty-two years!
I'm still involved in my sorority work, and Lloyd has been
developing land. One piece here by Vancouver Lake and
the same in Battle Ground. I'm looking forward to
our class reunion. Hope to see you there.

As life goes by, Millie passed away from pneumonia on July 3, 2014, after her five-year battle with Alzheimer's. Our son Doug wrote her eulogy, and we reprint it here in her memory:

Millie was born in Deer River Minnesota to hard-working parents, but grew up in Butte, Montana, and moved to Vancouver in 1945 at the age of 14, to a neighborhood where many were related, a loose-knit but extended family, living on small acreages where self-sufficiency was the order of the day.

In high school she met Lloyd Kessler, who affectionately describes her as a bit wild. "We were both wild," he says. "Or we'd have never met that night. She and three other good-looking girls were dragging the streets in a Model "A" coupe with the top off. She just wanted to have fun. And she did. We did." A diary entry of the time reads, "Got home at 6am. Slept 4 hours and went to St. Paul's to take communion."

After marriage Millie and Lloyd moved around the Northwest to wherever work could be found. Maxine was born in Enumclaw, WA, Karen in Vancouver, Doug in Richland, WA, and Joanne back in Vancouver. But after a few years, they bought a home on Vancouver Lake in the family neighborhood. Millie gave up her vagabond life to raise her children while Lloyd continued working out of town.

Millie shone as a young mother. Her children remember her nonstop program of swimming and gymnastics lessons, of library visits and day trips to interesting places. She pushed church and school, and making things with one's own hands. She loved singing. She raided junk stores, fabric stores, and lumber yard for toys and records, for supplies and books, and puzzles, bikes, and oddities to keep them occupied. She was was utterly devoted to the notion that the business of children is play, and she encouraged a level of adventurousness that would have been scandalous in almost any age. "We're riding our bikes to Oregon. We're rafting across the lake. We're building a bonfire and roasting our own lunch." "Well, be home for dinner. You won't be seven years old forever." She was a queen of the domestic arts of sewing and knitting, of cooking and baking, and made sure her children knew how to make almost anything from scratch. She seemed determined that her children be competent and self-sufficient.

She was sociable to people met by chance, with humor and an easy conversational skill. She was known as a striking beauty that sold Avon out of a car full of kids. She was an asset to her children's school – her work and multiple PTA presidencies earned her an honorary lifetime membership in the Washington PTA. She organized school carnivals and was an active leader in the Camp Fire Girls. She taught her children to work early. At a time when parents were expected to send their children to work on local farms she came along as a field boss.

The late sixties were a time of transition for Millie. Her children were in junior high and high school at a time when wildness was the norm, and Lloyd decided he'd had enough of working for other people and came home to start the long process of establishing his own contracting business. When things got tight, Millie helped hold things together by going to work, first as a teachers' aid at Lincoln School, then as a line worker at Bemis bag. She made it pay off while keeping up a home: there were always clean clothes, and dinner on the table. She was always there.

The payoff was sweet. She helped launch Lloyd's construction, both with material assistance and by brooding over the books, and costs and payrolls. And she thrived in a rising tide of prosperity. She enjoyed sporty red cars, trips abroad, plays and movies, the fresh company of her sorority sisters. She made the holidays, pure magic for a tide of grand and great grandchildren, and became a master of the riding lawn mower. But mostly she seemed to use the time to read, and think, and to make things and work in her garden.

Her obituary was published in The Columbian:

MILLIE KESSLER
August 29, 1931 ~ July 3, 2014

Mildred Irene Kessler was born to Robert and Inez Wille in Deer River, MN, on Aug. 29, 1931. In 1945 she moved with her family to Vancouver, WA. Here she met and married Lloyd Kessler, her surviving husband, and here they spent 64 years in a beloved home on Vancouver Lake. She died July 3, 2014.

Though no stranger to the working world, it pleased her more to raise a family at home, and later to help Lloyd begin a successful construction company. She remained a member of St. Paul's Lutheran Church her entire adult life. A 45-year member of Beta Sigma Phi sorority, she took pride in her Lifetime membership.

She was clever and artful with her hands, loved sewing, knitting, and reading. She valued laughter, friendship, independence, and self-sufficiency above most things.

Her survivors also include her four children and spouses, Maxine (Rick) Adams, Karen Kessler (Rex Jackson), Doug (Beverly) Kessler, and Joanne Kessler. She enjoyed nine grandchildren, and twelve great grandchildren. She was preceded in death by her brother, Clifford Wille.

A memorial service was held at St. Paul's Lutheran Church, on Friday, July 11, 2014 at 11:00 a.m. In lieu of flowers donations can be made to the church.

Lloyd and his family wish to express appreciation to the Highgate Senior Living facility for its loving attention to Millie in her final days.

As it turned out, our family was the pot of gold at the end of the rainbow. Millie and I found it and we kept it.

September, 1951.

What are the chances of all this happening to me, considering that I never planned any of my life? What are the odds? Or was this the work of the Almighty?

The End

Appendix

A few words from team members who helped write this book:

JUST ABOUT THE TIME I thought my career days were over and retirement was here, Lloyd's son-in-law Rex, a long-time friend and fellow massage therapist, approached me with the idea that I could help an elderly man write his autobiography. I thought it would take no more than 4 weeks or so for a short one. Then I met Lloyd H. Kessler (Nov. 1, 2012).

This is Now: May of 2015, some 30 months later, finishing a project that has spawned a better story-teller and historian of his own works than the one who began to tell it more than two years ago. What began as a mission with a total stranger has evolved into a vividly detailed, complete publication...and a fine friendship. We couldn't have been more suited for working together—complementing each other's strengths and weaknesses.

I learned that my seldom-exercised patience was now critically necessary in order to maintain silence for several minutes periodically while he formulated his sentences and watched them emerge on my laptop screen as I typed. Lloyd learned to take my advice; I learned to sometimes shut up! He learned the difference between editing his words on-screen and seeing them printed. I learned when to interrupt with a suggestion and when not to. And...he discovered what hard work editing really is! He persevered every 5-day work week for over two years, whether he felt like it or not. Some days we didn't make much progress, but mostly we did what we could with those regular morning sessions—sometimes amid many intrusions.

Lloyd was careful to explain a term or technique unfamiliar to those of us not acquainted with construction vernacular (other than the occasional cat-calls when I was young). His devotion to Millie during this time held stressful issues that often punctuated our sessions until her death. He juggled several projects and challenges for long periods of time, yet he continued to work each day during our allotted time. He was determined to capture as many memories as possible, get each detail correct, and do a LOT of research to find information long lost to anyone's memory. He did that as much for the historical perspective as for the personal. He allowed me to contact my cousin for her specialized genealogical research in sensitive areas—to me, a sign of dedication to the goal he envisioned. He trusted me to help him reorganize his home to accommodate the loss of his wife's presence and to find the treasures Millie had stashed away from the earlier years in which the command of their home was totally hers. I am grateful for that trust.

Our association with Heather produced a team effort that we all have enjoyed. Heather's sharp sense of sequence and familiarity with the construction business helped him write about those experiences in a way that even I could understand. I was the graphics and grammar police, and together we have produced a book worth reading!

I've never seen anyone work as diligently for such a long period of time on a project of so much accomplishment. So even though I've barked at him occasionally, I've come to admire this man—the tenacious 87-year-old seigneur who is alive and well inside that wiry body. He's my Friend. It was an honor to help him tell his story.

Lyn Z. Page

ONCE IN A GREAT WHILE, you get to work with someone on a project that has the distinction of providing you a chance to learn as much about them as you do about yourself. I had known Lloyd for a few years through my husband before Lloyd invited me to join his book project. The hours I've spent with Lloyd through over 150 separate writing sessions, while we sat overlooking Vancouver Lake or tucked away in his office out in his shop have revealed many, many things. I've come to appreciate the many decades-long history that Lloyd has in his industry and I appreciate him as a contractor who has left his mark on the region. I've seen him interact as a father, a husband, a grandfather and a friend.

I've come to thoroughly enjoy the wisdom that has come out of those intersections where the work and the personal have intersected. I've seen Lloyd through two years of changing seasons, bearing witness to success and frustration, grief and joy. I'm especially grateful that Lloyd thought to bring me into his writing partnership with Lyn. What a gift to partner with someone who can pick up where you left off and vice versa, both of us juggling whatever challenges Lloyd threw our way! We're still here writing, still smiling and enjoying the friendship and occasional glass of wine that has cemented a bond that transcends any differences in age. Overall, as this project comes to a conclusion, I see in Lloyd an intrepid spirit that still seeks to learn new things and embrace adventure wherever he encounters it. I consider it a privilege to call Lloyd a dear friend, and look forward to seeing where his adventures take him next.

Heather Deringer

CPSIA information can be obtained
at www.ICGtesting.com
Printed in the USA
FSOW03n0432230615
8087FS

9 781934 956663